VIOLETTE LEDUC:
MOTHERS, LOVERS, AND LANGUAGE

by
ALEX HUGHES

Published by
W. S. MANEY & SON LTD
for the
MODERN HUMANITIES RESEARCH ASSOCIATION
1994

Published by
W. S. Maney & Son Ltd
for the
The Modern Humanities Research Association

HONORARY TREASURER, MHRA
KING'S COLLEGE, STRAND
LONDON WC2R 2LS
ENGLAND

ISBN 0 901286 41 9

© The Modern Humanities Research Association 1994

Printed in England by
W. S. MANEY & SON LIMITED
HUDSON ROAD LEEDS

To My Parents

MODERN HUMANITIES RESEARCH ASSOCIATION

TEXTS AND DISSERTATIONS

(formerly Dissertation Series)

VOLUME 37

Editor

GRAHAM CHESTERS

(French: Modern)

VIOLETTE LEDUC:
MOTHERS, LOVERS, AND LANGUAGE

CONTENTS

ACKNOWLEDGEMENTS

A number of friends and colleagues gave me invaluable help and advice when I was writing my PhD thesis and transforming it subsequently into this study. I should like to take the opportunity to thank them here. During my time as a postgraduate student at Royal Holloway and Bedford New College, London, my thesis supervisor Harry Cockerham provided constant and enthusiastic support. In his company, supervision sessions were always a thoroughly enjoyable and enriching experience, and I remember them with much pleasure. I was also lucky enough to profit from the intellectual stimulation and friendship offered by two fellow postgraduates, Louise Robbins and James Williams. Without them, and without the reading group we formed, I should have found research a lonely business. My thanks go also to Martin Hall, of King's College, London, who was unfailingly supportive of me during the time I was a PhD student and afterwards, and to Ghyslaine Charles-Merrien, who not only allowed me to read her excellent (sadly, unpublished) thesis on Violette Leduc, but also introduced me to other 'Leducians' in France and provided many helpful insights and comments as far as my own work was concerned. Since I have been lecturing at the University of Birmingham, Professor Jennifer Birkett has given me a great deal of useful advice about thesis writing and revision, and I am most grateful to her. Ceri Crossley and Dennis Wood have also offered me the benefit of their own experience of research and writing, which has proved illuminating and for which I should like to thank them. I should like too to thank Professor Michael Sheringham of the University of Kent for allowing me to read his (at the time unpublished) work on Leduc, which I found most interesting, and Professor Graham Chesters for editing my study with such painstaking care. Lastly, and above all, I wish here to acknowledge the enormous debt of gratitude I owe to Elizabeth Fallaize, whose enthusiastic encouragement helped me to see this monograph through to publication.

University of Birmingham, 1993   A.H.

INTRODUCTION

During the eighteen years that followed the publication of her first novel, Violette Leduc's work drew critical esteem from a small group of intellectuals and fellow writers, but was otherwise largely ignored. During the sixties and early seventies, in the wake of the furore that accompanied the appearance of *La Bâtarde*, she achieved a degree of popular success which barely fell short of notoriety, and the originality of her writing was finally widely acknowledged by reviewers and critics. Sadly, however, interest in Leduc's texts waned once more after her death in 1972, and it is only recently that she has re-emerged from literary exile, thanks primarily to work that has been done on her writing in the United States. This monograph seeks to extend and refine a body of critical analysis by scholars who have brought to Leduc's *œuvre* the attention and recognition it deserves. A brief account of Leduc's life and, more importantly, of the critical responses her texts have elicited will guide the reader towards an understanding of the nature and scope of my project.

A LIFE IN WRITING

Violette Leduc was born in Arras on 7 April 1907. She was the illegitimate daughter of Berthe Leduc and André Debaralle, the son of a rich Protestant family in Valenciennes, in whose home Berthe had been a servant. Never legitimized by her father's family, Violette was brought up by her mother and her beloved maternal grandmother, Fidéline. Her impoverished, unhappy childhood, marred by the stigma of illegitimacy and by her mother's acts of unkindness, provided material for her first novel *L'Asphyxie* (1946), and is described in detail in *La Bâtarde* (1964), the first of what were to be three autobiographical *récits*. In 1913, Violette, Berthe, and Fidéline returned to Valenciennes. Fidéline's death in 1916 led to a strengthening of the already powerful bond that existed between Leduc and her mother. In the years that followed, during which Violette and Berthe lived together in relative isolation, Leduc received from her mother the warnings against men and pregnancy which reflected Berthe's experience of single motherhood, but which left her daughter with a fear and mistrust of the male sex she never entirely lost ('Nous prenions notre petit déjeuner, ma mère m'entretenait des laideurs de la vie. Elle m'offrait chaque matin un terrible cadeau: celui de la méfiance et de la suspicion. Tous les hommes étaient des salauds, tous les hommes étaient des sans-cœur' (*La Bâtarde*, p. 39)).

In 1919, Leduc became a *pensionnaire* at the *collège de Valenciennes*. The following year Berthe married Ernest Dehous. Violette experienced her mother's marriage as a betrayal, and never came to terms with her stepfather's presence. She remained a boarder in Valenciennes, despite the proximity of her mother's new home to the *collège*, until Dehous moved his business and family to Paris, at which point she entered the *collège de Douai*. During the academic year 1924–25, she began her first lesbian relationship with a class-mate, Isabelle, whose real identity has remained a mystery. The liaison ended when Isabelle left the school and the lovers lost contact. The following year, Leduc became involved with a *surveillante* at the *collège*, whom she calls Hermine in *La Bâtarde* and whose name, in reality, was Denise Hertgès.[1] When the affair was discovered, Denise lost her job and Leduc was subsequen-tly expelled. Having joined her family in Paris, Violette continued to see Denise, now working as an *institutrice* in the provinces. She studied at the *lycée Racine*, which she attended between 1926 and 1927, and met Jacques Mercier, the man she would eventually marry and whom she names Gabriel in her autobiographies.

In 1927, Leduc passed the written part of her *baccalauréat* but failed the oral. Her passion for reading helped her to find employment with the publishing house Plon where, in a sense, her career as a writer began, since her work involved the composition of 'news-items' (*échos*) into which she had to introduce references to authors published by Plon. Although still involved with Denise Hertgès, she continued, for a time, to see Jacques Mercier. Leduc recounts the curious, triangular situation which resulted in *La Bâtarde*, and it also inspired parts of her third novel, *Ravages* (1955). Forced by ill-health to leave Plon in 1931, Leduc was supported by Hertgès until the end of their relationship in 1934.

After her break with Hertgès, Leduc found work as a telephonist and receptionist with the film producer Denise Batcheff. During this second period of employment, she made the acquaintance of the homosexual writer Maurice Sachs, who was the first to recognize and nurture Leduc's literary talent. In 1939, she also met Jacques Mercier again, and subsequently married him, although the marriage was never a happy one. When war was declared, she lost her job. Encouraged by Sachs, with whom she was deeply infatuated, she took up magazine journalism and made a success of it. However, her troubled relationship with Mercier deteriorated, and a suicide attempt and an abortion (she was by now pregnant by Mercier) followed.

In 1942, Violette accompanied Sachs to Normandy and began, once again at his instigation, to write the text which would eventually be published as *L'Asphyxie*. After Sachs went to Germany as a *travailleur volontaire*, she became a black marketeer, continuing her highly profitable activities until the Liberation. Returning to Paris after the war, she met Simone de Beauvoir. This decisive encounter effectively launched Leduc's literary career. She was already an ardent admirer of Beauvoir's; in 1945 the two women were introduced, and Beauvoir read Leduc's manuscript and liked it.[2] She encouraged Leduc to rewrite parts of the novel, arranged for extracts to appear in the recently founded review *Les Temps Modernes* and ensured that Camus published *L'Asphyxie* in Gallimard's *Espoir* series. In Leduc's eyes, Beauvoir came to assume almost superhuman status.[3] She offered support, stimulation and constructive criticism until Leduc's death, even though the passionate devotion she inspired in her protégée remained unreciprocated. Leduc's second novel, *L'Affamée*, published in 1948, constitutes a fictionalized, surreal and often violent account of her feelings for her muse and mentor, whom she addresses as 'Madame'.

In 1947, Leduc was divorced from Mercier and received, apparently from Gallimard but in reality from Beauvoir, a monthly allowance which enabled her to go on writing. Genet introduced her to Jacques Guérin, a wealthy homosexual industrialist who became her patron. Like Sachs and Beauvoir, he was the object of Leduc's unrequited passion; in his case, however, her attachment turned into an obsession which played a key part in her later breakdown. Leduc's mental equilibrium was further disturbed in 1955, when Gallimard refused to publish her third novel, *Ravages*, until its first section, which chronicled the adolescent, lesbian relationship of two *collégiennes*, was removed. The novel appeared without this and other, shorter parts, and consequently only recounts the adult sexual relationships of its heroine, Thérèse. In order to console Leduc, Guérin financed a visit to Ibiza, during which she rewrote the rejected pages on delicate Chinese paper, creating a 'brouillon artificiel' which Guérin had published, as a gift, in an *édition de luxe*.

Gallimard's act of censorship exacerbated Leduc's recurrent delusions of persecution. In the latter part of 1956, she spent six months in a psychiatric clinic in Versailles, undergoing a sleep cure. During her period of hospitalization, she wrote *La Vieille fille et le mort*, the tale of an initially satisfying but ultimately hopeless passion a lonely old woman conceives for a corpse she finds one evening in her *café-épicerie*. In common with many of Leduc's texts, the novella emphasizes the fundamental solitude of the human individual and the transitory nature of love. *La Vieille fille et le mort* was published in 1958, together with *Les Boutons dorés*, another short narrative which, like *L'Asphyxie*, deals with the theme of childhood unhappiness. In the same year, Leduc discovered Faucon, the remote village in Provence to which she eventually retired, and met a stonemason, René Galet. Their relationship, which seems to have been Leduc's most successful heterosexual liaison, is described in her third autobiographical *récit*, *La Chasse à l'amour* (1973). In 1960, Gallimard published *Trésors à prendre*, the account of a journey through southern France that Leduc made at Beauvoir's suggestion. This journey represented a kind of pilgrimage, designed to affirm Leduc's almost mystical adoration of Beauvoir. As Isabelle de Courtivron argues, *Trésors à prendre* 'is a homage to the same unattainable Madame of *L'Affamée*, a hymn to her spirit',[4] and displays the poetic, lyrical quality which characterizes much of Leduc's most compelling writing.

Although Leduc had been a published author since 1946, commercial success had eluded her. Between 1960 and 1964, however, she wrote *La Bâtarde*, the text which, temporarily at least, brought her the recognition Beauvoir knew she deserved. Extracts from the *récit* appeared in *Les Temps modernes* in 1961 and 1963, and it was finally published in 1964, accompanied by a laudatory preface by Beauvoir. The work, which impressed readers with its startlingly honest exploration of human — and more particularly sexual — concerns, sold well, was considered for the Goncourt and Fémina literary prizes, and brought Leduc into the public eye for the first time. In the years that followed, she was able to buy the house she had rented in Faucon and to embrace an extravagant, fashionable lifestyle, which compensated in part for the penury and solitude she had previously endured. Another novella, *La Femme au petit renard*, which tells the story of a destitute woman's joyous obsession with a fox fur she finds in a dustbin, was well received by the critics in 1965.

In 1966, Gallimard brought out Leduc's modified version of the section of *Ravages* they had excised eleven years before, under the title *Thérèse et Isabelle*. This text differs from both Guérin's *édition de luxe*, twenty-five copies of which were published in 1955, and from the account Leduc gives in *La Bâtarde* of her relationship with the mysterious Isabelle, although all three versions inevitably display certain similarities.[5] In the same year, Leduc underwent radiotherapy for a tumour in her left breast; the treatment was unsuccessful, and the breast was eventually removed.

Leduc left Paris and settled permanently in Faucon in 1969. In 1970, *La Folie en tête*, her second autobiographical *récit*, appeared. The text covers the years following the end of the war and recounts some of the most significant and traumatic events of Leduc's life: her encounter with Beauvoir, the publication of her first novel, the obsession with Guérin which aggravated her mental collapse, and the rigorous creative process through which the opening section of *Ravages*, subsequently cut by Gallimard, came into being. The following year *Le Taxi*, a short erotic dialogue between an incestuous brother and sister, was published. In 1972, after a period in hospital in Avignon, Leduc succumbed to cancer and died in Faucon, on 28 May. The last of her autobiographies, *La Chasse à l'amour*, in which she describes her affair with René and the writing of *La Bâtarde*, was edited by Beauvoir and was published posthumously by Gallimard in 1973.

Despite the literary reputation she had acquired in the last decade of her life, Leduc's writing soon lapsed into obscurity.

LEDUC AND THE CRITICS

Leduc's life and personality were far from unexceptional, and furnished the stuff of much of her *œuvre*. Not unexpectedly, the majority of critics who have taken her work seriously have chosen to analyse the nature of her autobiographical project, and to examine the textual strategies she employs in order to construct her self in writing. The theoretical approaches critics adopt in their explorations of Leduc's autobiographical corpus vary widely. An early, Existentialist analysis of Leduc's autobiographical writing is contained in Beauvoir's preface to *La Bâtarde*. She presents the heroine of *La Bâtarde* as an individual dominated by guilt and shame, annihilatory sentiments reinforced by the accusing gaze of the Other, personified for Violette by her mother. According to Beauvoir, other people, whether the mother or Leduc's various lovers, are a source of torment; if present and accessible they ravage her, while their absence constitutes rejection. Salvation lies in acts of self-affirmation which free Violette from their domination: her black-marketeering and, more importantly, her literary endeavours. Writing permits moreover 'l'impossible synthèse de l'absence et de la présence' which escaped Leduc in her personal relationships but which her text allows her to enjoy in her relation with her reader.[6] Beauvoir's analysis led the authors of several works dealing with modern French literature to suggest that Leduc's writing might have Existentialist implications. The most compelling of these studies is contained in Michael Sheringham's recent exploration of French autobiographical writing, *Devices and Desires*.[7] Sheringham offers, *inter alia*, a remarkable analysis of the dynamic Leduc establishes with her reader, and of the transformation this undergoes as she moves towards liberation.

An article published in 1982 by Jean Snitzer Schoenfeld adopts a psychoanalytic approach to Leduc's first autobiographical *récit*.[8] Schoenfeld's point of departure is the Lejeunian notion that 'l'autobiographie [. . .] doit avant tout essayer de manifester l'unité profonde de la vie'.[9] He suggests that in Leduc's case, guilt and anguish at her illegitimacy which, transposed into a literary leitmotif, were meant to act as structuring forces providing continuity and cohesion, in fact function as destabilizing agents that ensure her quest for unity fails. He goes on to discuss the various strategies the narrator-heroine of *La Bâtarde* adopts within the text in order to mend the psychic divisions of which she is a victim, and concludes that while writing does not ultimately serve as a perfect unifying medium, it does permit Leduc to come to terms with her fragmented psyche — a more problematic but also more rewarding achievement than the creation of a superficial, aesthetic unity.

Martha Noel Evans's 'La Mythologie de l'écriture dans *La Bâtarde* de Violette Leduc' presents Leduc's autobiographical writing in terms of a search for a stable identity and origin, achieved via the textual rebirth of her own self.[10] Evans suggests that in *La Bâtarde* Leduc pursues an inauthentic identity by associating herself with each of the poles between which she oscillates: the legitimate world of her father, which is also that of writing, and the visceral, feminine sphere, of which her bloody, illegitimate birth is a symptom. Leduc's quest for identity takes the form of a quest for paternal and maternal models of authorship, the first involving an attempt to use the literary space to usurp the procreative power of the father, and the second a transformation of the text into a site of idyllic affection of the kind Leduc received from her grandmother. However, neither model of selfhood/writing proves valid or acceptable, and so Leduc is eventually forced to confront difference, which functions as the basis both of identity and of the language she creates in her *récit*. *La Bâtarde*, for Evans, ultimately involves a movement toward the evolution of a discourse in which femininity and masculinity play together, engendering 'un brillant tissu de mots'.[11] Evans's deconstructive reading gives a less than complete account of the text, but her ideas are interesting and are developed in several later essays.[12]

The degree of feminist analysis in Beauvoir's preface to *La Bâtarde* is limited. This should not surprise us, given that she wrote it at a time when, in spite of the success of *Le Deuxième Sexe*, feminist thought was not accorded the importance that it is today. However, other critics — including Elaine Marks,[13] Margaret Crosland,[14] and Germaine Brée[15] — have read Leduc's texts from a gynocritical/feminist perspective, and Brée includes Leduc in a list of women writers who have engendered 'l'explosion d'une littérature féministe qui cherche sa voie propre'.[16] Amongst those analyses of Leduc's writing that are gender-related, particular studies stand out. In a stimulating article on *L'Affamée*, Michèle Respaut argues that the novel's account of the relationship between its narrator and 'Madame' undermines the dualistic angel/monster stereotype so frequently discernible in representations of femininity, and generates a subversive discourse from which new visions of the feminine might emerge.[17] Leduc's explorations of the feminine condition and of feminine intersubjectivity have elicted a good deal of interest amongst feminist scholars. Marilyn Yalom and Colette Hall, for example, both include Leduc in discussions of French women authors who focus on the complex, troubled mother/daughter bond.[18] These critics indicate that Leduc's autobiographical writing provides insights of universal as well as personal significance into female kinship and interaction. Leduc's accounts of feminine homoeroticism in *Ravages*, *La Bâtarde* and *Thérèse et Isabelle* have led some critics to explore her treatment of lesbian bonding.[19] Jane Rule includes a chapter on Leduc in *Lesbian Images*,[20] and Leduc's handling of the lesbian theme is examined in detail in Elaine Marks's impressive essay 'Lesbian Intertextuality'.[21] Marks seeks to establish Leduc's place in the history of writing by and about lesbians, and to evaluate her contribution to it. She suggests that, like Colette, Leduc played a part in the revolutionary creation of 'a language capable of speaking the unspoken in Western literature — female sexuality with woman as namer'.[22] Marks views Leduc as a forerunner of Monique Wittig, hinting that the combination of sexual/textual rhythm in *Thérèse et Isabelle* represents an attempt to transpose body into text which prefigures the hymn to the lesbian body constituted by Wittig's *Le Corps lesbien*. Like Respaut, Marks indicates that Leduc helps forge a new discourse in which femininity may be represented with greater authenticity than was previously possible.

The critic who has undoubtedly done the most to ensure that Violette Leduc's work is not forgotten is Isabelle de Courtivron. Like the feminist scholars mentioned above, de Courtivron is attuned to the need to bring an awareness of issues of gender and sexuality to bear on readings of the Leducian corpus. In her doctoral thesis and in a later article published in *L'Esprit Créateur* in 1979, she analyses Leduc's exploration, in *L'Affamée* in particular, of the depths of the self and the experience of insanity, and examines her transposition of this inner voyage into an artistic form which reflects the chaos she confronted.[23] De Courtivron suggests that Leduc is one of the few women writers who have dared, like Rimbaud and Baudelaire, to penetrate the abysses of the self and in so doing has moved away from 'acceptable' models of feminine literary discourse — hence the unsettling nature of her work. In a further essay in *Yale French Studies*, which deals with *L'Affamée* and *Trésors à prendre*, she examines the literary account Leduc gives of the quasi-religious devotion she felt for Beauvoir, and speculates upon the role Leduc may have played in Beauvoir's life.[24] Finally, de Courtivron's monograph *Violette Leduc*, which appeared in 1985, provides a detailed, succinct introduction to Leduc's *œuvre*.[25] It includes a discussion of the differences between the work of male and female autobiographers and an analysis of aspects of Leduc's writing which, taken as evidence of her 'female imagination', place her within a specifically female literary tradition. The only other full-length study devoted to Leduc's work is *Œdipe Masqué*, by Pièr Girard.[26] In an absorbing if clinical psychoanalytic account of the connections between infantile and adult neuroses, Girard analyses Leduc's exposition in *L'Affamée* of her passion for Beauvoir and relates this to the primordial relationship between Leduc and her mother Berthe, as it is described in *La Bâtarde*.

WRITING THE FEMININE

As my (by no means exhaustive) overview of existing interpretations of Leduc's work suggests, most critics have concentrated on its autobiographical aspect, dwelling particularly on *La Bâtarde*. One consequence of this is that three of her texts, *L'Asphyxie*, *Ravages* and *Thérèse et Isabelle*, which deal with similar areas of female experience to those chronicled in *La Bâtarde* and may therefore be regarded in some measure as the *récit*'s fictional companion pieces, have either been ignored or have been treated as mere extensions of Leduc's autobiographical corpus. This view is widespread amongst Leducian critics, one of whom comments that:

Entre les romans et les récits on ne trouve aucune différence essentielle, chaque roman n'étant que la mise en œuvre de tels ou tels épisodes de la vie de l'auteur, à peine déguisés, et qui seront plus ou moins repris dans le premier récit franchement autobiographique. [...] Ce qui veut dire que les premiers livres sont l'approximation ou les fragments d'un livre total, les premières tentatives héroïques d'une percée au grand jour.[27]

If *L'Asphyxie*, *Ravages* and *Thérèse et Isabelle* are treated simply as elements of a homogeneous, albeit segmented, autobiographical whole, critical responses to them will inevitably be coloured by the account Leduc gives of herself and her experiences in *La Bâtarde*. Viewing these texts as mere 'fragments d'un livre total' can give rise to readings which obscure or disregard their individual qualities. My intention here is to approach these novels from a different angle. I aim to provide a close textual analysis of *L'Asphyxie*, *Ravages* and *Thérèse et Isabelle* which constitutes 'un travail qui s'installe *dans* l'œuvre', i.e. a reading that focuses exclusively upon the material contained within the texts in question, rather than one that is circumscribed by information and insights furnished by *La Bâtarde*.[28]

My decision to limit my exploration of Leduc's writing to a study of these particular novels, and to approach them as works of fiction rather than as autobiographical fragments which may be assimilated into *La Bâtarde*, can be justified in a number of ways. Firstly, like other Leducian texts, they have (undeservedly) received less critical attention than the autobiographical *récits*. Secondly, although clearly inspired at least in part by the experiences Leduc recounts in *La Bâtarde*, each has a unique flavour, and cannot therefore simply be dismissed as a segment of a divided but uniform autobiographical portrait. Furthermore, with regard to *L'Asphyxie* and *Ravages*, Leduc herself explicitly stated that she did not seek to create mere 'mirror-texts', in which sections of *La Bâtarde* are reproduced or magnified. As she analyses the history and behaviour of her mother Berthe in *La Bâtarde*, Leduc observes:

Ma mère s'était surpassée en courage, en énergie, en magnanimité quand elle avait quitté la maison d'André. Elle ne pardonnait pas aux autres hommes ce qu'elle avait fait pour un seul. J'ai parlé de cela autrement dans *Ravages*, dans *L'Asphyxie*. J'ai mêlé la vérité au roman. (p. 40)

Similarly, when she apostrophizes her ex-husband 'Gabriel' in the *récit*, she makes a clear distinction between the text she (or, more accurately, the narrating self she has created) is weaving and *Ravages*, in which the central male character, Marc, displays many of 'Gabriel''s traits: 'Archange, j'ai été injuste avec toi dans *Ravages*. C'est un roman, c'est notre roman, c'est romancé' (p. 125).

Both of these statements suggest that the *romans* to which they refer are autonomous works, which stand apart from Leduc's more directly autobiographical texts. It is true that elsewhere in *La Bâtarde* Leduc draws the attention of her readers to *Ravages* in order to avoid a lengthy re-narration of events which are depicted in that novel and which she wishes to describe once more. This simply suggests that *Ravages* incorporates autobiographical material, but does not mean that the novel is just an account of Leduc's life which parallels that contained in *La Bâtarde*. The above comments indicate that we need not and should not blithely assume that Leduc's early novels represent nothing more than preparatory sketches for her first autobiographical *récit*.

A further aspect of the three texts under scrutiny here justifies my decision not to read them through *La Bâtarde*. The latter text charts the development of Violette, a solitary female subject, whose destiny seems pre-determined by her illegitimacy, and whose experience of life is characterized by marginalization and alienation. A variety of encounters and relationships, invariably both painful and formative, enable the narrator/protagonist of the work to reach a point from which she is able to write retrospectively about her life and to gain access to the *salut* represented, if Beauvoir and other analysts of Leduc's writing are to be believed, by literary creation. In *L'Asphyxie*, *Ravages* and *Thérèse et Isabelle*, however, the focus seems different. Each novel may be read as an exploration of the complex (familial or sexual) ties which exist between female subjects. In these fictional works, in other words, Leduc appears more concerned with the dynamics of feminine interaction, whereas in *La Bâtarde* the emphasis is upon the evolution of a single female subject and, more particularly, on her artistic evolution. *L'Asphyxie*, *Ravages* and *Thérèse et Isabelle* may then, for all the foregoing reasons, be approached as a cohesive body of texts which merit separate analysis.

Existing studies of Leduc's work indicate that her account of feminine interaction occupies a central place within her *œuvre*. I seek to bring fresh insights to bear upon Leduc's representation of the mother/daughter and lesbian bonds and to interrogate certain assumptions made by critics about her vision of these relationships. Consequently, chapters 1–3 of my discussion will be concerned with Leduc's treatment of female bonding in the three novels I have chosen to focus on. Chapters 1 and 2 examine her depiction of the mother/daughter tie in *L'Asphyxie* and *Ravages* and chapter 3 offers an analysis of her portrayal, in *Thérèse et Isabelle*, of lesbian love.

In *L'Asphyxie* and *Ravages*, Leduc does more than denounce maternal inadequacy of the kind she undoubtedly encountered in her relationship with

Berthe. It has been claimed that *L'Asphyxie* simply offers an emotional, highly subjective critique of 'a harsh, egocentric woman, who inspires nevertheless fascination in her daughter', and represents a cry of rage, uttered by a daughter/writer unable to forget the pain of the past, at the cruel inflexibility of her mother.[29] This assessment is unjustifiably limited. *L'Asphyxie* in fact contains a systematic denunciation of a sexually unequal sociocultural order which emerges as a key source of the violence to which the daughter-heroine of the novel is subjected by her mother. Furthermore, *L'Asphyxie* may be interpreted as a symbolic account of the unconscious ambivalence felt by its heroine toward a maternal figure whose reality remains hidden. The Kleinian reading of the novel I offer in the concluding section of Chapter 1 locates this ambivalence as the stimulus for the fantastic, oppositional configuration of 'good' and 'bad' mothers contained in *L'Asphyxie*.

Leduc's third novel, *Ravages*, has been read as the tale of the damaging effect upon a daughter's psychosexual and social development of a restrictive maternal embargo against heterosexuality and maternity.[30] While Leduc certainly confronts the problems inherent in the mother/daughter dynamic in *Ravages*, she also creates a powerful critique of a (Freudian) model of feminine evolution, according to which the female subject must shatter her primordial attachment to her mother and take up her place in a phallocentric sexual economy, in which she is exiled and made subordinate to the male. Moreover, *Ravages* reveals Leduc to have been instinctively attuned to the need — subsequently foregrounded in the theoretical writings of Luce Irigaray — to remove the mother/daughter bond from the limbo of non-representation to which it has been consigned in our androcentric culture, and to articulate the absence of/need for a 'maternal genealogy'.[31]

Chapter 3 of my study deals with Leduc's account of feminine homoeroticism in *Thérèse et Isabelle*, and illuminates the visionary, utopian character of her lesbian discourse in this short text. In *Thérèse et Isabelle*, the lesbian bond between Leduc's adolescent heroines emerges as a seemingly perfect — if ultimately vulnerable — erotic union. My argument in this chapter is that Leduc's efforts to represent a very positive lesbian dynamic, which neither mimics a heterosexual, potentially unequal relationship nor simply functions as an extension of the mother/daughter bond, are indicative of a desire on her part to envision a new and different order of feminine sexuality and inter-subjectivity.

First and foremost, my reading of feminine interaction in *L'Asphyxie*, *Ravages* and *Thérèse et Isabelle* has been influenced both by (French) feminist theory and by psychoanalysis, since an initial examination of existing interpretations of Leduc's texts suggested that approaches which engaged with feminist and/or psychoanalytic discourse proved to be the most illuminating. It has been pointed out that Leduc's own ambivalent attitude towards feminism — and, more specifically, her apparent belief that literary activity affords women access to a (privileged) virility they otherwise lack — means that her writing cannot justifiably be treated as a 'revanche féministe'.[32] Critics must, however, take care to avoid oversimplification. For one thing, the relatively dormant state of feminism in France at the time when Leduc's *œuvre* came into being means that it stood little chance of representing a 'revanche féministe' of the kind which younger, more politicized women writers have created in recent years, and which is easily identified by today's reader — but this does not mean that Leduc's texts cannot be interpreted as feminist productions. Furthermore, we need not take Leduc's equation of virility and (women's) writing as proof positive that her work lacks a feminist dimension. This is because those parts of her *œuvre* which imply a conviction on her part that women accede to 'masculinity' via literature arguably constitute the expression of a feminist consciousness which lacked the vocabulary or intellectual sophistication to articulate itself in a more plausible form. In any case, even if we find Leduc herself politically 'dubious', we should not forget that 'ce que palpent nos antennes de lecteur, ce sont les intentions de l'œuvre plutôt que les intentions de l'auteur',[33] and that it is both possible and productive to make a coherent feminist reading of Leduc's writings. It seems clear, therefore, that this kind of interpretation of her texts is valid and valuable, whatever her own position *vis-à-vis* feminism may have been.

Critics who apply psychoanalytic theory to a literary text may do so in order to discover something about its author, its characters or the culture which has engendered it, or may choose instead, if they adopt a less traditional approach, to concentrate on the structural workings of the text, treating its language as the mirror of a non-personal psyche which is structured in an identical way to language.[34] For those scholars who stress the personal, autobiographical character of Leduc's writing, it is Leduc herself who becomes the analysand of the critical reader, whose task it is to scan her works for evidence of her unconscious desires and obsessions. Rather than treating Leduc's texts as documents attesting to the most secret workings of their author's psyche, this study, in so far as it exploits insights provided by psychoanalysis, will seek to interpret the unconscious conflicts and impulses her writing stages, primarily through an examination of the actions and motives of the characters she creates. The fact that the works which constitute my corpus are narrated in the first person will evidently necessitate some discussion of the relationship between the characters whose psychical complexities are revealed in *L'Asphyxie*, *Ravages* and *Thérèse et Isabelle* and the narrators whose voices reveal them. However, the extent of Leduc's own personal identification/ involvement with the protagonists and narrators she creates is not at issue here.

The fourth and final chapter of my study offers an analysis, informed once again by feminist thought but also by a more traditional, formalist perspective, of the language Leduc employs in *Thérèse et Isabelle*. My decision to restrict discussion to an investigation of *Thérèse et Isabelle* reflects the fact that in *La Folie en tête* Leduc implies that it was her efforts to write the first version of this work which led her to confront the limitations inherent in language. This chapter will include an account of some of Leduc's own observations concerning the (woman) writer's craft. This is intended to help establish whether (and in spite of claims critics have made regarding her belief in the 'virilizing' function of literary activity) Leduc pursued, and achieved, the creation of a language of feminine bonding which was itself somehow 'feminine gendered', or whether the figurative, highly poetic discourse contained in *Thérèse et Isabelle* was intended to serve a different purpose. Although her texts predated the radical feminist analyses of language which emerged in France in the 1970s, the possible relevance of these theoretical discourses to Leduc's *œuvre* will be examined, and the extent to which *Thérèse et Isabelle* constitutes an example of *écriture féminine* will be assessed. The limitations of an exclusively feminist critical approach to Leduc's writing will emerge from this concluding section of my study.

NOTES

1. This information was given to me by Carlo Jansiti, Leduc's biographer, in a letter dated 3 November 1987.
2. 'Au cours de l'automne, je rencontrai, dans la queue d'un cinéma des Champs-Elysées, en compagnie d'une relation commune, une grande femme blonde, élégante, au visage brutalement laid mais éclatant de vie: Violette Leduc. Quelques jours plus tard, au Flore, elle me remit un manuscrit. "Des confidences de femme du monde", pensais-je. J'ouvris le cahier: "Ma mère ne m'a jamais donné la main." Je lus d'un trait la moitié du récit; il tournait court, soudain, la fin n'était qu'un remplissage. Je le dis à Violette Leduc: elle supprima les derniers chapitres et en écrivit d'autres qui valaient les premiers; non seulement elle avait le don, mais elle savait travailler.' Simone de Beauvoir, *La Force des choses* (Paris: Gallimard, 1963), p. 30.
3. Leduc's idolization of Beauvoir is indicated by the terms in which she describes the feelings she experienced on making her acquaintance: 'C'était plus attachant, c'était plus bouleversant qu'une amitié, c'était plus angoissant qu'un amour, c'était plus exigeant qu'une morale, c'était plus fort qu'un inceste, c'était plus asservissant qu'une religion mais cela ne dépendait que de moi, c'était plus sévère qu'un devoir de fidélité, c'était de ma part, un fabuleux entêtement, c'était un renoncement qui dépassait mon imagination, pour lequel j'arrivais au monde, ce n'était rien, c'était la passion', *La Folie en tête*, p. 50.
4. Isabelle de Courtivron, 'From Bastard to Pilgrim: Rites and Writing for Madame', *Yale French Studies*, 72 (1986), 133–48 (p. 140).
5. Information regarding the evolution of *Thérèse et Isabelle* was provided by Ghyslaine Charles-Merrien, author of *Violette Leduc ou le corps morcelé* (unpublished *thèse de doctorat*, Université de Haute Bretagne, Rennes II, 1988). The version of *Thérèse et Isabelle* I analyse is, obviously, the edition published by Gallimard in 1966. Charles-Merrien's study is the most stimulating exploration of Leduc's work that has appeared to date, and I will refer to it from time to time, even though it has not yet been accepted for publication.
6. *La Bâtarde*, p. 12.
7. Michael Sheringham, *French Autobiography: Devices and Desires* (Oxford: OUP, 1993). For other Existentialist readings of Leduc's autobiographical discourse, see Maurice Nadeau, 'L'Existentialisme et ses à-côtés', in *Le Roman français depuis la guerre* (Paris: Gallimard, 1970), pp. 133–35, and Jacques Brenner, 'Destin et liberté', in *Histoire de la littérature française* (Paris: Fayard, 1978), pp. 228–29.
8. Jean Snitzer Schoenfeld, '*La Bâtarde*, or Why the Writer Writes', *French Forum*, 7 (1982), 261–88.

9.   Philippe Lejeune, *L'Autobiographie en France* (Paris: Colin, 1971), p. 21.
10. Martha Noel Evans, 'La Mythologie de l'écriture dans *La Bâtarde* de Violette Leduc', *Littérature*, 12 (1982), 82–92.
11. Ibid., p. 92.
12. Martha Noel Evans, 'Writing as Difference in Violette Leduc's Autobiography', in Shirley N. Garner *et al.* (eds), *The (M)other Tongue: Essays in Feminist Psychoanalytic Interpretation* (Ithaca and London: Cornell University Press, 1985), pp. 306–17 and 'Violette Leduc: The Bastard' in Evans, *Masks of Tradition* (Ithaca and London: Cornell University Press, 1987), pp. 102–22.
13. Elaine Marks, 'I am my own Heroine: Some Thoughts about Women and Autobiography in France', in Sidonie Cassirer (ed.), *Female Studies IX: Teaching about Women in the Foreign Languages* (New York: Feminism Press, 1975), pp. 1–10.
14. Margaret Crosland, *Women of Iron and Velvet* (New York: Taplinger Publishing Company, 1976), pp. 201–10.
15. Germaine Brée, *Women Writers in France* (New Brunswick, New Jersey: Rutgers University Press, 1973), p. 69, 81.
16. Germaine Brée, *La Littérature française* (vol. 16: le XXe siècle II, 1920–70) (Paris: Arthaud, 1978), p. 266.
17. Michèle Respaut, 'Femme/Ange, Femme/Monstre', *Stanford French Review* (Winter 1983), 365–74.
18. Marilyn Yalom, 'They Remember Maman', *Essays in Literature*, 8 (1981), 73–90; Colette Hall, 'L'Ecriture Féminine and the Search for the Mother in the Works of Violette Leduc and Marie Cardinal', in Michel Guggenheim (ed.), *Women in French Literature* (Saratoga: Anma Libri, 1988), pp. 231–38.
19. Two anthologies of erotic writing include extracts from Leduc's work in which lesbian lovemaking is depicted: Jean-Jacques Pauvert, *Anthologies des lectures érotiques (de Félix Godin à Emmanuelle)* (Paris: Ramsay, 1980), pp. 14, 197, 448, 669; Claudine Brécourt-Villars, *Ecrire d'amour: anthologie de textes érotiques féminins* (Paris: Ramsay, 1985), pp. 45, 50, 283, 287.
20. Jane Rule, 'Violette Leduc', in *Lesbian Images* (Garden City, New York: Doubleday, 1975), pp. 139–46.
21. Elaine Marks, 'Lesbian Intertextuality', in George Stambolian and Elaine Marks (eds), *Homosexualities and French Literature* (Ithaca and London: Cornell University Press, 1979), pp. 353–77.
22. Ibid., p. 363.
23. Isabelle de Courtivron, *'Androgyny, Misogyny and Madness': Three Essays on Women in Literature* (unpublished Ph.D. thesis, Brown University, 1973); Isabelle de Courtivron, 'Violette Leduc's *L'Affamée*: the Courage to Displease', *L'Esprit créateur*, 19 (1979), 95–102.
24. 'From Bastard to Pilgrim: Rites and Writing for Madame', *Yale French Studies*, 72 (1986), 133–48.
25. Isabelle de Courtivron, *Violette Leduc* (Boston: Twayne's World Authors Series, 1985).
26. Pièr Girard, *Œdipe Masqué* (Paris: Des Femmes, 1986).
27. Dominique Aury, 'Violette Leduc', *La Nouvelle Revue française* (March 1974), 114–16 (p. 114).
28. Roland Barthes, 'Les Deux Critiques', in *Essais critiques* (Paris: Editions du Seuil, 1964), pp. 246–51 (p. 251).
29. Colette Hall, op. cit., p. 233.
30. Charles-Merrien talks of a 'malédiction maternelle' against heterosexual sex and motherhood which she perceives as destructive and which is most in evidence in *Ravages*. Charles-Merrien, op. cit., p. 69 and passim.
31. The concept of a maternal genealogy is central to the work of Luce Irigaray. Its significance and relevance to *Ravages* will be explored at the end of chapter 2.
32. Both Evans and Charles-Merrien argue that Leduc's unconscious need to occupy the place of her absconding, dead father caused her to perceive writing — traditionally deemed a male activity, particularly because of the conventional pen/penis equation — as a means to acquire a 'virile' or paternal/procreative status. According to Evans, 'for Leduc [...], literary creation becomes a strategy [through which] she usurps and steals the creative power of men' (*Masks of Tradition*, p. 107). Charles-Merrien suggests that writing represented for Leduc an 'accès à une virilité autonome et autorisée' (Charles-Merrien, op. cit., p. 360). Charles-Merrien argues further (on the grounds of denigratory comments Leduc makes in *Trésors à prendre* about the 'femininity' of George Sand's novels) that although Leduc was aware of the

unequal relationship between the sexes and viewed the *venue à l'écriture* of women as a means to combat sexual inequality, her belief in the male character of literary/creative activity and of the women who pursued it means that neither she nor her writing may be considered wholeheartedly feminist: 'Toute l'ambiguïté des relations de Leduc avec le féminisme se résume ainsi: les femmes doivent écrire, elles peuvent rivaliser avec les hommes, mais seules les femmes viriles en sont capables! [. . .] L'Écriture est donc pour Violette le moyen d'accéder à la virilité en rompant avec le destin d'une femme soumise et dominée par l'homme, mais elle est surtout le moyen d'*arborer* cette virilité. En effet, il ne s'agit pas tant d'exister comme une femme libre et reconnue, que de jouer à l'homme. Et c'est en ce sens qu'on ne peut pas proprement parler de revanche féministe' (Charles-Merrien, op. cit., pp. 372–74). Chapter 4 will show that matters are more complex than these critics allow.

33.   Jean Rousset, *Forme et signification* (Paris: José Corti, 1962), p. xvi.
34.   For a comprehensive overview of different psychoanalytic approaches, see Elizabeth Wright, *Psychoanalytic Criticism: Theory in Practice* (London and New York: Methuen, 1984).

CHAPTER 1

L'ASPHYXIE:
THE DOUBLE FACE OF MATERNITY

The twenty-one tableaux which make up *L'Asphyxie* describe the dealings of its heroine, a child of indeterminate age, with her mother, her grandmother and a host of curious and frequently grotesque individuals who inhabit the provincial French town in which the work is set. The organization of the novel's episodes is associative rather than chronological, and seems (at least initially) to indicate that the narrator's memory is ranging in an unsystematic way over events which took place during her childhood.

The text engendered by the narrator's retrospective activity is equivocal in status. Although (superficially) realistic, the oddness of many of the individuals encountered by its heroine and the seemingly disconnected nature of its episodes means that at times it resembles an extended dream-sequence. Moreover, while the tale we are told is clearly the creation of an adult who is recalling her past, it frequently appears, despite the passage of time, to be coloured by the perceptions and responses of the child she once was. In other words, the distance between narrating and narrated/protagonistic selves seems somehow to be erased.[1] This is not always the case, since there are moments when it is evident that the narrative perspective of the novel is exclusively that of the heroine's older self. In the first chapter, for example, the way in which the different concerns of the little girl's vain, ultra-feminine mother and her unaffected, gluttonous grandmother are suggested indicates that the narrator is a mature adult, who can revive and describe the past with humorous detachment:

Quand nous rentrions, [ma grand-mère] offrait une bouchée à sa fille qui la refusait.
– Allez vous coucher, ça conserve.
Se trouvant suffisamment conservée, ma grand-mère commençait de modeler un chausson aux pommes. (*L'Asphyxie*, p. 10)

However, for much of *L'Asphyxie*, the analytic or ironic perspective of the unnamed, older narrator seems to be submerged by that of the novel's naïve, unworldly child-heroine, so that there is a blurring within the narrative of the distinction between her outlook and that of her adult persona. This characteristic of the novel makes it quite different from *La Bâtarde*, in which Leduc's narrator Violette periodically employs the present tense in order to digress from her retrospective account and comment upon her past or present circumstances, or even to address her readers directly — a strategy which emphasizes her separate narrating presence and draws our attention to the gulf that exists between her older and younger selves. Given the ambiguity surrounding the narrative focalization in *L'Asphyxie*, it is safe to assume that the novel's account of its heroine's relations with what are in fact two maternal figures, her mother and her grandmother, somehow amalgamates a youthful and an adult vision of these relations. This chapter seeks to examine some of the different ways in which Leduc's portrayal of mother/daughter interaction in the novel may be read.

The Text as Accusation: the Mother on Trial

Existing critical explorations of *L'Asphyxie* have assumed that its heroine is Violette Leduc herself, or rather the child she once was, and that the mother and grandmother in the work are thinly disguised versions of her own mother and grandmother. Furthermore, critics who approach the text from a biographical perspective have tended not only to concentrate more or less exclusively on the account we are offered of its heroine's unhappy relationship with her mother, but also to suggest that *L'Asphyxie* contitutes a passionate condemnation of Berthe Leduc by her daughter Violette. Colette Hall observes, for example, that in *L'Asphyxie* 'the uncaring mother is crucified', and argues that for Leduc, in 1946 at least, 'writing becomes a cathartic experience during which the mother is immolated'.[2] Reading *L'Asphyxie* simply as a *roman-procès* ignores the complexities of what is a rich and polysemic text. However, the accusatory dimension of the novel, since it is the one to which (biographical) critics have responded most readily, requires elucidation.

   Two aspects of maternal inadequacy emerge from Leduc's description of the central mother/daughter relationship in *L'Asphyxie* and, initially at least, seem to justify reading the work as an attempt to put the mother portrayed within it on trial. The dual nature of the mother's 'wickedness' is established in the first of the novel's twenty-one tableaux. Firstly, she appears here as the embodiment of denial, because of the physical and affective deprivation to which she exposes her daughter. Maternal denial takes various forms. The bitterly poignant opening sentences of *L'Asphyxie* indicate that a fundamental and very obvious feature is the mother's determined refusal of the comfort of physical contact:

Ma mère ne m'a jamais donné la main. . . Elle m'aidait à monter, à descendre les trottoirs en pinçant mon vêtement à l'endroit où l'emmanchure est facilement saisissable. Cela m'humiliait. (p. 7)

In this tableau, physical communication between mother and daughter is rendered impossible by the mother's consistently rejecting attitude. Even when the child, realizing that her mother is distressed and herself in need of comfort, attempts to provide this, she faces repudiation:

Ma mère répétait entre ses sanglots:
  – Nous n'arriverons à rien, à rien!
  J'accourus et je me jetai dans ses bras. Elle me repoussa:
  – Pieds nus sur le carrelage! Tu veux me faire mourir de chagrin . . .? (p. 13)

The mother's extreme preoccupation with her appearance means that her child is exposed not only to physical and emotional deprivation, but also to rejection of a more pernicious kind. Overweening maternal vanity ensures that the mother's gaze is almost always focused on her own image, rather than upon her daughter. The little girl, admiring but excluded, is left to watch her mother watching herself in her mirror, and suffers, in consequence, from a damaging lack of maternal recognition:[3]

Elle avait l'habitude de poser son chapeau sur sa tête quand elle était encore en pantalon, chaussée de bottines lacées jusqu'au dessous du genou. Elle avançait, reculait, en se préoccupant seulement devant la glace de son visage et de cette immense galette qui basculait sur son chignon perdu. [. . .] Le sac perlé et l'ombrelle à la main, elle séduisait le miroir. C'était la répétition générale. (p. 8)

The other feature of maternal conduct which seems to be the object of Leduc's ire in *L'Asphyxie* is the mother's capacity for rage and for punitive violence. The 'regard dur et bleu' which she directs at her daughter acts as a cipher for the maternal anger and its paralysing effects which are constantly evoked in the text. In the first tableau, and in those that follow it, the *regard maternel*, on those occasions when it is trained upon the little girl, functions as an annihilatory force, rather than a source of comfort and reassurance:

Cette fois, on bougeait dans la chambre de ma mère. Nous avions peur.
  Elle ouvrit la porte. Un ouragan.
  – File te coucher, me dit-elle, avec son regard dur et bleu.
  Je filai mais je laissai la porte ouverte. Ainsi je restais en contact avec ma grand-mère. Nous nous protégions à distance. (p. 12)

Denial and punitive rage continue to be associated with the child-heroine's mother throughout the novel. Individual chapters in which the mother appears stress one or the other of these fundamental aspects of her responses to her daughter. In the fifteenth and eighteenth tableaux, it is the mother's capacity for anger which is the key focus. Her rage becomes so extreme in these episodes that she appears not only as a persecutory but also as a destructive and life-threatening figure. In the the final tableau, on the other hand, Leduc foregrounds the deprivation to which the child is exposed by her mother, and the paradoxical role this plays in the little girl's intense attachment to her. It is clear from the language employed at this point in the novel that the narrative voice recalling the events which followed the mother's decision to leave her daughter in school during a public holiday is that of the heroine's adult, analytical self:

Après la messe, nous avions acheté des gâteaux. Nous fîmes une pause sur un banc de la place Verte pour les manger. La surveillante les avalait en lisant. Je n'existais que pour moi et c'était monotone. Ma mère m'occupa. Je désirais sa présence mais si elle était passée à proximité du banc, j'aurais peut-être tourné la tête d'un autre côté. N'était-ce pas l'impossible en elle qui me passionnait plus qu'elle-même?

(pp. 181–82)

The combination of maternal denial and retributive fury to which she is subjected generates the feeling of *écrasement* that the child experiences in her mother's company. This feeling assails her with such frequency that the last words of *L'Asphyxie*, 'C'était une mère irréprochable' (p. 188), inevitably seem, on first reading at least, to be highly ironic. The little girl's perception of her mother as a destructive force is intense, and explains the emphasis that has been placed upon the accusatory aspect of *L'Asphyxie*. However, despite the presence of a body of 'evidence' which seems to vindicate interpreting *L'Asphyxie* as an attempt at maternal denunciation/crucifixion, such an inter-pretation is unnecessarily restrictive. For one thing, it obscures the political, polemical dimension of the novel, a dimension which effectively exculpates the mother, and considerably attenuates the irony permeating the concluding words of the text. Underlying the account we are offered in *L'Asphyxie* of mother/daughter interaction is a powerful if implicit critique of sociosexual oppression, which Leduc appears to have woven into her narrative with considerable care. The presence of this critique — which is illuminated by a feminist reading of *L'Asphyxie* — reveals the superficiality of those interpre-tations that deal solely with the expressions of daughterly pain and accusation contained in Leduc's first novel.

Since it allows *L'Asphyxie* to constitute more than an exercise in personal, autobiographical retrospection, and therefore extends the scope of the work, a feminist, sociopolitical analysis of the novel is undoubtedly more helpful than the biographical approach delineated above. However, like the biographical approach, this model of interpretation provides only a partial account of the text. In the next section of this chapter, the nature — and drawbacks — of a political reading of *L'Asphyxie* will be examined.

THE TEXT AS POLEMIC: AN ASSAULT ON PATRIARCHY?

The central mother-figure of *L'Asphyxie*, like Leduc's own mother Berthe, has been seduced and abandoned by a wealthy young man. In the course of the novel, it becomes apparent that she has been left with a daughter who resembles her father, is consequently a constant reminder of his betrayal, and is a focus for the mother's frustration and despair ('—Tu n'en feras jamais d'autres. Ses défauts, tu les as tous. Sans tête, sans cœur', p. 50). Maternity is presented in the work as a state fraught with tensions, and as a source of grief rather than satisfaction to the woman who has given birth to its heroine.

The simple inclusion of this information may allow the reader to gain some understanding of the mother's (reprehensible) conduct towards her child but it cannot, if taken in isolation, be considered as proof that in L'Asphyxie Leduc is actively seeking to exculpate the mother. None the less, it is possible to read her text as a feminist work, in which the underlying cause of 'bad' maternity are teased out, and in which it is patriarchy rather than maternal inadequacy that is ultimately condemned. The feminist subtext of L'Asphyxie emerges from key passages in which manifestations of the mother's cruelty towards her child are juxtaposed with indications that the society inhabited by mother and daughter is governed by a system of institutionalized masculine privilege which oppresses and frustrates women. The resultant explanation of the heroine's mother's deficiencies in terms of the existence and consequences of sexual (and social) inequality is reinforced by the novel's account of a failure on the part of other women characters evoked in the text to be 'good' mothers. This failure, Leduc hints, like that of her heroine's mother, is due to the particular social order circumscribing the lives of these women, an order which appears to preclude harmonious and equal relations between the sexes.

The political/feminist aspect of L'Asphyxie, which is intuitive rather than didactic, is particularly apparent in the eighteenth tableau, one of the lengthier and more important episodes in the novel. In this chapter, the heroine, who has lost her umbrella, is subjected to an assault by her mother whose violence verges on the annihilatory:

– Dire que je me crève pour ça. Elle nous mettra sur la paille. Un parapluie tout neuf. Le plus beau de la ville. Ça n'est pas digne de ce qu'on fait pour elle. Ça n'a rien dans le cœur, ça n'a rien dans le ventre. Maboule! Espèce de maboule.
Elle secouait mes épaules, elle secouait mes bras. Elle me projetait en avant, elle me projetait en arrière. Elle me jetait sur le côté. C'étaient autant de gestes qui me mettaient à l'Assistance, mais elle ne lâchait pas mon bras . . . (pp. 127–28)

In the course of the attack, the child becomes almost incapable of thought or action. Eventually, she is reduced to a state in which her vulnerability is compared to that of a lilac tree battered by the storm raging outside:

Elle me fit tournoyer comme notre petit lilas au fond du jardin. Je me pliais, je me relevais en même temps que lui. Mes pleurs coulaient partout, comme les gouttes d'eau qui s'égrenaient de ses feuilles en forme de cœur . . . J'étais épuisée. (p. 129)

A biographical critic would undoubtedly view the pathos conveyed by this passage as part of Leduc's indictment of a mother/monster who victimizes her daughter. It is noticeable however that in the above extract, the emphasis is on the child's sufferings rather than on the mother's cruelty. Absence of explicit reproach suggests that Leduc's depiction of 'bad' maternity may be more complex than critics have allowed, and that she is preparing the ground for an exculpation of the mother. A number of aspects of the 'umbrella episode' indicate that this is indeed the case.

The significance accorded by Leduc to the umbrella, whose loss is the immediate cause of the mother's anger, is one of the means by which exculpation is suggested. This object does not function simply as the stimulus for yet another display of maternal violence. The way in which Leduc describes it, and the place in the narrative at which its loss is evoked, also ensure that our attention is drawn to the mother's unfortunate situation (the actual source of her cruelty toward her daughter) and, more importantly, to the child's father — who, together with the social/sexual order he represents, is responsible for the circumstances in which mother and child find themselves.

The mother's position, which she resents, results from her seduction and her status as an unmarried parent, and is characterized by marginalization and poverty. In the light of this, the fact that the umbrella she gives her daughter is no ordinary *parapluie*, but rather one which is 'tout neuf', and 'le plus beau de la ville' (p. 127), is telling. Her decision to buy it suggests an attempt on her part to transcend the opprobrium accorded to women with illegitimate offspring and to offer her child a symbol of the (inaccessible) luxury she associates with the world inhabited by her aristocratic seducer, the world of the rue des Foulons ('la rue la plus imposante de la ville', p. 39), which has remained closed to herself and her daughter because her former lover has refused to legitimize them. The loss of the umbrella, on the other hand, signals (to her and to the reader) the fruitlessness of her efforts. By presenting an apparently neutral object in terms which must remind us, however implicitly, of the mother's problematic situation and her incapacity to improve her own lot or that of her child, Leduc goes some way towards mitigating what seems initially to be an exclusively denigratory portrayal of 'bad' motherhood.

Leduc's exculpation of her heroine's mother in this episode is reinforced by her description of an apparently coincidental encounter between the little girl and the man whom we know to be her father. The mother's seducer appears for the first time in the eighth tableau, in which he is portrayed as an 'homme lâche' (p. 46), who has more or less abandoned his former mistress and their child, and has been able to do so because he belongs to a sex and class which place him above reproach. In the eighteenth tableau, the heroine meets this man once more, after she has discovered that she has lost her umbrella and shortly before she falls victim to the rage its loss provokes in her mother. The encounter occurs as she returns home with a schoolfriend, trembling at the prospect of what awaits her there:

Alors l'homme de la rue des Foulons surgit: il s'adressa à Mandine:
– Qu'est-il arrivé à cet enfant?
– Elle a perdu son parapluie.
Il s'éloigna, rassuré, pressé, dégagé. (p. 124)

The reappearance here of the mother's seducer is highly significant. By placing the meeting between child and father where she does, Leduc is able both to draw our attention once again to the mother's difficult situation and to hint strongly that her subsequent mistreatment of her daughter is an expression of her own helplessness, a helplessness caused by the sufferings she has endured at the hands of an indifferent, heedless male. In other words, Leduc constructs this tableau in such a way that maternal sadism is shown to be a concomitant of the mother's exposure to sexual and social injustice, and is therefore somehow excused.

Our sense that Leduc uses contextualization in order to exculpate the mother and to make a 'political' point is intensified by an observation made to the child by her grandmother after the mother has abandoned her assault upon the little girl and has retired in order to repair her damaged appearance. This completes the 'frame' into which the scene of maternal violence is inserted, and reinforces the denunciation of sexual inequality contained in this chapter:

– Je crois que ça ne va pas avec lui. C'est pour ça . . . Elle n'arrive pas à ce qu'elle veut . . .
Pendant l'orage, j'avais donc servi de double à l'homme qui ne cédait pas.
(p. 132)

We can deduce that the 'lui' to whom the grandmother refers here is not the mother's seducer but rather a second male character, who also appears for the first time in chapter eight. The mother hopes that this man will marry her, in spite of the burden she carries. He is evidently refusing to legitimize their relationship, and it seems likely that it is the mother's stigmatization by and within a social order that condones men who father bastards but not the women who bear them which has provoked his refusal. Leduc indicates, through the grandmother's words, that the anger the mother directs at her child during the 'umbrella episode' is certainly exacerbated and probably caused by the intractability of her new suitor — hence the heroine's perception that she has become the 'double' of the individual concerned.

Leduc's account of her mother's violence is therefore placed between references to not one but two denying male figures, both of whom frustrate the mother's efforts to resolve her difficulties. By situating the horrific exchange between mother and daughter within this framework, Leduc strengthens our sense that *L'Asphyxie* constitutes an instinctively feminist text, which exposes the social inequities to which women are subject. Her framing technique means that the mother's cruelty emerges as the consequence of a damaging disequilibrium between the sexes, which women cannot hope to combat. The reader's impression that the mother is as worthy of pity as the child whom she mistreats is reinforced by a remark the narrator makes as she recalls the grief her mother's enraged behaviour provoked in her. Her tears, she implies, were caused as much by her sense of her mother's pain as by her own sadness:

Alors le chagrin me prit en main. C'était une sève qui circulait en moi comme l'eau dans les nochères... J'oubliai ma mère et moi-même en pleurant de toutes mes forces pour nous deux. (p. 130)

The stories the heroine of L'Asphyxie is told about other mother/daughter relationships intensify our feeling that Leduc contextualizes 'bad' motherhood in such a way that she ultimately produces a feminist critique of sexual inequality rather than an impassioned outburst against maternal monstrosity. The 'readings' the heroine's mother and grandmother make of their own backgrounds and of the women who gave birth to them reveal that the little girl is the descendant of three powerless and victimized mothers, who were all brutalized by their partners and were consequently, to a greater or lesser degree, unavailable to their daughters.[4] On one level, the narrator's inclusion of these narratives-within-the-narrative simply serves to explain the failure of both her mother and grandmother to achieve wholly 'good' maternity in terms of the model of inadequacy each inherited from her own mother — a phenomenon likened by Adrienne Rich to the continuation, from generation to generation of Chinese women, of the practice of footbinding.[5] However, the stress Leduc places in L'Asphyxie on the link between male selfishness and 'bad' motherhood means that this explanation, although relevant, does not go far enough. Her account of the circumstances which generated the form of maternity adopted not only by her heroine's mother but also by her grandmother and great-grandmother transforms her novel into a kind of chronicle of suffering motherhood. In L'Asphyxie, Leduc is quite clearly endorsing the point made by Beauvoir in Le Deuxième Sexe that 'il n'existe pas d'instinct maternel: le mot ne s'applique en aucun cas à l'espèce humain. L'attitude de la mère est définie par l'ensemble de sa situation et la manière dont elle l'assume',[6] and is clearly blaming masculine exploitation for the maternal failings she delineates. Consequently, it is naïve in the extreme to suggest, as one critic has done, that 'il n'y a pas dans l'œuvre de Violette Leduc de dimension politique ou idéologique'.[7]

The ideological aspect of Leduc's novel inflects her account of the men her heroine encounters, and is particularly apparent in her descriptions of their sexuality. If the mother's seducer, in spite of his cavalier behaviour, is portrayed with a modicum of sympathy, M. Pinteau, M. Panier and the anonymous individual who exposes himself in the fourth chapter are presented as grotesque sexual deviants, whose aberrant eroticism is frightening. Male non-desire is also depicted as damaging to women: Georges Dezaille and

M. Barbaroux (who remains 'off-stage') not only subject female characters to sexual denial but appear to take a perverse delight in doing so.[8] The brutalization of women by men is all too usual within the universe Leduc creates in *L'Asphyxie*. An encounter between a young woman and an unknown male at a fair, witnessed by the child-heroine early on in the novel, emblematizes this aspect of the relations between the sexes. The stranger's 'playful' attempts to suffocate the young woman (which look forward to M. Pinteau's semi-strangulation of the heroine herself, as he assaults her in his greenhouse), symbolize the harm done to women by men, and give us one possible indication of why Leduc chose to entitle her first novel *L'Asphyxie*. The only male character of any significance who deviates from the pattern of oppressive, damaging behaviour displayed by other men is Fernand, the *contrebandier*. This seductive personage is described sympathetically by the narrator — yet, in the ninth tableau, she suggests strongly that his gentleness and incapacity to hurt stem from an unarticulated desire to achieve a devirilized state, rather than from an effort to adopt a non-harmful stance *vis-à-vis* the opposite sex.[9]

With the exception of Fernand (and several minor male characters), men appear in *L'Asphyxie* in a negative light, and the female characters consistently emerge as their victims. There are only two women in the novel who escape this fate, and offer its heroine a less discouraging model of femininity than that incarnated by the female members of her family circle. Both are encountered in the final tableau. One is the young pianist, whose playing inspires the child's imagination. The other is the teacher who comforts her after her mother has left her in the empty school, whose intelligence and independence stand in stark contrast to the passivity and impotence the little girl has observed in other women, and who indicates to her that there are means through which an apparently ineluctable feminine destiny of suffering and dependency may be avoided:

– Tu iras à la bibliothèque. Tu trouveras un livre sur la table. Tu le liras. Tu ne comprendras pas. Ça ne fait rien. Ça déposera. Tu pleures comme une femme, il faut abandonner les gamineries littéraires. Si le chagrin ne sert à rien, il est grotesque. Je ne veux pas que tu sois grotesque. Embrasse-moi et tiens-toi droite.
(p. 176)

Clearly, then, *L'Asphyxie* cannot be read simply as a work of disguised autobiography in which a mother (Berthe Leduc) is put on trial, because it also constitutes a forceful feminist critique of the society in which the central, unsatisfactory model of maternity depicted within it evolves. Leduc's exegesis derives its power primarily from her explanation of the deficiencies displayed by her heroine's mother in terms of the latter's unfortunate relationships with men, and from her evocation of other maternal figures who are at once inadequate and victimized. Leduc's denunciation of sexual inequality is extended by her presentation of the male characters with whom her heroine comes into contact as figures of oppression, and by her depiction of femininity as a state of asphyxiating subjugation, from which only a few women are able to escape.

Since it enables us to gain a broader understanding of *L'Asphyxie*, and of the nature of the relationship between the heroine of the novel and her mother, a 'political' interpretation of the kind outlined in the preceding pages seems more satisfactory than a biographical reading. None the less, the sociopolitical approach still fails to tell the whole story. In the last analysis, this sort of interpretation must be considered limited because it allows no room for the elucidation of a fundamental aspect of *L'Asphyxie*, that is, the dialectical, oppositional vision of maternity the text offers the reader. The account given in the novel of the child-heroine's relations with not one but two, radically different, maternal figures, whom she perceives respectively as her 'good' and 'bad' mothers, is an essential part of Leduc's tale. Neither a biographical interpretation nor a feminist reading of *L'Asphyxie* provides a complete explanation of the maternal opposition which exists in the text, and of the role played by the subjective responses of the heroine herself in its formation. A psychoanalytic approach to the novel, on the other hand, does illuminate this key facet of the work.

THE MOTHER DIVIDED

The maternal opposition of *L'Asphyxie* is created by the systematic juxtaposition of positive and negative images of motherhood, which are embodied by the child's grandmother and by her mother. Its fundamental significance is suggested by the fact that it not only represents a major thematic strand of *L'Asphyxie*, but also appears to influence the way in which the novel is constructed. The organization of the work's tableaux and of the subsections within them seems, initially, to be more or less random. However, a careful examination of the text rapidly reveals that the structure of the tale reflects its heroine's extreme preoccupation with her two mothers, and her need to measure them against each other. Throughout the novel, episodes involving the little girl's (bad) mother alternate with others in which her (good) grandmother is evoked, so that the narrative focus constantly shifts between one maternal figure and the other. This oscillation continues to determine the organization of the narrative even after the seventh tableau, in which the death of the grandmother is recounted. In other words, 'external', chronological time is superseded in the text by a more idiosyncratic, private order of temporality that reflects the heroine's overwhelming concern with the nature of, and differences between, the two models of maternity to which she is exposed.[10] The emphasis upon maternal dualism in *L'Asphyxie* is, in consequence, intense.

The maternal opposition is established in the opening tableau of *L'Asphyxie*. Our awareness of its existence is due primarily to the stress placed on the very different treatment the heroine receives at the hands of the two mother-figures with whom she interacts. As the opening section of this chapter indicated, if she is with her mother, the little girl experiences denial, rejection and alienation, especially when exposed to the mother's averted or annihilatory gaze. The grandmother, on the other hand, provides the little girl with the nurturing and attention she craves. She shares with the child the sugary treats forbidden by the mother, treats which the old woman and her granddaughter enjoy conspiratorially. She also gives the child the physical affection that the latter is unable to obtain from her mother. Her unremarkable, sexless appearance ('elle ressemblait à un curé sans âge', p. 13), unlike that of her coquettish, narcissistic daughter, is a source of reassurance to the heroine of the novel. Her gaze, in contrast to the 'regard dur et bleu' of the mother, holds no terrors for the little girl, since it is a 'lac de douceur' (p. 13), which comforts the child. Her stories afford her granddaughter the stimulation her youthful imagination requires. The grandmother's caresses, the kindliness and concern she displays toward the little girl, her readiness to entertain and protect her all mean that she represents a form of maternity which differs considerably from that embodied by the child's harsh, self-absorbed mother.

Maternal dichotomization is reinforced in more complex ways in *L'Asphyxie*. Rather curiously (at least for the reader unfamiliar with the fluid, shifting nature of gender identity in the Leducian creative universe), both mothers have a 'male' aspect, but the masculine traits each displays are antithetical. The child's mother's authoritarian character and more particularly her harsh, penetrative gaze afford her a phallic aura which stands in direct contrast to the priestly (and therefore, for Leduc, emasculated) persona of the gentle grandmother.[11] The maternal opposition is further strengthened by the existence in the novel of other women who function as maternal doubles, extensions of one or the other of the two pivotal mother-figures portrayed in the text. The 'badness' of the 'bad' mother is mirrored by Mme Bave's heedless treatment of her daughter Clémence in the nineteenth tableau, and by the cruelty manifested toward a fragile butterfly by Mandine, the heroine's friend.[12] We are reminded of the heroine's 'good' mother by the café-owner, Juliette, who offers the child the sweet things she loves and who 'se coiffait deux fois par semaine, mais qui avait une bouche si bonne et si nette' (p. 42), by Mme Barbaroux's greedy enjoyment of cakes and *absinthe*, and also by the comforting schoolmistress encountered by the little girl in the final chapter, with her 'chaussures d'homme' and 'opulente tresse grise' (p. 176). Even the female characters in the silent films the heroine adores emerge as the cinematic counterparts of the two polarized maternal figures between whom she oscillates. The division of these characters into 'anges gardiens' or 'démons féminins [que les acteurs] séduisaient facilement' (p. 78) turns the account of the child's trip to the picture palace with her grandmother into a *mise en abyme* which subtly but forcibly recalls the dialectical vision of motherhood contained in *L'Asphyxie*. Despite its centrality, however, the maternal *clivage* which Leduc's narrator creates cannot be taken at face value. Although the novel's account of its 'good' and 'bad' mothers appears on first reading to be reliable, there are a number of indications in the text that this is not in fact the case.

There are, for example, various signs which suggest that the maternal figures portrayed in *L'Asphyxie* are fantasies, creations which are devoid of objective truth. The fantastic aspect of the heroine's mothers is suggested by the exaggerated way in which their contrasting characteristics are depicted. In the eighteenth tableau, the force with which the cruelty displayed by the 'bad' mother is evoked ('Elle m'attendait, paisible comme un commissaire dans l'esprit duquel vadrouillent des abominations', pp. 127–28) and the extravagant description of the environment in which the scene of maternal violence occurs ('Le temps faisait de la mise en scène. Sur les façades des maisons, c'était théâtral', p. 124) mean that the account of maternal wickedness offered to the reader lacks credibility. The unreality of the 'bad' mother is also hinted at in the description we are given in the first tableau of her self-absorbed parade before her mirror:

Elle avait l'habitude de poser son chapeau sur sa tête quand elle était encore en pantalon, chaussée de bottines lacées jusqu'au-dessous du genou. Elle avançait, reculait, en se préoccupant seulement devant la glace de son visage et de cette immense galette qui basculait sur son chignon perdu. Le dressage de la voilette était fantastique. Elle la choisissait parmi des flots de tulle dans une boîte. Elle devait adoucir ou souligner ses traits.
– Qu'est-ce que tu penses de celle-ci?
Je répondais que je trouvais joli ce fin treillis gris et ces petites abeilles plus irréelles que la voilette elle-même dont on l'avait décorée.
– Je te demande ce que tu penses par rapport à moi.
Par rapport à elle, je ne pensais rien. (p. 8)

On one level, this extract simply reveals the mother's narcissism, and the sense of alienation her vanity arouses in her daughter. The closing words of the passage, which suggest that the veiled coquette has somehow ceased to seem real to her child, can be taken merely to indicate the heroine's feelings of exclusion. However, the fact that the mother's face *is* veiled, and that the veil which obscures it is a 'voilette . . . *fantastique*', decorated with 'abeilles *irréelles*', may also constitute a signal that in this passage (in which the mother is described for the first time), and perhaps throughout the novel as a whole, we are being shown a personage whose face is no more than a fantastic mask and who should not, therefore, be taken at face value.

The (objective) truth of the heroine's 'good' mother is also cast into doubt. In the opening chapter, a passage of description relating to the grandmother draws our attention both to the unparalleled beneficence the little girl associates with the old woman and, simultaneously, to her fundamental unreality:

Je me couchai et m'endormis. Quand j'ouvris les yeux, je vis au plafond une tache qui se déplaçait. Grand-mère entrait dans la chambre, le quinquet à la main. Dans sa longue chemise de nuit, elle ressemblait à un curé sans âge. Je ris tout haut, je sautai à pieds joints sur la natte. Je la secouai, je m'ébrouai contre elle.

Je levai la tête. Son regard était un lac de douceur. Son regard comblait mon élan.

Ses cheveux cendrés, son visage serein me fascinaient. Il me semblait qu'elle se mouvait au-dessus de la carpette, qu'elle venait jusqu'à nous grâce à un fil de la Vierge. (p. 13)

In the above extract, the grandmother, enveloped in a soft, enfolding glow, becomes an ethereal, disembodied being, a vision of serenity and gentleness. The reference in the passage to a 'fil de la Vierge' establishes an oblique analogy between the 'good' mother of *L'Asphyxie* and the Virgin Mary, Western culture's most complete symbol of perfect motherhood. The idealization of the old woman which emerges from the above account and the disincarnation to which she is subject attenuate the credibility of her portrait to such an extent that we are encouraged to perceive her, like the child-heroine's mother, as a fantasy.

If certain elements of *L'Asphyxie* hint strongly that its maternal figures are illusory entities, others indicate that the *clivage* separating them is less complete than it at first appears. A series of tiny but important similarities in dress and gesture reduce the gulf dividing the mothers, leaving the reader with the feeling that the maternal split is somehow artificial.[13] Furthermore, there are two passages in the novel in which the ambiguity surrounding the 'elle' employed in order to evoke one of the novel's maternal figures makes it temporarily impossible for the reader to see which mother it is. This ambiguity contributes considerably to the demolition of the maternal opposition. The first of these passages occurs at the end of the third tableau, as the narrator describes the stranger she and her mother met at the fair and his efforts to impress:

On reprenait *Les Pas des Patineurs*. Je donnai mon ticket au garçon de manège. De nouveau, l'étranger était près de moi. Il lançait des serpentins à proximité de ma mère. Il regardait au-delà des choses et des gens. Il cherchait encore à plaire à ma mère en m'installant dans une gondole. Il descendit en marche aussi bien que le personnel. Elle se serait assise à côté de moi. Nous aurions sucé de grosses pralines. Elle m'aurait montré les personnes que nous connaissions. Elle aurait dit que nous allions manger des frites chez la fille de la chaisière de Notre-Dame, que les cornets étaient petits, mais les frites bien en chair. Puis elle m'eût fait monter sur un manège modeste et m'eût souri à chaque passage . . . (p. 22)

In this extract, it seems initially that 'elle' refers to the mother. The narrative appears to suggest that she would have joined her child in the *gondole* and offered her treats, had it not been for the presence of the stranger whom, we learn earlier on in the chapter, she finds attractive and seeks to please. The references to 'pralines' and 'frites' and to the smiles that 'elle' would have directed at the child indicate however that the woman evoked here is the grandmother, whose company would have afforded the child a greater degree of pleasure than that of the 'bad' mother. By omitting to preface the second part of the passage with an explicit conditional phrase (for example, either 'Si l'étranger n'avait pas été là et que ma mère ne l'eût pas préféré à moi-même' or 'Si ma grand-mère avait été avec moi') Leduc leaves room for the ambiguity which diminishes the *clivage* between the two mothers.

The same technique is employed at the beginning of the fourteenth episode. The account of the heroine's acute discomfort as her clothes and face are cleaned and inspected recalls the description given in the opening chapter of the daily rituals to which she is subjected by her mother, so that it seems at first that it is she, rather than the grandmother, who is the 'elle' referred to here:

– Assieds-toi.
Elle me déchaussa, tourna mes souliers, racla les semelles avec le couteau rouillé. Des languettes de boue séchée tombèrent sur un journal. Enfin, elle frotta le dessus mais la propreté des semelles la captivait.
Elle me poussait contre le dos de la chaise. Elle vérifiait mes yeux: avec un doigt, elle désirait emmener ces petites saletés dans la courbe de mes cernes. Pour mieux inspecter mes oreilles, elle enfonçait presque son nez dedans. Elle se penchait sur ma robe. Avec un ongle, elle décolla deux confettis de sucre fondu. Ils étaient transparents comme du tulle extra-fin. Cette robe fut flagellée. Elle brossait fort. Malgré les couches de vêtements, ma peau se hérissait. (p. 83)

A number of aspects of this extract lead us to suppose that the child is in the company of her 'bad' mother. The preoccupation with being clean and impeccably dressed displayed by 'elle', the roughness with which the little girl is treated, the reference to her 'robe . . . *flagellée*' all remind us of the mother and her habitual conduct towards her daughter. Consequently, the third paragraph of the tableau comes as something of a surprise:

Je ne reconnaissais plus grand-mère. Cette propreté d'exaspérée n'était pas dans ses habitudes. Elle devait subir une influence. (p. 83)

The ambiguous and confusing nature of the 'elle qui flagelle' reflects the fact that the actions of the 'good' mother recalled by the narrator at this stage in her tale were, for once, uncharacteristic. The child's failure to recognize her grandmother and her perception that the old woman is in the grip of some alien influence emphasize this point. Yet the fact remains that the employment of an inexplicit 'elle' temporarily adulterates the distinction between the heroine's two maternal figures, even though the narrator rapidly re-establishes the maternal *clivage*. Indeed, the ironic observation 'elle devait subir une influence', which is undoubtedly intended to remind the reader of the gulf separating the two mothers, effectively makes us more aware that this gulf has been dissolved, albeit briefly.

The fact that both the reality of the maternal figures portrayed in *L'Asphyxie* and the rigidity of the divide separating them are called into question means that while it is tempting to accept without challenge the novel's account of 'good' and 'bad' mothers, to do so is unjustifiable. It is, however, possible and indeed logical to approach the maternal figures of *L'Asphyxie* as 'object doubles' fantastically decomposed facets of a single, whole mother whom the reader never actually sees but whose 'invisible' presence we may, and do, intuit. If we read the 'good' and 'bad' mothers in this way, we must attempt to understand what it is that provokes the decomposition of which they are the product.

In his psychoanalytic study of literary doubles, Robert Rogers observes that object doubling is 'subjective in origin (the split symbolizing conflicting attitudes on the part of the perceiver rather than significant dualities in the object)' and that it derives from 'the perceiver's ambivalence toward the object'.[14] He also comments that 'whenever we encounter decomposition in a literary work we may expect to find that the splitting depicts, in one way or another, some very elemental division in the human mind'.[15] Rogers's remarks help us to see that the existence in *L'Asphyxie* of two polarized and essentially fantastic mothers can be taken not only as a sign that the text involves object doubling but also as a symptom of the unconscious — and destabilizing (because inwardly divisive) — ambivalence felt by its central character towards a maternal figure who is the focus of both her love and her hate. In other words, the dualistic vision of motherhood offered by the novel may be interpreted as an indication of its heroine's contradictory responses to a woman whose reality is effectively hidden *behind* the text. The maternal figures depicted *within* the text may be viewed as phantasms, symbolic projections of these responses, whose only 'truth' is that conferred upon them by the child-heroine's psyche.[16]

If we accept that the maternal split dominating *L'Asphyxie* is a function of the child-heroine's subjectivity, and more specifically of the conflicting unconscious feelings she harbours towards her mother, then we obviously need to establish the source of these decompository sentiments. It is helpful at this point to refer to the writings of Melanie Klein. In Klein's work, the splitting by the human child, in response to its exposure both to maternal nurturing and to maternal denial, of its mother (and particularly of the maternal breast) into good and bad, gratifying and denying entities, is a central theme. As the Kleinian analyst Hanna Segal explains, 'quite early, the [infantile] ego has a relationship to two objects; the primary object, the breast, being split into two parts, the ideal breast and the persecutory one. The phantasy of the ideal object merges with, and is confirmed by, gratifying experiences of love and feeding by the real external mother, while the phantasy of persecution similarly merges with real experiences of deprivation and pain'.[17] Arguably, the heroine of *L'Asphyxie* manifests unconscious reactions which are not dissimilar to those of the Kleinian child, even though she is no neonate. Consequently, it is possible to read the novel, from a Kleinian perspective, as an extended and fundamentally infantile psychic fantasy, transposed into literary narrative — particularly since, as Juliet Mitchell observes, in the unconscious (as theorized by Klein) 'infancy is a perpetual present' and 'the past and the present are one'.[18]

Given that the heroine's 'good' mother is associated in the novel with food and pleasure, she may logically be read as a projection of the little girl's appreciation of maternal gratification. This explains the idealization of the old woman which permeates the novel, particularly since, in Kleinian terms, 'idealization is bound up with the splitting of the object' and 'springs from the power of the instinctual desires which aim at unlimited gratification and therefore create the picture of an inexhaustible and always bountiful breast'.[19] The little girl's idealization of her 'good' maternal object and her attempts at identification with her are of such magnitude that she seeks, on occasion, actually to incorporate the 'good' mother within herself, thereby achieving a lasting unification of self and good object.[20] Introjecting the 'good' mother is made possible through the consumption of the cakes and sweets the grandmother offers the child. These are perceived by the little girl as the very essence of the beloved maternal object:

Dans la nuit, nous mangions la moitié de ce chausson remarquable. On retrouvait ma grand-mère dans sa pâtisserie simple et légère. Elle avait le don. (p. 10)

The remarkable character of the pastries evoked here reflects the fact that they constitute an extension of the grandmother and allow the child to take her into her own body. Nevertheless, the cannibalistic pleasure she experiences as she introjects her good object is ultimately adulterated, since in the end introjection arouses guilt. Guilt is provoked by the connection the heroine makes between her loving consumption of her 'good' mother and the latter's frailty and eventual demise. The child's anguished sense of this connection is suggested in the tenth tableau, which reinforces Klein's point that the infant who has introjected its good object, initially out of a desire to protect it, 'dreads that he [sic] has forfeited it by his cannibalism'.[21]

In this episode, the little girl, who is staying with her aunt in the country, learns of the death of a class-mate's grandmother. The news distresses her because her own grandmother has recently died, and her distress is intensified by her friend Olga's apparent absence of grief. The reproaches the heroine expresses to the other child when she sees her eating instead of mourning, and the anxiety she experiences during their encounter, are indicative of a deep-seated belief on her part that her desire to internalize her grandmother has somehow contributed to the disappearance of the old woman:

– Pourquoi ne pleures-tu pas, Olga?
– Pourquoi veux-tu que je pleure?
– Tu as oublié?
– Mais non, puisque je vais chez le menuisier. Elle semblait invulnérable. Je l'enviai.
– Tu ne la regrettes pas?
– Qui?
– Elle.
Elle sortit de sa poche un écheveau de jujube. Elle introduisait les lacets dans sa bouche à la façon d'un charmeur de serpents. Je la secouai:
– Ne mange pas de jujube aujourd'hui.
– J'en mange tous les jours.
– Olga, n'en mange pas.
Un rire robuste secoua son petit corps d'athlète. Ses dents, ses joues, ses mollets resplendissaient. Elle mâchait le jujube avec application. Elle s'éloigna, superbe de vie. (p. 63)

The heroine's extreme preoccupation here with the jujube, which reminds us of the treats offered by her 'good' mother and of her perception of these as the means by which she might achieve introjection, indicates that the anguish she feels stems from an unspoken awareness that her efforts to incorporate her 'good' maternal object have harmed the latter. Consequently, the vulnerability displayed by the 'good' mother throughout the novel may be read as a projection of the guilt the heroine's attempts at internalization cause her to experience, just as the kindliness and nurturing embodied by the grandmother can be taken to reflect the child's appreciation of maternal gratification.

The excessively denying aspect of the 'bad' mother means that it is equally logical, once we approach L'Asphyxie from a Kleinian standpoint, to view her as a phantasm generated by the little girl's paranoid response to maternal deprivation. The retributive rage the mother frequently displays can be explained in a similar fashion, even though the connection between the heroine's own unconscious reaction to maternal denial and the 'bad' mother's capacity for anger may initially appear obscure. This connection is illuminated in the fifteenth tableau. In this section of the novel, we learn of the 'bad' mother's refusal to keep her daughter at home. The child, who is being sent to boarding school, is taken here to purchase items of school clothing. The essential focus of the episode is therefore, once again, her experience of maternal deprivation and denial. Faced once more with this prospect, the heroine is filled with an anguish which is so intense that it fills her whole body ('J'étais gonflée de peine comme une nacelle qui va monter', p. 101), and which provokes an outburst of maternal fury almost as extreme as that described in the eighteenth tableau:

– Mais qu'est-ce que tu as? Réponds, sauvage. Tu m'énerves! Si tu savais comme tu m'énerves!
Ce crescendo durait. Elle grinçait des dents. Elle me jetait sur une chaise. (p. 101)

The rage displayed here by the 'bad' mother may simply be understood as a sign of the irritation she feels at the sight of her daughter's embarrassingly public unhappiness. However, in Kleinian terms it constitutes a more complex phenomenon. Towards the end of the tableau, as she describes her mother's anger at the spectacle of her tears, the narrator comments: 'J'étais dans une cage, délivrée de ma peine mais livrée à elle' (p. 101). This observation is significant, since it establishes a vital link between the distress the heroine experiences as she faces the possibility of maternal deprivation ('J'étais gonflée de peine'), her projection of this suffocating, invasive distress into the outside world ('J'étais [. . .] *délivrée* de ma peine') and the fury her 'bad' mother subsequently manifests ('J'étais [. . .] *livrée* à *elle*'). The narrator's remark effectively implies that the enraged violence of the 'bad' maternal object is ultimately the consequence of a kind of 'projective identification', a defence mechanism by means of which the anguish felt by the child as she confronts maternal rejection, and the unspoken rage which undoubtedly accompanies it, are externalized, and are transmuted in the process into *maternal* anger.[22] In other words, it is the subjective reaction of the child-heroine herself that is the real source of the fury described here, a fury which is her own but which she effectively projects onto her 'bad' mother, with the result that a hated maternal figure becomes a hateful and persecutory mother. The guilt the little girl experiences as she witnesses her mother's actions ('Je me sentais coupable. Elle serait de plus en plus en colère', p. 101) reinforces our impression that it is the child herself who is responsible for the annihilatory rage she imputes to her 'bad' maternal object.

In the eighteenth tableau, there are further signs that maternal rage is the result of 'projective identification'. Here, the loss of the mother which is the source of the heroine's pain, is figured, symbolically, by the loss of the famous umbrella, a gift the child has received from her mother. Significantly, the umbrella is not explicitly named until the seventh page of the chapter, a fact which intensifies our sense that there is more at stake here than the disappearance of an everyday, insignificant object. Once again, exposure to a form of maternal deprivation, signalled by the absence of the umbrella, causes the little girl to feel intense, invasive anguish ('Alors le chagrin me prit en main. C'était une sève qui circulait en moi comme l'eau dans les nochères . . . [. . .] J'étais gonflée de lui', p. 130), and, once again, it seems that her expulsion of her own, harmful anguish somehow engenders the maternal violence to which she is subjected in this episode:

Elle s'était jetée sur moi. C'était le commencement de la délivrance. La catastrophe venait au monde. Je l'avais sortie de moi-même, la catastrophe me soulageait. L'angoisse plierait bientôt bagages. (p. 127)

At this point in her story, the heroine seems to be so much in the grip of the projective impulse that it is not only her 'bad' maternal object but also the environment in which mother and daughter find themselves which appears hostile and persecutory — and, moreover, quite fantastic:

> Les nuages courroucés nous suivaient. (p. 124)
> Le ciel blasphémait avec sa couleur. (p. 125)
> [...] le temps s'énervait. (p. 127)
> Une pluie méchante piquait la terre. (p. 128)

All of the above endorses a Kleinian reading of *L'Asphyxie*, which frames the novel as a symbolic, subjective account of the ambivalence provoked in its daughter-heroine by her conflicting experiences of maternal deprivation and gratification. It is these experiences which, arguably, constitute the true source of the dichotomous vision of maternity that dominates the text. The maternal opposition appears to remain largely unresolved in Leduc's heroine's mind, since her 'good' and 'bad' phantasmic mothers still figure in the final tableau of *L'Asphyxie*. However, there is some evidence in the text of a movement towards a synthesis of its divided maternal figures, and therefore of a more realistic relationship with the 'hidden' mother on the part of its heroine. Since the maternal split portrayed in the novel is indicative also of a profound division within her own psyche, maternal synthesis is, in fact, a step the child-heroine must ultimately make, if she wishes to overcome inner fragmentation.[23] As Segal observes, for Kleinians at least, 'as the mother becomes a whole object, so the [...] ego becomes a whole ego and is less and less split into its good and bad components. The integration of both ego and object proceed simultaneously'.[24] A nascent acceptance of synthesis is revealed in the 'umbrella episode', which we must now re-examine.

Paradoxically, the maternal *clivage* seems at its most intense here. The scene of 'bad' maternal violence, which is the focus of the opening section of the chapter, is immediately followed by another, very different episode, in which the heroine, in the company of her grandmother, enjoys once again the experience of maternal gratification. The juxtaposition of these two scenes brings the 'good'/'bad' mother split into sharp relief. In the second one, the nurturing aspect of the 'good' mother is stressed:

J'appuyai ma joue contre son épaule couverte de lustrine noire. Je posai ma main sur son genou de femme éteinte. *Le temps coulait comme du lait.* (p. 132, my emphasis)

> On pouvait tout se permettre. Je pris grand-mère par la main.
> – Promets que tu te laisseras faire.
> – Promets que tu n'as pas mal...
> Elle était mon sauveur et ma compagne. (p. 133)

The identification which the child-heroine consistently seeks to establish between herself and her good object, and her intense need (also evidenced by her earlier, introjective activities) to protect and preserve the old woman, are indicated here by her efforts to become a 'mother' too — which further complicates the kaleidoscope of maternal doubles *L'Asphyxie* contains. The little girl's desire to accede to 'maternity', and the confusion between 'good' maternal object and daughter which this desire produces, are suggested in the section of the text in which her attempts to nourish her grandmother are described:

Je vis les fraises qui faisaient le gros dos sous les feuilles bombées. J'en cueillis beaucoup. Je préparai les tartines, j'écrasai dessus les fruits. Je saupoudrai et je déposai les nourritures sur une assiette précieuse. Je courus avec.
   – Si tu la casses, nous sommes perdues!
   Mais le bonheur n'est pas maladroit. (p. 133)

The love the little girl feels for her 'good' mother is made most apparent when she offers her a gift of roses. The giving of these flowers symbolizes the harmony which exists between the child and her 'good' maternal object, and the liquid, refreshing 'scintillements' they exude suggest once more that, for the moment, the boundary between the roles of *nourrisson* and *nourrice* is being blurred:

Elle m'accompagnait du regard. J'étais deux fois plus légère . . . Je cueillis d'abord la plus grosse. Je la tenais comme un cierge. Je prenais des précautions pour la lui donner avec des scintillements dessus. Elle la regarda et la posa sur ses genoux.
   – Mets-la grand-mère!
   – Je suis trop vieille . . .
Je pensais qu'elle était plus jeune que tout le monde mais je ne savais pas le lui dire.
   J'en cueillis avec cet acharnement qui me prenait quand je volais de la luzerne pour nos lapins . . . Je ne laissai que les malheureuses. Je les avais déposées dans mon jupon de dessus pour ne pas salir ma robe. Je préparai mon élan. Je réussis à les jeter toutes sur son écourt qu'elle creusait pour les recevoir.
   Nous nous baissâmes en même temps. Je frottai mon visage sur tous les pétales. Elle avait seulement appuyé sa tête sur la mienne. Sous cette tendre protection, je respirai le parfum qui se faufilait profondément en moi. Les scintillements rafraîchissaient les lèvres, les paupières, le lobe des oreilles . . . (pp. 134–35)

Leduc's opposition of positive and negative models of motherhood emerges so strongly in this tableau that a synthesis of her two mother-figures seems out of the question. Nevertheless, fusion does eventually take place, albeit temporarily. This occurs once the 'bad' mother resurfaces in the text, in the form of the 'naine du quartier', whose characteristics indicate that she, like Mandine and Mme Panier, is one of the 'bad' maternal doubles of the novel. The parallel between the *naine* and the heroine's mother is hinted at as the dwarf chides the grandmother for her lack of interest in the recipe for rabbit pâté she has brought her. It is established through references to her (grotesquely) coquettish, ultra-feminine aspect and through the employment of the verb 'accoucher' which suggests that she too is a (displaced) maternal figure:

–Je venais vous dire que mon pâté de lapin est au four. Si vous voulez le voir . . .
–Je n'y tiens pas, répondit grand-mère qui pensait peut-être à notre évasion impossible.
–Je vous trouve bizarre . . . Il est vrai que l'orage agit sur les personnes de nos âges . . .
La naine repoussait le sien avec une coquetterie grotesque.
–Vous ne dites rien. Décidément, je vous répète que l'orage ne vous réussit pas.
Grand-mère contemplait le corps de ballet formé par la lessive qui séchait, qui dansait, qui suppliait dans le jardin de nos voisins.
–On te parle, grand-mère.
La naine accoucherait-elle encore d'une autre phrase du genre féminin?

(pp. 135–36)

The two maternal objects, the 'good' grandmother and the 'bad' maternal double, the coquette/dwarf, are symbolically conjoined by the child's decision to give the *naine* the roses she has picked for her grandmother. The transfer of the flowers from one mother to the other establishes a kind of union between the two maternal figures which briefly erases the *clivage* between them:

La naine tapa du pied.
–Vous m'agacez avec vos mystères.
Notre bonheur m'inspira.
–On a cueilli ça pour vous.
Elle m'embrassa. Sa fine moustache couchée me souleva le cœur.
–Vous vous êtes dévalisée pour moi?
–Votre recette valait ça, enchaîna grand-mère qui me donnait enfin un coup de main.
–Des fleurs. C'est la première fois que ça m'arrive . . . (pp. 136–37)

It is obviously possible to interpret the gift of the flowers merely as a tactic adopted by the child-heroine in order to resolve an awkward moment. At a deeper level, however, it signals her unconscious integration of two previously divided, antithetical maternal phantasms. The heroine's own happiness in this section of the eighteenth tableau indicates that she may be in the process of healing a profound psychic rift within herself. Once she returns to school, however, the synthesis she has achieved breaks down. That fusion is rapidly replaced by renewed fragmentation and separation is suggested in a passage in which the narrator recalls how her teacher instructed her to sit between two fellow pupils. The contrast between these two girls, who are presented simply as 'la brune' and 'la blonde', together with the fact that they are also described as 'twins' by the schoolmistress, indicates that they too are substitutes for the artificially divided mother/objects of the novel, mothers who have been integrated by and within the psyche of its heroine but who are, by this stage, being pulled apart once more. The way in which the 'twins' are told to 'se desserrer' makes it possible to interpret an apparently anodine incident both as a reminder of the child-heroine's recent attempt to fuse the maternal phantasms her unconscious has generated and as a sign of her (stronger) need to maintain, for the moment at least, the phantasmic maternal *clivage*:

– Desserrez-vous les jumelles. Elle se mettra entre vous deux... Vous la surveillerez...
Je me plaçai donc entre les gendarmes. J'éprouvais l'équilibre d'une pendule entre deux chandeliers. L'une brillait par l'intelligence et l'application, l'autre par un coup de crayon extraordinaire. On revisait les croisades. Je me contentai de croiser les bras. (p. 138)

The heroine's sense of well-being here indicates that however satisfying her earlier movement towards synthesis has been, she is enduringly wedded to her familiar vision of maternal fragmentation, and remains therefore in the grip of inner division. We must consequently read *L'Asphyxie* not only as a literary representation of the depths of its daughter-heroine's psyche, but also as the account of an inner duality which, in the last analysis, is unresolved. It is impossible to establish definitively whether the narrator whose voice conveys the psychical rift to which her younger, protagonistic self was subject has herself achieved total integration. As Shlomith Rimmon-Kenan observes, 'narration-as-repetition seems [...] double-edged: it may lead to a working through and an overcoming, but it may also imprison the narrative in a kind of textual neurosis, an issueless reenactment of the traumatic events it narrates'.[25]

It should be quite clear by this stage that the reader is under no obligation to interpret *L'Asphyxie* simply as a work of personal retrospection in which Violette Leduc's traumatic bond with her mother Berthe is the central focus. Both the sociopolitical/feminist and the psychoanalytic interpretations delineated above reveal the richness of the novel's treatment of the mother/daughter dynamic, and enable us to see that *L'Asphyxie* represents much more than a literary *procès* in which Berthe Leduc's maternal shortcomings are revealed and denounced. Since it is a psychoanalytic, and specifically Kleinian, approach which allows the reader to gain the fullest understanding of the intricate system of parallels and *dédoublements* lying at the heart of the text and of the heroine's complicated relations with the maternal figures with whom she interacts, this final reading appears the most satisfactory. As my next chapter will indicate, psychoanalytic theory — of a different kind — also enables the reader to penetrate the complexities of the account of mother/daughter bonding offered in Leduc's third novel, *Ravages*.[26]

NOTES

1. '*L'Asphyxie* is an impressionistic text composed of fragments of memories, tidbits of conversations, brief appearances by assorted characters, and isolated images (of a fairground, a schoolroom, a concert). Though selected and conveyed by an older narrator, they nevertheless retain the character they had when perceived by the child. [...] Seldom does the older narrator, who seeks to re-create these early impressions, intervene directly.' (Isabelle de Courtivron, *Violette Leduc*, p. 18.)

2. Colette Hall, op. cit., p. 233. Hall also describes *L'Asphyxie* as a 'text dripping with hate', and observes that in the novel 'Leduc unleashes unabashedly her hate for a mother who "never held her hand"' (ibid.).

3. Ronnie Scharfman describes the relationship between the heroine of *Wide Sargasso Sea*, Antoinette, and her mother in terms which illuminate the similarities between Jean Rhys's text and *L'Asphyxie*: 'Self-absorbed, [the mother] is imprisoned in a destructive narcissism. Antoinette, who is fascinated with her mother's beauty, watches it more than she interacts with it. She watches her look at herself in the mirror, watches her sleep, watches her when she brushes her hair, watches her when she dances. But she never sees herself reflected there. Her mother's concern for Antoinette is mainly as a disappointing, narcissistic extension of herself. Although the daughter desperately seeks the sense of safety which an acknowledged identification with her mother might confer, the mother bars her from this feeling of unity and dooms her to a sense of fragmentation' (Ronnie Scharfman, 'Mirroring and Mothering in Simone Schwarz-Bart's *Pluie et vent sur Télumée Miracle* and Jean Rhys's *Wide Sargasso Sea*', *Yale French Studies*, 62 (1981), 88–106 (p. 100)).

4. The heroine's mother tells in tableau 8 that she was more or less abandoned by her mother, the child's grandmother, because the latter, married to an unfaithful husband whose uncaring attitude and premature death left her unprepared for the rigours of life, was incapable of looking after her daughter ('–... Maman était molle. Veuve à vingt et un ans. Ses parents m'élevaient. Ils m'ont fait entrer chez les Sœurs', p. 51). In tableau 17 the little girl's grandmother tells her that her own mother also 'failed' her by turning to drink, but did so because the man she lived with mistreated her, disregarded their child, and never stopped hoping that the wife who had left him would return and displace her ('Il nous privait de tout. Ma mère se mit à boire, un peu, pour oublier cet éternel mari abandonné, ma naissance désordonnée', p. 116).

5. 'A mother's victimization does not merely humiliate her, it mutilates the daughter who watches her for clues as to what it means to be a woman. Like the traditional foot-bound Chinese women, she passes on her own affliction.' (Adrienne Rich, *Of Woman Born: Motherhood as Experience and Institution* (London: Virago, 1977), p. 243.)

6. Simone de Beauvoir, *Le Deuxième Sexe* II (Paris: Gallimard, 1949), pp. 323–24.

7. Hall, *Les Mères chez les romancières du XXe siècle* (unpublished PhD dissertation, Bryn Mawr College, 1983), p. 237.

8. Mme Barbaroux's obsessive need to clean and polish, described in tableau 14, is the concomitant of the sexual denial to which she is subjected by a husband who, the narrator implies, is either terrified of his wife's sexual overtures or, more probably, is a sadist who enjoys frustrating her. Once the tramp Georges Dezaille understands in chapter 11 that the heroine's adolescent friend Mandine is seeking some kind of sexual gratification from him, he too takes pleasure in withholding the satisfaction she craves. Clearly, in the world of *L'Asphyxie*, sexual contact with men, whether imposed or refused, is problematic for women.

9. Charles-Merrien (who reads *L'Asphyxie* as an autobiographical fragment, hence her decision to refer to its anonymous heroine as Violette) finds evidence of Fernand's desire for devirilization in the ninth tableau. She attributes it to a sense on his part of an incurable impotence which can be relieved only by total castration: 'Malgré sa séduction naturelle, il est en effet habité par une "impuissance à faire quelque chose", impuissance derrière laquelle il faut entendre, une incapacité de prouver sa virilité. La petite Violette, après avoir dansé avec lui, essaie de le rassurer, lui répétant "qu'il l'a blessée" en la serrant trop fort. Ainsi, elle le réconforte sur son impuissance, lourde à porter, dont une castration le libérerait: "Il était désespéré, vaincu éternellement, quoique vainqueur dans l'aventure, la tête et la nuque offertes à un bourreau qui ne viendrait pas."' (Charles-Merrien, op. cit., p. 191).

10. John Sturrock's remarks about the distinction, in the *nouveau roman*, between chronological, objective time and personal or individual time, are helpful to an understanding of *L'Asphyxie*: 'What the imagination has to work with are public facts that have been absorbed into private consciousness and retained in the memory. [...] We can, and invariably do, examine our past in a different order to that in which it was actually given to us. This new order will, inevitably, be a more personal and revealing one, it is the order which the psychoanalyst must try to extract from his patient by techniques of verbal association' (John Sturrock, *The French New Novel* (London: Oxford University Press, 1969), p. 23).

11. According to Freud, the unconscious establishes a 'substitutive relation between the eye and the male organ which is seen to exist in dreams and myths and phantasies' — which, he argues, means that 'the self-blinding of the mythical criminal, Œdipus, was simply a mitigated form of the punishment of castration' (Freud, 'The Uncanny', *SE*, 17, p. 231). The existence

of the eye/penis equation, and the association of scopic activity with the phallus — both of which are firmly entrenched in our (post-Freudian) culture — makes it hard not to view the mother of *L'Asphyxie*, with her 'regard bleu et dur', as virile, or, as Charles-Merrien puts it, as a 'femme phallique' (op. cit., p. 197). Charles-Merrien suggests that on those occasions when the child-heroine is with her mother, 'elle ressent constamment [sa] virilité, surtout à travers "le bout menaçant" de ses bottines' (ibid.). Virility, therefore, becomes associated with 'bad' motherhood in *L'Asphyxie*. 'Good' maternity on the other hand, embodied by the grandmother, when given a 'masculine' form, assumes one which is clearly devirilized (i.e. which is that of the 'curé sans âge'). Leduc's linking of 'good' motherhood and neutered, sacerdotal maleness resurfaces in *Trésors à prendre*, in a description she gives us of her own grandmother. Here, she explains her valorization of the castrated/priestly masculinity she discerned in Fidéline in terms of the fear of men and pregnancy her mother instilled in her: 'Ma grand-mère, ma folie. [. . .] Je l'ai aimée parce que sa longue robe noire ressemblait à une soutane, parce que la soutane est une robe d'homme, parce que les hommes en robe ont un sexe qui a disparu dans l'ampleur de l'étoffe, parce que ma grand-mère était longue, plate comme un prêtre, parce que je croyais qu'un prêtre n'était pas un homme. Craignant ma mère qui me séparait d'avance des autres en me décrivant des monstres, craignant ces monstres, je me suis tournée vers celle qui ne ressemblait ni à un homme, ni à une femme' (*Trésors à prendre*, pp. 111–12).

12. The way in which Mandine, once she finally traps the butterfly in tableau 18, is described as 'un aigle avec une proie' (p. 121) and the account of how she holds the insect ('Avec la main gauche, elle saisit une aile qui se croyait libre. Elle le brandissait à bout de doigt, comme un acrobate qui en élève un autre à la force du poignet', p. 121) recall descriptions of the 'bad' mother's treatment of her child, especially in tableau 1 ('Elle [. . .] me souleva de terre comme un poulet qu'on enlève par une seule aile', p. 7). Earlier parallels between Mandine and the mother emerge in tableau 11, where Mandine's efforts to seduce Georges Dezaille (p. 71) remind us of the scene in tableau 8 between the 'bad' mother and her seducer (p. 45). Since the mother's former lover is described in tableau 8 as a 'fuyard' (p. 47), who is as hard to entrap as the butterfly Mandine pursues in tableau 18, and since the French verb 'papillonner' has sexual connotations, we can find another link — between the 'bad' mother's seducer and Mandine's 'papillon' — which further reinforces the Mandine/'bad' mother parallel. The fact that the butterfly, tormented by Mandine, also functions as the double of the child–heroine herself indicates the richness and flexibility of Leduc's exploitation of *dédoublements* in this text.

13. The reader can find identificatory parallels between the 'good' and 'bad' mothers by tracing references to the hairpins (pp. 8, 36), boots (pp. 8, 86) and plain garments (the grandmother has a 'jupe ample de curé', p. 85, while the mother has a 'jaquette monacale', p. 73) each wears. Both mothers make an identical, curious movement before the child–heroine which strengthens their identification: at the fair in tableau 3, the 'bad' mother draws 'arabesques' in the litter of streamers at her feet (p. 21), while the 'good' mother designs figures of eight in the dust of her attic floor in tableau 17. The blue of the mother's 'regard' is reflected in the grandmother's blue apron — which sets up a further (surprising) parallel.

14. Robert Rogers, *A Psychoanalytic Study of the Double in Literature* (Detroit: Wayne State University Press, 1970), p. 109.

15. Ibid., p. 44.

16. Hall comments that 'the pattern of love and hate in *L'Asphyxie*, dissociated in the two figures of the Mother and the Grandmother, embodies the ambivalent nature of maternal love which can be a positive and a negative force at the same time' ('L'Ecriture Féminine and the Search for the Mother', p. 235). While helpful, her account of ambivalence/splitting in the novel remains unsatisfactory, because it does not pinpoint the relationship between maternal division and the instinctual desires of the child-heroine herself, and focuses solely on the dualistic character of mother-love.

17. Hanna Segal, *Introduction to the Work of Melanie Klein* (London: Hogarth Press, 1988), p. 26.

18. Juliet Mitchell, 'Introduction', in Juliet Mitchell (ed.), *The Selected Melanie Klein* (Harmondsworth: Penguin Books, 1986), pp. 9–32 (pp. 26, 27).

19. Klein, in ibid., p. 182.

20. In Kleinian terms, this process is one of introjection. Introjection signifies the infant's efforts to internalize/identify with the good object. It is the consequence of the fact that the infant 'fears internalized persecutors against whom he [sic] requires a good object to help him [sic]' and of the infant's 'phantasy that the loved object may be preserved in safety within oneself' (ibid., p. 119).

21. Ibid.
22. Juliet Mitchell explains this mechanism as follows: '*Projective identification* was first described by Klein but has been developed much more fully by Kleinians subsequently. In this the ego projects its feelings into the object which it then identifies with, becoming like the object which it has already imaginatively filled with itself. [. . .] Its own destructive feelings — emanations of the death drive — make the baby very anxious. It fears that the object on which it vents its rage (e.g. the breast that goes away and frustrates it) will retaliate. In self-protection it splits itself and the object into a good part and a bad part and projects all its badness into the outside world so that the hated breast becomes the hateful and hating breast' (ibid., p. 20). Segal observes that 'projective identification has manifold aims: it may be directed towards the ideal object to avoid separation, or it may be directed towards the bad object to gain control of the source of danger. Various parts of the self may be projected, with various aims: bad parts of the self may be projected in order to get rid of them as well as to attack and destroy the object' (op. cit., p. 27), and comments also that 'the projection of bad feelings and bad parts of the self outwards produces external persecution' (ibid., p. 30).
23. It is a key Kleinian point that the splitting of the maternal object is indissociable from the splitting of the ego. Laplanche and Pontalis comment: 'le clivage des objets s'accompagne d'un clivage corrélatif du moi en "bon" et "mauvais" moi, le moi étant pour l'école kleinienne essentiellement constitué par l'introjection des objets' (J. Laplanche and J.-B. Pontalis, *Vocabulaire de la Psychanalyse* (Paris: PUF, 1967), p. 67). That auto-division is the inevitable corollary of maternal splitting is suggested in *L'Asphyxie* by the way in which the child-heroine is identified both with the 'bad' mother and with her opposite, the 'good' grandmother. The 'doubling' of child and 'good' mother emerges time and again in the novel, for example in tableau 5, where the little girl, 'imprégnée de [sa grand-mère] comme nous le sommes d'un parfum' (p. 26), mimics her cough ('Je pensais que je ressentirais son mal, que j'attirerais son attention', p. 28). Child/grandmother doubling is also apparent when the heroine imagines herself at school, dressed in 'tabliers de serge ou de lustrine' (p. 99) — her grandmother habitually wears a 'tablier' and in tableau 18 she is clad in 'lustrine noire' (p. 132). Identificatory parallels between child and grandmother are particularly palpable in the scene in the garden in tableau 18, where the two characters seemingly exchange roles. The identification of the child with her 'bad' mother is indicated by the little girl's activities before a mirror in tableau 2 ('J'enfonçai mon pied dans l'espadrille, j'avançai, je reculai devant l'armoire à glace, croyant rectifier ma démarche', pp. 15–16), by the fact that she finds herself draped by M. Pinteau in the same 'tulle' which covers her mother's hats ('Il se pencha en avant, ouvrit un tiroir, sortit du tulle vert et le drapa autour de mes épaules découvertes', p. 34) and by the way that she tugs at her grandmother in tableau 12 ('Je tirai grand-mère par la manche, mais elle était partie fort loin', p. 7), since this reminds us of the mother's usual method of obliging her child to move ('Tout à coup, elle pinça le tissu de mon manteau à l'endroit où l'emmanchure est facilement saisissable', p. 43). The child's decision to offer her grandmother a pile of *tartines* in chapter 18 (p. 133) recalls the 'bad' mother's preparation of her daughter's snack in tableau 8 ('Elle me préparait une tartine de saindoux qu'elle agrémentait de sucre', p. 40). All of the above indicates that the maternal split reflects division within the ego of the child herself, which requires healing. Her inner fragmentation seems at one stage to be articulated explicitly in the text. This occurs as the narrator recalls the confusion she felt as she listened to her ailing grandmother groan, in a passage in which the questionable character of the maternal opposition is also indicated again: 'Elle gémit. Était-ce bien elle qui gémissait? On gémit encore. *Je me pliai en deux pour écouter*. Ce n'était pas elle. Ma mère?' (p. 27, my emphasis).
24. Segal, op. cit., pp. 68–69.
25. Shlomith Rimmon-Kenan, 'Narration as Repetition: the Case of Günther Grass's *Cat and Mouse*', in Rimmon-Kenan (ed.), *Discourse in Psychoanalysis and Literature* (London and New York: Methuen, 1987), pp. 176–87 (p. 178).
26. A shorter, earlier version of the argument contained in this chapter appeared in *The Modern Language Review*, 88 (October 1993), 851–63.

4

CHAPTER 2

RAVAGES: THE DAUGHTER'S DEFECTION

As I demonstrated in chapter 1, *L'Asphyxie* may be interpreted from both a political/feminist and a psychoanalytic perspective. Leduc's first novel does not however invite the kind of critical approach that is generated by the (uneasy? belligerent?) 'marriage' of psychoanalysis and feminism. *Ravages* on the other hand lends itself to precisely this kind of reading. For the feminist critic who seeks to employ insights provided by psychoanalytic theory in order to understand what gender means, the processes whereby it is constructed, and the way in which gender relations function, the novel represents a rich source of interest.

In *Ravages*, the dynamics of the mother/daughter bond are scrutinized even more closely than in *L'Asphyxie*. It has been suggested that the novel tells the story of a mother and daughter who 'struggle from dominance to coexistence, from symbiosis to separation'[1] within a patriarchal order that makes women into rivals instead of allies. Although issues of female symbiotic bonding and autonomy are central to *Ravages*, this reading obscures the complexities and ambiguities of a text which cannot be treated as the straightforward chronicle of a passage from symbiosis towards an individuation that is achieved via a daughter's liberatory 'refusal of her mother'.[2] Interpreting *Ravages* as the tale of the ultimate defeat of its heroine, Thérèse, by a mother who denies her daughter independence and maturity, is (for reasons which will become apparent) equally restrictive.[3] It is more productive to approach *Ravages* as containing not only an analysis of the problems inherent in the mother/daughter bond but also a forceful critique of a (Freudian) model of feminine psychosexual evolution which is predicated upon the destruction of the daughter's primal bond with her mother, and which constructs 'normal' femininity around the phallus. It is this latter aspect of the novel which generates its feminist dimension.

In this chapter, the causes of Thérèse's problematic relationship with her mother, the nature of her attempt to liberate herself from the mother's sphere of influence, and the 'phallocentric' character of the feminine identity she pursues throughout much of *Ravages* will be examined. In addition, the complexities of the model of maternal conduct depicted in the text will be discussed. Finally, I intend here to explore the possibility of reading the conclusion of *Ravages* as a utopian moment, in which a form of femininity that has proved to be profoundly damaging is finally abandoned by Thérèse, in a way which enables her to regain access to (aspects of) a lost, 'pre-œdipal' bond with her mother.

Ravages is a more hermetic work than *L'Asphyxie*. At its most simple level, the novel describes a young woman's quest for independence, which involves her in a lesbian and a heterosexual relationship, and leads her eventually to abort the child she is carrying. Her story is told by a first-person narrator who, we sense, is less undetached from her past and her younger self than the narrator of *L'Asphyxie*. *Ravages* may also however be read as a symbolic account of the primordial process through which a 'normal', œdipal gender identity is achieved (and ultimately rejected) by a developing female subject, and consequently exemplifies Barthes's contention that 'tout récit ne se ramène-t-il pas à l'Œdipe?'.[4] The novel conflates infantile and adult, conscious and unconscious levels in an extremely subtle way. It constitutes, in part, the artistic expression of an infinitely complex psychic reality which, because it is so complex, requires careful and prolonged unravelling. The 'unconscious' aspect of the work is particularly noticeable in a series of present-tense monologues (distinct from the occasional intrusions of the historic present elsewhere) which erupt into, and disrupt, the narrative. In these sequences, which are usually lyrical and oniric, and in which the voice of Thérèse's younger self seems (briefly) to take over the narrating function, her innermost desires are exposed. The longest of these monologues, the 'bébé-de-la-ruelle' episode, is of central significance to the novel and will be discussed at length below.

Characterization adds to the complexity of *Ravages*. The entities of mother and daughter are treated as problems to be explored, rather than as self-evident categories. On occasion, Thérèse and her mother display characteristics which reveal the fragility of the boundary between the positions they occupy, and erode the rigidity of the mother/daughter distinction. *Ravages*, in other words, offers ample confirmation of the point made by Marianne Hirsch that 'to study the relationship between mother and daughter is not to study the relationship between two separate, differentiated individuals, but to plunge into a network of complex ties, to attempt to untangle the strands of a double self, a continuous multiple being of monstrous proportions stretched across generations, parts of which try desperately to separate and delineate their own boundaries'.[5] The situation is further complicated by the presence of Cécile, Thérèse's lesbian lover, who functions as a double of, or substitute for, Thérèse's mother.[6] Cécile's maternal aspect is ultimately of greater significance, as far as Thérèse's evolution is concerned, than her position as Thérèse's lesbian partner. The relationship between Thérèse and her 'mother/lover' Cécile, like the bond she shares with her biological mother, involves a degree of identity confusion which is particularly evident in the later parts of section two of the novel. The way in which the daughter and mother(s) depicted in *Ravages* appear, on occasion, to exchange roles and functions may be attributed to the peculiar, symbiotic nature of the bond which unites them, and to the problems of non-differentiation and entanglement which issue from it. An initial discussion of mother/daughter symbiotic identification is vital to an understanding of the account of feminine interaction contained in *Ravages*.

THE SYMBIOTIC BIND

Symbiotic identification between a mother and her child is essentially a pre-œdipal phenomenon, constituting that phase in an infant's development at which its sense of fusion with the maternal figure is so intense that it has little grasp of the distinction between self and other and 'no sense of its own body boundaries'.[7] It has also, however, been theorized less as a stage through which an individual passes than as part of 'an interpersonal field of relationships internalized by the infant and therefore configurative in the adult personality'.[8] Its effects tend to be more significant and enduring in feminine relationships, in which the primal identification between mother and daughter is frequently stronger than that which exists between mother and son. The greater intensity of mother/daughter symbiosis has been attributed by Nancy Chodorow in her work on object relations theory to the different treatment sociocultural norms lead mothers to offer their female and male offspring. For Chodorow, 'mothers and women tend to identify more with daughters and help them differentiate less, [so] that processes of separation and individuation are made more difficult for girls', whereas 'a mother tends to identify less with her son, and to push him toward differentiation and the taking on of a male role unsuitable to his age'.[9] Freud remarked upon the unique character of the (pre-œdipal) mother/daughter bond, but never discussed it in depth. More recent psychological and psychoanalytic studies which have appeared in the United States and in France[10] have however, in their different ways,[11] explored the complexities of the mother/daughter relationship in much greater detail.

The conclusions drawn by French and American theorists suggest that the mother/daughter bond, by virtue of its excessively identificatory nature, is characterized by interpenetration and entanglement, rather than by separation. Within it, initial non-differentiation of 'I' and 'not-I' easily continues to prevail, which, for Chodorow, leads to 'experiences of boundary confusion or equation of self and other', and can cause a mother and daughter to feel 'guilt and self-blame for the other's unhappiness, [or] shame and embarrassment at the other's actions'.[12] The continuous character of the relationship between a mother and her daughter can leave the latter with an abiding sense of non-separation from her parent, which prevents her from knowing, precisely, where the borders and limits of her own self lie.[13] One consequence of this may be a feeling on the part of the daughter that she is somehow imprisoned within the maternal/filial bond; another may be her impression that she is no more than the mirror-image of a mother whose identity and development she is doomed to reproduce. The 'specularity' that is intrinsic to the mother/daughter tie is the focus throughout Luce Irigaray's short text *Et l'une ne bouge pas sans l'autre* (1979), the opening lines of which convey the feelings of paralysis and stasis daughters can experience in relation to their mother/mirror: 'Avec ton lait, ma mère, j'ai bu la glace. Et me voilà maintenant avec ce gel à l'intérieur. Et je marche encore plus mal que toi, et je bouge encore moins que toi'. [14] Mother/ daughter identification may also arouse an unconscious sense of boundary confusion in the mother herself, which can cause her to blur the distinction between her role and that of her child and can provoke conflict and disharmony. In other words, the mother/daughter bond is potentially highly problematic, and can involve difficulties which are absent from other interpersonal relationships.

L'Asphyxie offers some indication of the symbiotic dimension of the mother/ daughter relation and the problems it is liable to engender — the heroine of the novel declares in tableau ten that she wishes to 'devenir une autre' (p. 64) *vis-à-vis* her mother, and claims in the final chapter that her mother's presence encloses her in a 'corset de fer' (p. 188) — but does not explore this aspect of feminine bonding in detail. However, mother/daughter symbiosis and its attendant complications is a key focus in *Ravages*. The problematic nature of the maternal/filial bond is made evident in the first of the novel's three parts, in which Thérèse returns to her mother's home after spending an initial, inconclusive night with the man she eventually marries, and in the second section of *Ravages*, which deals with her relation with her 'mother/lover' Cécile. Given the parallels established in the work between Thérèse's bond with her biological mother and her relationship with Cécile, the two unions will be treated here as different facets or stages of a *single* mother/daughter relation.

The difficulties experienced by the daughter–heroine of *Ravages* as a result of the identificatory bond which links her to her mother(s) are suggested in a number of ways. On several occasions, we are given descriptions of engulfing, oppressive spaces which enclose Thérèse, spaces which are tacitly associated with the maternal figure(s) with whom she interacts, and which convey the restrictions the mother/daughter relation imposes upon her. The first of these is the cinema auditorium where Thérèse encounters Marc, her future husband. This environment, described in the opening pages of *Ravages*, is presented as a uterine space, an enclosing domain which Thérèse instinctively perceives as threatening and even life-denying. The 'résonance antique' (*Ravages*, p. 11) which assails her inside the picture house conveys its womb-like character, as does the account of her exit from the auditorium, which resembles a kind of birth ('Je descendis l'escalier avec une fausse désinvolture, je bravai la salle de cinéma, je reçus dans le hall une giclée de vitalité', pp. 12–13).

The desire to free herself from the gloomy cinema/womb and to make it clear that she has done so ('Je roulais des épaules, je voulais [. . .] prouver que je m'étais libérée de la salle de cinéma', p. 13) announces to the reader the problems of individuation her relationship with her mother(s) involves, and her need to resolve them. The 'salle de cinéma' is only one of several symbolic milieux that emblematize the mother/daughter relation and the feelings of suffocation it arouses in Thérèse. Another is the 'maison', which is evoked on a number of occasions in the first and second parts of *Ravages*.

The 'maison' is the most significant and flexible of the symbolic environments whose description conveys Thérèse's feelings of engulfment within and by her mother(s). At first, it is presented as something which is of value to Thérèse. In the 'bébé-de-la-ruelle' episode, a dream-like sequence during which Thérèse recalls (or seems to recall) events from her childhood, the 'maison' functions as a cipher for the exclusive relationship she used to share with her mother, and for the joys this dyadic bond afforded her in the past ('Je penserai d'abord à la maison. A notre maison. Je lui ai bien lavé son carrelage tout à l'heure. J'aime bien travailler pour elle. Oh! que j'aime travailler pour elle', p. 58). The association of the 'maison' with feminine intimacy also emerges from the account Thérèse gives Marc, in part one, of the house in Auvigny inhabited by Cécile ('Elle a une maison. J'y vais chaque samedi, chaque dimanche. Elle aura sa nomination, nous habiterons dans un pavillon', p. 41). In the second part of *Ravages*, however, once Thérèse has started to find her relationships with her biological mother and with Cécile, her maternal substitute, intolerably restrictive, the significance of the symbolic space is modified. The 'maison' ceases to be a site of unity and pleasure, and comes instead to represent for Thérèse a source of unease. On the opening page of part two, she informs her 'mother/lover' that the house they share has begun to terrify her ('J'ai peur dans la maison', p. 75). As the two women discuss the fleas which have infested their home and which, significantly, torment only Thérèse, she suggests to Cécile that her continued habitation of the 'maison' will threaten her reason:

Elle vint s'asseoir sur une marche.
"Si tu dormais, tout changerait. Pourquoi n'arrives-tu pas à dormir? C'est calme ici.
– Calme! Et les puces? Elles me tuent ces puces!"
Cécile baissa la tête.
"Regarde. Le droguiste m'a dit que cette fois ce serait radical."
Elle s'agenouilla près de la chaise. Elle serra mes mains dans les siennes.
"Il n'y a pas que les puces, cette maison me rendra folle. (p. 76)

Thérèse's feelings of asphyxiation within a 'maison' she is increasingly eager to abandon are much in evidence in the opening section of part two of *Ravages*. Later on in this part of the novel, after Marc has become ill and she temporarily loses sight of the possibility of escape he embodies, Thérèse's resentment of the 'maison' becomes intense. As she inwardly articulates this resentment, the link between her relationship with Cécile, her 'mother/lover', and their 'maison' becomes more explicit:

Je me racontai dans l'autobus qui me ramenait en banlieue que j'avais une maison, une amie, que cette amie faisait partie des fondations, que l'on pourrait vivre sans aimer, que c'était supportable [. . .]. Je ne croyais pas un mot de ce que je me disais et je voulais être près de Cécile pour l'accabler. [. . .] Mes efforts pour me rapprocher du pavillon m'écœuraient [. . .]. (p. 132)

The descriptions she gives of the 'salle de cinéma' and the 'maison' and of the sense of entrapment these milieux aroused in her younger self represent one means by which the novel's narrator is able to convey the stifling character of the bond that linked her to her mother(s). Its problematic nature is also highlighted by references to mirrors and reflections. These references, although oblique, enable us to understand more clearly that it is because it is an identificatory, specular relation that the mother/daughter union depicted in *Ravages* is experienced by Thérèse as oppressive.

The account given in part one of *Ravages* of the dynamics of mother/daughter mirroring is both complex and telling. In the course of the row which follows Thérèse's nocturnal escapade with Marc, her mother demands to know where and with whom she has spent the previous evening. At this stage in the story, we gain a strong sense that the particular nature of the relationship she shares with her mother means that Thérèse comes to function as a kind of maternal reflection, and that this impinges upon her own liberty and individuality:

– Tu n'as pas traîné toute une nuit sans quelqu'un. On verra la suite! dit-elle à ses mains jointes.
– J'ai écouté un clarinettiste. Je ne vois pas où est le mal. J'ai écouté un clarinettiste à se mettre à genoux devant lui. De la moelle, maman.
– Innocente! dit-elle à un berger d'Arcadie que reflétait le miroir en face de son lit. (pp. 49–50)

As Thérèse's mother speaks to her daughter here, she simultaneously addresses an image caught inside the mirror facing her bed. In consequence, Thérèse and the reflection within the glass are implicitly bound together, becoming one and the same. The image the mother apostrophizes in the mirror is at once an ornamental statue, a 'berger d'Arcadie', and, given the particular position of the mirror, the mother's *own* reflection (significantly, parallels are established elsewhere in the text between statues and the mother-figure).[15] Consequently, Thérèse emerges in the extract both as a mirror-image of her mother and as a static, lifeless entity, i.e. the 'berger' (whose Arcadian simplicity stands in ironic contrast to the complexity of the mother/daughter dynamic which is being depicted here). The double transformation to which Thérèse is subject makes us conscious not only of the specularity inherent in the relation that binds her to her mother, but also of the restrictive, paralysing effect that mother/daughter mirroring has upon her.

In the pages that follow the exchange I have just analysed, the complexities of mother/daughter mirroring continue to provide a key focus. Thérèse's mother is presented as a kind of human mirror, a reflective surface whose presence her daughter cannot escape. The narrator infers that this aspect of Thérèse's relationship with her mother considerably increases her sense of engulfment within it, and exacerbates the problems she experiences as she moves towards independence and individuation:

– Tu t'es mariée, tu as de bons moments. Je ne découche pas tous les jours.
– Je le saurai que je suis mariée! dit-elle avec colère. Ça voit loin une mère, ça réfléchit une mère!
J'en avais par-dessus la tête. (p. 53)

Elle mourra. Je ne m'y habitue pas. Je me dis elle mourra: je frissonne. C'est un grand moment d'amour.
Elle vivait et elle réfléchissait. (p. 52)

In the first of the above extracts, Thérèse's need for separation and autonomy — which her mother does her utmost to frustrate — is conveyed by her use of the verb 'découcher'. The mother's references to her own ability to 'voir loin' and, more importantly, to 'réfléchir' (to ponder but also to mirror) suggest that her efforts to prevent Thérèse's pursuit of autonomy are facilitated by the mirror-like nature of their bond and by the power that she, the mother/mirror, derives from this — the implication being that she can see, and see into, her daughter, even at a distance, precisely because Thérèse is her mirror-image, an image caught within the maternal mirror. In the second passage, the independence Thérèse seeks is tacitly equated with the death of her mother, the prospect of which excites Thérèse ('Je me dis elle mourra: je frissonne'). Since however her mother is very much alive, this independence seems, here, to be out of Thérèse's reach. Significantly, the mother's continued existence, which entails Thérèse's continued imprisonment within the mother/daughter relation, is associated once again with the mirror-function the mother/daughter bond bestows upon the mother ('Elle vivait et elle réfléchissait'). In other words, in both of the above extracts, as in the account of the mother's apostrophization of the 'berger', the specular character of Thérèse's relationship with her mother is highlighted, in such a way that the essential contribution made by the phenomenon of mother/daughter mirroring to the problems of individuation Thérèse encounters in her bond with her mother becomes apparent.

Since the mother/daughter relationship emerges as a bond which is both asphyxiating and excessively identificatory, the need Thérèse feels in parts one and two of *Ravages* to bring to an end her attachment to her mother(s) is understandable. However, her movement towards detachment is not accomplished easily, or without regret. If she senses that she must abandon the 'maison', it also represents a powerful magnet to which she remains drawn. In part one, after Thérèse has encountered Marc and spent the night with him, she seems eager to achieve separation and liberation. However, the narrator's recollection of the conversation which subsequently takes place between Thérèse and her mother suggests the fragility of her determination to do so:

"Je m'en vais: tu boudes. Est-ce que je peux déjeuner?
–..."
J'entrouvris la porte, je simulai un départ pour l'effrayer, comme si elle était mon bébé. Je revins près de son lit:
"Tu rumines?"
Leur femme de ménage nettoyait le tapis de leur salle à manger avec l'aspirateur. Il y avait une âme plaintive dans l'appareil.
"Tu ne veux pas me répondre? Tu étouffes sous le drap.
– Cette fois, je m'en vais. Au lieu de se dire bonjour, au lieu de s'embrasser!"
Je ne pouvais pas m'arracher de son lit. (p. 47)

In the second part of *Ravages*, after Marc has temporarily rejected Thérèse, the ambivalence she feels about emerging from the maternal orbit resurfaces in the text. Despite her by now considerable dissatisfaction with it, Thérèse is at this stage almost tempted to preserve her intense attachment to the maternal figure (embodied here by Cécile):

C'est près d'elle que je devrais être, c'est près d'elle que je devrais être... Je m'éterniserai aux pieds de Cécile. Je l'aimerai, je serai dans la ligne. Elle existe, Cécile, elle va et vient dans la maison. J'ai Cécile, j'ai une maison, des fondations, je ne devrais pas être triste. Elle était libre et je l'ai laissée. J'arriverai: elle ne me reprochera rien. Comme je vais rattraper le temps perdu... (p. 143)

The authenticity of the need to remain close to her mother(s) which Thérèse experiences here, since it is occasioned by Marc's defection and by her resultant feelings of pique, is somewhat questionable. None the less, the above passage does indicate the profound ambivalence which accompanies Thérèse's pursuit of individuation. Throughout the first and second parts of *Ravages*, she appears torn between a desire to remain within the maternal sphere and to continue to be nurtured by her mother(s) — evidenced by her enduring need to be 'accueillie' and 'rafraîchie' by her 'mother/lover' Cécile (p. 143) — and a wish for an autonomous existence. Her 'painful bind'[16] is most apparent in part two, even as her relationship with Cécile is coming to a close. She clearly both longs for and dreads the severance of the maternal/filial bond, symbolized here by the 'chambre' she shares with her 'mother/lover':

Ce soir-là, je sortis dans le jardin. Ce serait moins morne. Cécile avait tiré les doubles rideaux, elle devait se déshabiller. La fenêtre de notre chambre me passionna. "Je ne partirai pas, cette fenêtre chaque soir me nourrira", me disais-je sans y croire. Je tombai dans l'herbe. Partir, ne pas partir, je n'en peux plus, dis-je à la feuille de géranium que je serrais dans ma main. (p. 152)

Although Thérèse is increasingly keen to end her bond with her mother(s), detachment remains problematic, with the result that her actions and desires are consistently marked by contradiction. Despite the ambivalence she feels, she none the less appears to succeed in breaking the tie that binds her to the maternal figure(s) of the novel. That a break occurs, and that this break is her doing, is suggested in the highly complex scene which takes place between Thérèse and Cécile, her 'mother/lover', in the hotel room Thérèse rents at the end of part two of *Ravages*. Superficially, this episode records *Cécile*'s rejection of *Thérèse*, a rejection occasioned by her disillusionment with her lesbian partner and by the fact that she has fallen in love with another young woman. Cécile's repudiation appears, on the surface at least, to be profoundly unwelcome to Thérèse, who seems to wish to *maintain* her symbiotic relation with her lover and to revive their fading love — hence her dogged efforts to relive the past ('Je t'aime. Tout est possible. Buvons le champagne, mangeons les framboises comme à Auvigny', p. 175). However, the hotel room scene also contains indications that another, more profound separation is occurring, a separation instigated by *Thérèse*, which is the consequence of her determination to *shatter* her oppressively symbiotic relation with her mother(s). In other words, in the course of the hotel episode, two contrasting *ruptures* take place concurrently. If the focus of the episode appears, on first reading, simply to be the severance of a lesbian, adult bond (brought about by Cécile, in defiance of Thérèse's wishes), there is evidence that it simultaneously chronicles the breaking (by Thérèse) of what is essentially a maternal/filial tie.

We are reminded of Cécile's maternal aspect early on in the scene, in a passage in which her new love and her consequent abandonment of Thérèse are evoked:

Cécile me regardait comme si j'étais une photographie. Un être que l'on finit d'aimer ne s'évanouit pas comme une bulle. Elle accouchait de son nouvel amour pour l'autre, elle m'aimait encore en aimant ailleurs. (p. 176)

The use of the verb 'accoucher' in the above lines helps us to realize that while the episode we are witnessing seems merely to involve the painful parting of two women lovers, it also, at a deeper level, constitutes a decisive encounter between a daughter and her 'mother'. Significantly, the latter stages of the scene between Thérèse and her 'mother/lover' take place before a mirror. The inclusion of this object in the description of what occurs in the hotel room increases our impression that we are being shown a maternal/filial exchange, since the glass evokes the problems (illustrated in part one of *Ravages*) caused by the specular character of the mother/daughter bond, and reminds us once more of Thérèse's reasons for shattering symbiosis. The conversation which takes place in front of the mirror between Thérèse and Cécile suggests that by this point in the narrative, she has opted definitively to do so:

[Cécile] sortit le peigne de poche de l'étui, elle peignit ses cheveux devant la glace. Elle soignait son avenir.
   "Regarde-toi, regarde-nous!"
   Je la poussai en avant de toutes mes forces. Son front heurta le beau miroir de l'hôtel. Cécile pleurait sans larmes, le tumulte dans sa gorge ressemblait à un rire sans éclat. Ce sont les coups donnés aux autres qui nous abattent le plus. Je lui pris son peigne, je la coiffai doucement devant le miroir. Cécile fermait les yeux.
   "Regarde, Cécile, mais regarde donc. Oui, toi, moi. Et tu voudrais que nous formions encore le même tableau!
   – C'est toi que me le demandais."
   Le grand lit dans le miroir me donna le vertige.
   "Je t'aimais, je t'aime encore. Que faire?" demanda Cécile. (p. 180)

For much of the hotel episode it is Cécile who is presented as the sole seeker of separation. However, the above exchange indicates that Thérèse is also realizing a form of *sevrage*, and that in her case it is the undifferentiated, identificatory relation which has attached her to her mother(s) that she is bringing to an end, before the mirror which emblematizes the specularity of the mother/daughter bond. That she is doing so is conveyed through the positive emphasis she places in the latter stages of the extract on the separate, singular pronouns 'toi' and 'moi', by her implicit refusal to continue to be part of a homogeneous 'nous', and by her determined rejection of the unified 'tableau' she and her 'mother/lover' have formed hitherto. These elements of the passage suggest strongly that, by now, Thérèse is leaving behind her a mother/daughter bond of an engulfing and essentially infantile nature, and progressing toward a state of independence and autonomy *vis-à-vis* the maternal figure (embodied here by Cécile). If she still feels some nostalgia for the comfort maternal/filial symbiosis has afforded her ('Le grand lit dans le miroir me donna le vertige' implies this, since it recalls the observation Thérèse makes regarding her biological mother in part one: 'Je ne pouvais pas m'arracher de son lit'), she is concerned above all here to reject her mother(s) and to emerge from the maternal orbit. This rejection does not occur in a vacuum. The novel's narrator makes it quite clear that Thérèse's movement away from the maternal sphere is both stimulated and facilitated by a decisive event which takes place at the very start of the novel: her encounter with Marc. Since he functions as the agent who provokes Thérèse into breaking symbiosis, Marc's significance and his role in Thérèse's development require careful examination.

THE FATHER'S SEDUCTION[17]

Taken at face value, Marc represents an intrusive suitor who disrupts Thérèse's relationships with her biological mother and with Cécile, and whom she eventually — and unwisely — marries. Since, however, much of *Ravages* can be read as a metaphorical account of a feminine œdipal trajectory, whose progress corresponds to that described by Freud in his late essays 'Female Sexuality' (1931) and 'Femininity' (1933), Marc may also be deemed to play a symbolic, quasi-paternal role within the narrative, particularly in parts one and two.[18] He possesses, in other words, a 'double face'. He is at once a lover and eventual husband who makes Thérèse aware of the unsatisfactory aspects of the relationships in which she is already involved and exacerbates her need to end them, and he is a phallic father-figure, who obliges Thérèse to confront feminine castration, seduces her away from her primordial attachment to a maternal object and leads her to substitute for this attachment a desire for him, and for his penis.

In the first two sections of *Ravages*, Marc is presented as a liberating force. During Thérèse's initial encounter with him in the womb-space of the cinema, she seems instinctively to sense that he will help her to break her attachment to her mother(s). This is suggested by her need to prove to him that she is capable of desiring and moving towards the freedom he appears to embody ('Il me suivait. J'avais une brûlure sur ma nuque, sur mes reins. Je roulais des épaules, je voulais lui prouver que je m'étais libérée de la salle de cinéma', p. 13). Thérèse's vision of Marc as a liberator is articulated more explicitly when she returns home after her first, 'innocent' night with him, to face her mother's reproaches. As she recalls the events of the previous evening, Thérèse reflects upon what she perceives as the tyrannical character of her mother's behaviour towards her. Marc appears to her at this point as the means by which she will be able to undermine the oppressive bond which exists between herself and her mother and obliterate the ascendancy that their relationship affords the older woman:

J'éteignais, j'allumais, j'éteignais, j'allumais. Elle veut me prendre ce dessinateur à la terrasse des cafés comme elle m'a pris Isabelle. Elle prend, elle supprime: c'est infaillible, c'est irrésistible.
   "Je m'en irai, je m'en irai le plus vite possible", dis-je dans l'obscurité.
   [Marc] m'appellera bonhomme dans un hôtel de passe et le règne d'une mère finira. (p. 54)

The precise character of the emancipation Marc offers Thérèse is complex, and reflects the dual nature of his role in *Ravages*. Superficially, Marc permits Thérèse eventually to accede (in part three) to a social and sexual conventionality which would have eluded her had she remained attached either to her mother or her 'mother/lover' Cécile. Her pleasure at the civic/heterosexual legitimization their union allows her is indicated by the delight she expresses, after she marries him, as she observes in a second hotel mirror the couple they form together. In this scene, which is clearly intended to remind the reader of Thérèse's earlier rejection (also before a mirror) of her symbiotic bond with

Cécile, Marc's negative response to his new wife, increasingly evident in the third part of *Ravages*, is already discernible:

"Comme tu te regardes! Qu'est-ce que tu vois?
— Je me vois", dit Marc.
Je l'ai pris par la taille, j'ai mis sa joue contre le mienne.
"Regarde . . . Nous sommes mari et femme. Tu le vois?
— Je vois que j'ai la même tête qu'hier", dit Marc.
Il tourna le dos au miroir, il lança nos bérets basques sur l'édredon. (p. 195)

Thérèse's need, when she marries Marc, to transform herself into his double indicates her longing to achieve a new identity, which lies outside the mother/daughter bond and which is unrelated to that relationship:

Nous avons crié plus fort que les autres dans la mairie. Nous avions les mêmes bérets basques, les mêmes imperméables, les mêmes cigarettes, la même boîte de suédoises dans nos poches pendant que nous signions sur le registre, pendant que j'abandonnais mon identité de jeune fille. Les boutons de cuir tressé de nos manteaux de pluie étaient les mêmes. Je me grisais avec ces ressemblances. (p. 193)

Thérèse is enchanted by the 'ressemblances' which link her to Marc because they signal her emergence from a form of selfhood which she associates with her mother(s) — her 'identité de jeune fille' — and make manifest the social and sexual status marriage to Marc has brought her. However, Marc's significance, and the significance of the 'liberation' he affords Thérèse, transcend the social. If he provides her with a civic respectability she seems to crave, he also emerges, at a deeper, symbolic level, as a 'paternal' figure who causes Thérèse to embark upon a psychosexual journey which leads her towards the acquisition of a 'normal' female gender identity. The 'œdipal' aspect of Marc's role is most apparent in parts one and two of *Ravages*. It is suggested by the events which take place in the very first hotel room Thérèse visits, a room in which she sees his alien, masculine body for the first time.[19] The fact that Marc is Thérèse's 'premier homme' (p. 39) and the powerful images employed by the narrator in order to evoke his sexual organ transform the scene into a primordial episode, in which a turning point in Thérèse's psychosexual evolution is clearly occurring:

Marc ramassa ses vieilles misères éparpillées. L'aiguille de pin bouffie de puissance oscillait, frappait et refrappait l'air vicié de la chambre, se cognait aux points cardinaux, divaguait de pesanteur. Marc avançait avec son sceptre bistre. (p. 42)

The sight of Marc's 'sceptre' evidently represents a moment of revelation for Thérèse. The account of her exposure to Marc's penis is expressed in such a way that the scene may be read not only as an initiatory, adult episode but also as a symbolic figuration of that stage of female psychosexual development at which, Freud suggests, the feminine subject first becomes aware of her own castration (and that of the mother to whom she has hitherto been libidinally attached) and begins to move towards the father and 'normal' femininity.[20] Implicit in the above passage is a recognition on Thérèse's part of the state of lack which, for Freud at least, is woman's sexual lot. If we choose to interpret what takes place in the hotel room in this (Freudian) fashion, then Thérèse's subsequent attraction to Marc — and her subsequent perceptions of her mother as unnaturally passive and impotent and of Cécile as physically flawed[21] — may be related to the 'castration complex' the episode engenders within her. In a comparable way, the path she follows after this initiatory moment may be understood in terms of her need to suppress her first attachment to her (equally castrated) mother(s) and to embark upon an œdipal trajectory which will enable her to compensate, up to a point, for her lack of the penis which Marc, for all his sexual ambiguity ('Marc à moitié déshabillé attirait le supplice. De tendres épaules, des avant-bras de femme-enfant', p. 42), possesses.

Marc's later actions assist Thérèse in this development. In Freudian terms, Marc's function is to detach Thérèse from her mother(s) and to destroy the 'maison' which represents the primal mother/daughter bond, so that she may make the transfer from mother-love to father-love which the female subject must achieve if the œdipal process is to be set in train and 'normal' femininity attained. His fulfilment of this divisive role and Thérèse's acceptance of his phallic intervention are strongly suggested in the second section of the novel:

"Il y a un homme dans la maison", me dis-je avec satisfaction. (p. 114)

La maison ne nous appartenait plus. Je me demandais si Marc se déchirait à la rocaille sous notre fenêtre ou bien si Marc pissait du sperme dans sa main, la tête haute, l'œil frotté d'étoiles. (p. 116)

La ceinture de cuir [qui appartenait à Marc] tomba sur le carrelage, le bruit de la boucle fit naufrager la maison. (p. 89)

The primal displacement of the maternal object in Thérèse's unconscious is presented in terms of a conflict between Marc and her mother(s) which becomes intense in part two of *Ravages*. Thérèse feels torn between Marc and her 'mother/lover' Cécile, and becomes the site of a psychical battle, during which symbolic maternal and paternal entities embark upon a struggle for control of her psychosexual allegiance. This struggle is implicit in the veiled challenges Marc makes to Cécile, which enable him to remind her of her (castrated) femininity and to vaunt his own (superior) phallic masculinity. It reaches a climax as Cécile suggests that she and Thérèse make love, in a gesture of defiance to the intrusive male who has come uninvited to their 'pavillon' and threatens its security. Thérèse is paralysed by her awareness of Marc's voyeuristic presence and of the erotic possession his scopic activity entails,[22] and refuses a sexual encounter (with Cécile) which, she senses, will transform her unconscious into a battleground, leaving her the victim of the œdipal conflict raging within her. The sexual character of Marc's voyeurism — which deters Thérèse from responding to her 'mother/lover' — is highlighted by the parallel that emerges here between his conduct and that of M. de Nemours, another phallic spy bent on erotic conquest as he watches outside Mme de Clèves's 'pavillon',[23] and by the way in which the Freudian eye/penis equation is foregrounded throughout *Ravages*, for example in the narrator's recollection of Marc's masturbatory activities ('Marc pissait du sperme dans sa main, [. . .] l'œil frotté d'étoiles', p. 116):

Il est sous la fenêtre, il attend comme Cécile attend, il le désire comme Cécile le désire. Si je cède, Marc et Cécile se trouveront en moi. Ils se cherchent à travers moi. Je me trompe, je veux me tromper . . .
"Serre-moi, Thérèse. C'est vrai: je deviens folle avec toi dans mes bras et lui sous la fenêtre.
– Du calme; sois calme, mon petit" dis-je sans assurance. Le Paris–Meaux me frôla l'épaule. Marc sifflait.
"Que c'est triste ce qu'il siffle . . .
– Demain je te le jouerai, dit Cécile. Tu me quittes?
– Nous ne pouvons pas l'abandonner. (p. 119)

This extract conveys Thérèse's feeling that the œdipal combat between old and new, maternal and paternal love-objects which is taking place will damage her in some way. This combat is extended and lengthy. For much of part two, Thérèse appears to oscillate between loyalty to each of her two objects, reflecting the point stressed by Freud that the female subject's movement from mother-love to father-love is circuitous. In the above passage, Marc has the upper hand, whereas elsewhere Thérèse hopes that her attachment to her 'mother/lover' will be preserved and that the Father/phallus will be vanquished ('"Elle a le dessus, c'est elle qui a le dessus", me dis-je', p. 108). The debilitating illness to which Marc succumbs represents, symbolically, the inner resistance Thérèse puts up against the displacement of her mother-object by a phallic/paternal one. His recovery from typhoid, on the other hand, signals that this displacement must none the less take place — hence Thérèse's eventual repudiation of her 'mother/lover' at the end of part two.

Thérèse submits to the object transfer Marc's phallic intrusion provokes partly because it liberates her from the asphyxiating relation which has bound her to her mother(s). The reader also senses, however, that she feels impelled to do so, once her exposure to Marc's penis has occurred, by an intense (if initially ambivalent) need to embrace a form of femininity to which father-love alone (signalled, in the text, by her eventual acceptance of a heterosexual relationship with Marc) affords her access. The 'phallocentric' character of this femininity, which Thérèse pursues for much, if not all, of *Ravages* and which is related to her lack of a penis, is made apparent in the 'bébé-de-la-ruelle' episode. Significantly, this oniric sequence occurs in part one of *Ravages*, not long after Thérèse has seen Marc's sexual organ for the first time. The events described in the dream sequence appear to be detached from those of the rest of the novel. They are however related both to Thérèse's discovery of the 'fact' of feminine castration, which precedes the 'bébé' episode, and to the choices she makes and the path she follows once it has taken place.

LE BÉBÉ DE LA RUELLE: THE PENIS REGAINED

Although it is presented as a memory, this episode resembles more closely a dream or phantasm.[24] Within it, the narrator seems to expose to the reader Thérèse's unconscious and the œdipal desires which dominate it. The primordial, infantile character of these desires is conveyed by the fact that the heroine of the passage is the child that Thérèse was long before the events of *Ravages* take place, rather than the young woman on whose activities the rest of the novel focuses. This substitution means that the incidents occurring in the phantasm stand outside the main temporal boundaries of the novel, and constitute a flashback. An analogy is therefore established between Thérèse's past and the buried realm of her psyche, which, we sense, is on display here.

The narrative perspective of the phantasmic passage is unusual. The episode is introduced by the words 'Je ne me reposai pas. Je me souvenais . . .' (p. 58), which suggest that the narrator is simply recalling her younger/protagonistic self's recollection of her childhood, and is reproducing the memories this activity generated. However, much of the rest of the monologue constitutes a kind of *discours immédiat* in which Thérèse's *childhood* self takes the place of the narrator and speaks directly to the reader.[25] This mimetic technique is employed elsewhere in the novel,[26] usually when Thérèse is in the grip of strong emotions, but the 'bébé-de-la-ruelle' incident represents the most sustained and absorbing example of it.

As the phantasm begins, Thérèse, now a small child, is supposed to be in the fields picking 'pissenlits' for her mother's rabbits. Instead of doing so, however, she has returned to a sinister 'ruelle' (a word used in the seventeenth and eighteenth centuries to denote the bedchamber of a lady of quality) where, for the last three days, she has been looking after an anonymous baby which has been given to her by its mother. Thérèse's return to the 'ruelle' is in defiance of her own mother, whose anger she fears. Yet she feels impelled to transgress by the hope that the baby will return, and by an obsessive need to pick the herbs she has collected on the previous occasions from the 'jardin aux mauvaises herbes' contained within the 'ruelle':

Il faut que je cueille mon herbe comme les autres jours. (p. 60)

Je cueillirai vite mon herbe. Je peux cueillir puisque c'est le jardin aux mauvaises herbes. Je prendrai l'herbe entre les pierres. (p. 58)

Il faut que je le cueille. (p. 58)

Maintenant il faut que je vole du persil dans le jardin. (p. 61)

In *Ravages*, a number of everyday objects are transformed into sexual symbols, either because they are conventionally associated with the erotic or because of the suggestive character of their names/appearance. The 'mauvaises herbes' (chervil and parsley) which grow in the 'ruelle' fall into this category of objects, since they function as phallic substitutes — a fact which enables the reader to relate the urgency with which Thérèse seeks them out during the phantasmic sequence to the need she has begun to feel, after she has confronted castration in Marc's hotel room, to gain access to the penis she lacks. The phallic character of the herbs is suggested in the course of the phantasmic episode itself, for example when Thérèse uses them to stroke ('balayer') the genitals of the baby girl whom she is attempting to 'amuse'. This can be read as a kind of penetration as well as a simple caress, particularly since, in French erotic slang, the noun 'balayette' has penile connotations[27] ('Le bébé ne voyait pas ce que je lui faisais. Il me regardait pendant que je balayais son amande avec mon cerfeuil', p. 61). The sexualization of the herbs is also made clear outside the phantasm, in the second part of the novel. This section of *Ravages* contains several descriptions of efforts made by Cécile to destroy some 'fines herbes'. Since her actions appear to constitute attempts to castrate, symbolically, the intrusive male who is destroying the 'maison' she shares with Thérèse, they strengthen the reader's awareness of the phallic character of the herbs:

Elle me chatouilla la joue avec le bouquet d'aigrettes vertes:
"Vous aimez la ciboulette? Coupe, coupe", dit-elle en regardant Marc.
Elle fourra la paire de ciseaux dans mes mains. (p. 112)
Elle m'avait donné les fines herbes, il était entre nous, elle me disait: "Coupe, coupe." (p. 147)

Since the word 'herbe' has traditionally been associated with the penis in French erotic discourse, the phallic nature of the 'mauvaises herbes' Thérèse discovers should not surprise us unduly.[28] Our sense of the phallic role played by the herbs she finds in the alley is further reinforced by their names. 'Cerfeuil' is suggestive of the penis because it juxtaposes, phonetically, 'cerf', which clearly connotes masculinity, and 'œil', a conventional phallic symbol. 'Persil', the other herb Thérèse picks, since it is a reversal of 'il perce', signals penetration and defloration. The fact that it is these particular herbs which Thérèse finds in the alley serves to confirm the reader's impression that they function as penile substitutes.

If Thérèse is authorized by her mother to pick dandelions in the fields (a 'pissenlit', although visually more penile than either 'cerfeuil' or 'persil', is semantically devoid of any phallic connotation and suggests rather a rejection of (hetero)sexuality), her search for the 'mauvaises herbes' is in defiance of maternal wishes, since Thérèse is not supposed to be in the alley at all. Early on in the passage, as she looks for the chervil, Thérèse tells herself: 'Il faut que je le cueille. Non. Je penserai d'abord à la maison. A notre maison' (p. 58). Her words imply that, in the extraordinary world of the 'ruelle', she finds herself faced with the need to choose between either picking the phallic herbs (an act of maternal rejection) or preserving her exclusive bond with her mother(s), for which the 'maison' is a symbol, by leaving the herbs untouched. Although clearly ambivalent about doing so, Thérèse continues her treacherous search for the phallic herbs.

The 'betrayal' of her mother and their dyadic relation which this search involves mirrors a similar betrayal by Thérèse's mother, which is also evoked in the 'bébé' sequence and seems to be one of the causes of Thérèse's own defection. The mother's betrayal is constituted by her imminent marriage. In the section of the phantasm in which the mother's decision to marry (i.e. to repudiate the exclusivity of her relationship with her daughter in favour of a man) is described, the confusion of maternal and filial identities apparent elsewhere in the novel resurfaces, for example, when Thérèse articulates her desire to work for and protect her mother — particularly since her 'Je veux qu'elle se repose, je veux qu'on m'embauche dans une usine' (p. 58) recalls words spoken by the mother herself just before the phantasm begins: 'Maintenant va te reposer et éteins' (p. 58). If Thérèse's mother emerges at this particular point in the dream-sequence as a defecting/œdipal 'daughter', the focus of the episode as a whole is, none the less, *Thérèse*'s daughterly defection, which takes place as she is drawn towards the herb/penis and away from the maternal orbit.

The exact nature of Thérèse's desire for the symbolic herb/phallus is complicated. Arguably, her rage at her own castration and her 'penis-envy' are so extreme here that she is seeking actually to *possess* for herself the phallic attribute she lacks, in its herbal form. If we read Thérèse's search for the 'mauvaise herbe' in this way, then it is tempting to view her activities in the 'ruelle' simply as an attempt at a kind of fantastic self-virilization, which suggests that she is in the grip of a strong masculinity complex.[29] This (Freudian) interpretation of her actions is supported by her 'penetration' of the baby girl with the chervil which, together with the other assaults she 'accidentally' makes upon the child's genitals, hints at a longing on her part to reject her castrated femininity, change gender identity and become masculine:

Je ne sais pas comment cela est arrivé mais cela s'est entrouvert, cela s'est enfoncé sur mon bras parce que le bébé n'a pas de culotte, parce que je le faisais sauter de plus en plus haut et qu'il retombait de plus en plus fort sur mon bras. (p. 60)

Chaque fois qu'il sursautait, mon bras s'enfonçait dans la fente. Je le portais. Ce n'était pas ma faute. (p. 61)

If, on one level, it can thus be taken as evidence that she is driven by a masculinity complex, Thérèse's pursuit of self-virilization in the 'ruelle' may also be understood in terms of her need to revenge herself against Marc. One of the most striking things about the baby in the alley is its curious hermaphroditism. Although it is 'une petite fille', it is also referred to as 'le bébé', 'il', 'lui', etc., so that its sexual identity seems to shift. One possible reason for this is that, in spite of its feminine gender, the baby also functions, in the later stages of the phantasm, as Marc's double. It becomes his double when it repeats the unwelcome oral penetration to which he previously forced Thérèse to submit in the taxi taking her to his hotel ('Le bébé m'a frappé sur le nez, il a enfoncé son doigt dans ma bouche. Il voulait que je la suce', pp. 60–61). The identification of Marc and the baby that is established here means that Thérèse's search for the phallic herbs can be read as a sign that she is motivated less by a masculinity complex *per se* than by a hidden urge to use the herb/phallus to 'get her own back'. By arming herself with the 'mauvaise herbe' and turning herself into someone who can penetrate the baby (who is effectively Marc), Thérèse becomes capable of committing a fantastic act of violatory vengeance, by means of which she can transform the man who imposed himself upon her into a passive victim, and can recuperate her earlier sexual defeat.

Conceivably, therefore, Thérèse simply picks the herb/phallus out of a desire to achieve an inverted, *masculine* gender identity, because she cannot acknowledge her own castration and/or because she is pursuing revenge. However, the phantasm suggests equally strongly that the impulses driving Thérèse inside the 'ruelle' correspond to what, in Freudian terms, are 'normal', *feminine* œdipal desires. Her assiduous search for the 'mauvaises herbes' can be taken to indicate that she wishes for heterosexual penetration by the herb/phallus, and for the *consequences* of penetration, rather than for an actual, unmediated *possession* of the penis. Her need to 'cueillir l'herbe', in other words, may be read as a sign of sexual maturation, and of a more 'realistic' attitude towards her own castration, on her part. Thérèse's movement toward feminine normality is suggested in the following section of the dream-sequence, which occurs near the start of the passage:

Je peux cueillir puisque c'est le jardin aux mauvaises herbes. Je prendrai l'herbe entre les pierres. Je ne prendrai pas l'herbe à la terre. C'est le jardin de personne mais ils verront qu'on a cueilli du cerfeuil. Je le vois. Une branche vendredi, une branche samedi, une branche dimanche. C'est clair au milieu de la touffe. [. . .] Si je cueille, dans cinq minutes mon panier sera plein. (p. 58)

Thérèse's incantatory description of her ritualistic culling of the tufts of chervil and her vision of the full 'panier' (vagina) which she will subsequently have are strongly suggestive of the penetration she longs for. Moreover, the 'touffe' left bare and open after the chervil has been picked symbolizes her physical (and psychosexual) state after defloration has taken place. If, however, the above lines indicate that she desires (and achieves) penetration by the herb/penis, other sections of the 'bébé-de-la-ruelle' passage suggest that this is not Thérèse's ultimate goal. Elsewhere in the monologue, it becomes clear that if she pursues penetration so keenly in the 'ruelle', it is because it represents the means by which she may acquire the *baby* that will make her femininity 'complete'. In the Freudian psychosexual schema, the wish for a baby is of paramount importance in the development of 'normal' femininity. According to Freud, the acquisition of a child is perceived by the developing female subject, once she has been exposed to the 'fact' of her castration, as the only effective way to overcome her state of lack and gain the equivalent of the penis she does not have — hence the intensity of the desire for maternity he attributes to her.[30] Aspects of the account of Thérèse's activities in the 'ruelle' indicate that it is indeed a baby, and the 'completed' femininity its presence will afford her, that she is really seeking throughout the phantasmic sequence as she looks for the herbs.

That Thérèse shares (here) the Freudian vision of feminine/maternal 'normalization' outlined above is suggested in the part of the sequence in which she describes the effect of her acquisition of the herbs. This occurs towards the end of the phantasm, when she defiantly tells her mother 'J'ai cueilli l'herbe. Je t'assure que j'ai cuelli l'herbe. C'est un bébé que je porte' (p. 61). Thérèse is implying here not only that penetration by the herb/phallus has proved fruitful, and that the baby she is carrying is its consequence, but also, more importantly, that it is maternity, and the phallic substitute with which motherhood will provide her, that she has ultimately been pursuing inside the 'ruelle', as she has sought out the 'mauvaises herbes'. There are indications in the monologue that the strange baby Thérèse is given becomes *her* baby and that, in her dream at least, she does accede to the form of femininity which Freud presents as both normal and complete — motherhood.

In the course of the 'bébé-de-la-ruelle' sequence, Thérèse (or rather her childhood self) appears then to move from an envious desire for the penis *per se* to a 'normal' feminine wish for the baby which represents the only form of the phallus she can realistically hope to possess. Although this movement does not evolve in a linear, sequential way, the phantasm conveys none the less an impression of development and maturation. Thérèse's willingness to embrace the œdipal process is suggested by the considerable number of imperatives contained in the passage, which indicate her sense of the ineluctability of the course she is following. The link between the events of the phantasm and those of *Ravages* as a whole is complex. On the one hand, the 'phallocentric' feminine identity pursued in the 'ruelle' by the child Thérèse was may be viewed as a distillation of the femininity sought by her older self, via her dealings with Marc, throughout much of the novel. On the other hand, since the Thérèse of the phantasm welcomes maternity while the adult Thérèse aborts at the end of the text, the dream-sequence is clearly not a *mise-en-abyme* of the work *in toto*. If, in other words, the phantasm helps the perceptive reader to understand more fully the nature of the gender identity Thérèse attempts to assume, particularly in parts one and two of *Ravages*, it does not tell us the whole story.

Thérèse's position *vis-à-vis* the feminine 'normality' she confronts in the 'ruelle' clearly changes by the end of her story, for reasons which I will examine presently. Her mother's, however, does not. The strength of the mother's resistance to Thérèse's pursuit of phallocentric femininity is made apparent by the description in the phantasm of her violent reaction when she discovers that Thérèse has acquired a child/penis:

> Maman a pincé la robe de laine.
> "Qu'est-ce que c'est que ça?
> – Un bébé.
> – Lâche ça, laisse ça. Défais-toi de ça. Je ne veux pas de ça.
> – Je ne peux pas. On me l'a confié."
> Elle est venue sur nous.
> Elle a essayé de me le prendre mais je lui ai résisté. Elle aurait dû comprendre puisque je lui disais:
> "Il faut que je le porte. On me l'a confié . . ."
> Plus je le répétais, plus elle voulait me l'enlever. Le bébé criait. Les doigts de maman s'emmêlaient dans la dentelle de laine de la robe. Elle a été la plus forte. Elle l'a arraché de mes bras, elle l'a jeté sur l'herbe. Elle m'a secouée, elle l'a dit trop près de mon visage.
> "Pas de ça. Tu entends: pas de ça."
> J'ai cru qu'elle l'avait tué mais il remuait la tête de notre côté. (pp. 61–62)

Thérèse's mother's efforts to deny her daughter access to feminine/maternal 'normality' have been interpreted in a negative way by Leducian critics.[31] While it is certainly possible to approach *Ravages* as another tale of inadequate motherhood, the account of maternal conduct the work contains, like that contained in *L'Asphyxie*, is complicated, and need not be read as a simple denunciation, by Leduc's narrator, of maternal oppression. Thérèse's mother's interdiction against feminine 'normality' can be taken less as a sign of maternal selfishness — although elements of the text justify viewing it as such — than as evidence that she is driven to shield her daughter from a feminine destiny predicated upon 'paramètres masculins'[32] which, she believes, will restrict and enslave Thérèse. In the remaining sections of this chapter, I will explore the ramifications of the mother's behaviour. I will argue, moreover, that the abortion Thérèse undergoes at the end of *Ravages*, rather than constituting an act of submission to a mother whose aims regarding her child are purely self-interested, can be interpreted as a radical, 'anti-œdipal' gesture, which enables Thérèse to envisage a different kind of femininity, to heal the divisions to which she and her mother are subject for much of the novel, and to enter perhaps into a genuinely intersubjective relation with her maternal parent.

THE MATERNAL INTERDICTION: TYRANNY OR LIBERATION?

In those sections of *Ravages* which focus on her dealings with her daughter, the embargo the mother places upon feminine normality is so strong that it seems to penetrate Thérèse's inner being, causing her to substitute her mother's desires for her own. Rather like Mme de Clèves, whom Marianne Hirsch views as another 'dutiful daughter' incapable of eluding an internalized, and denying, maternal discourse, Thérèse 'exists only in relation to her mother's advice and admonitions'.[33] This is made apparent in two present-tense monologues contained in part one of *Ravages*. The first erupts into the narrative after Marc tries to make Thérèse masturbate him in the taxi they take to his hotel. As she contemplates doing so, the reluctance she feels appears to be a consequence less of her *own* desire to avoid exposure to his penis than of the internalized influence of her mother:

J'ai honte sur la plage du poids de leur sexe sous le jersey du maillot de bain. Les hommes en robe me rassurent, un prêtre qui surveille la baignade d'une colonie de vacances me ravit. Je touche, je comprime ce qui me faisait honte, ce que j'évitais de regarder. Je ne lui fais rien, il ne me fera rien et c'est dangereux. Je veux tout de suite une règle de vie, je veux devenir un mannequin de pureté. Me lever à six heures du matin, me coucher à huit heures du soir. Je ne peux pas l'abandonner. Je suis allée le chercher, je lui ai donné de l'appétit. Je ne peux pas le reléguer.

Je suis soulagée quand ils s'élancent vers la vague, quand ils entrent dans l'eau, quand ils me tournent le dos, quand ils font demi-tour dans l'eau et que je ne vois que leur buste, leur visage. Je lis avec tranquillité lorsque la vague les habille amplement.

Qui m'a poussée vers lui au cinéma? Moi-même. Je l'ai choisi, je l'ai voulu. J'ai de la répulsion mais je ne peux pas me détacher. Je ne suis pas coquette. Je suis timide et je me suis trop engagée. Je ne suis pas honnête et je ne suis pas malhonnête. Je déteste et je ne déteste pas le sexe. Je suis une ennemie indécise. Je lis sur la plage, je crois qu'un chien fou envoie du sable mouillé sur mon livre, je lève la tête, je les revois: ils ont quitté la mer, ils accourent le slip sec, vers le bain de soleil. Le renflement est noir, luisant sous le jersey mouillé. C'est provocant. Je ferme les yeux, je me fiance avec moi-même. Pas d'homme: "A aucun prix il ne te faut de ça", a dit ma mère. (pp. 31–32)

In this curious passage, Thérèse seems, on the surface at least, eager to reject Marc and his penis. Her eagerness is conveyed by her reference to the chaste 'mannequin de pureté' she wishes to incarnate and by her longing for a 'règle de vie' which excludes all contact with men. Yet her reflections regarding the provocative spectacle of semi-naked youths on the beach and her disingenuous observation 'je suis allée le chercher [. . .] je ne peux pas le reléguer' reveal that she is also powerfully drawn to Marc, and to the normal, œdipal/heterosexual femininity to which she is being offered access at this point. Her contradictory feelings appear perplexing, until we reach the end of the monologue, with its evocation of her mother's determined instruction 'il ne te faut de ça'. The inclusion of this indicates that whilst Thérèse is instinctively drawn to

Marc and heterosexuality here, her attraction is being blocked by a prohibitive maternal voice, which exists deep inside her and prevents her from pursuing her own instincts.

The second monologue is more visionary than its predecessor, and interrupts the narrative at the point at which Thérèse is about to succumb to Marc's efforts to penetrate her. In it, the infiltration of Thérèse's unconscious by her mother's prohibitions is conveyed more obliquely than in the previous extract:

Je ne peux pas. Je me veux jeune fille jusqu'à la fin, je me veux séparée d'eux, je me veux hors d'atteinte. Je ne veux pas qu'ils entrent dans mon trésor. Quand Cécile sera partie je serai seule, j'irai avec ma pieuvre assoupie dans mes entrailles, j'entrerai dans l'eau, je marcherai au-devant des vagues qui se creuseront et me prendront. Je ne veux pas me joindre au troupeau, je ne veux pas me perdre, je ne veux pas m'oublier, je ne veux pas être leur carpette. Je m'aime jeune fille. Je veux être une tombe surplombant la mer. Une vierge en ébène en moi veille. Je veux être honnête avec elle. (pp. 43–44)

The use here of predominantly marine imagery — traditionally evocative of the maternal[34] — suggests the degree to which Thérèse's actions are determined by her mother's wishes. The intensity of her desire to repudiate Marc and to lose herself instead in the watery embrace of the *mer/mère* intimates to the reader just how willing Thérèse is at this point to accede to her mother's dictates, even though this threatens her with a kind of extinction ('Je veux être une *tombe* surplombant la mer'). Our awareness of the internalized presence of the mother and her admonitory discourse is further reinforced by the reference, at the end of the passage, to the 'vierge en ébène', who, Thérèse senses, watches inside her/over her, and to whom she desires to remain 'faithful'.

Even after marriage and accession to heterosexual femininity, Thérèse is still haunted by her mother's interdiction. It adulterates her erotic pleasure, and means that she is unable to give herself unreservedly to her husband, whose sexual gratification she is keen to assure, because of the fear of pregnancy her mother has instilled in her — a fear which she likens to 'la police dans mes ovaires' (p. 269). How should the reader interpret the prohibition Thérèse's mother imposes? If we adopt a biographical approach and read *Ravages* in conjunction with *La Bâtarde*, then we might argue that the mother's efforts to prevent her child from pursuing heterosexuality and maternity stem from a reluctance to relive her own, unhappy experience of motherhood. The fact that Thérèse perceives herself, once she becomes pregnant, as her mother's 'miroir aux déceptions' (p. 311) lends some weight to this interpretation. Since, however, *Ravages* (unlike *La Bâtarde*) contains few precise indications of the circumstances in which its heroine's mother became pregnant, this reading is unsatisfactory. Other explanations of the maternal embargo, the majority of which still lead us to view the mother's conduct negatively, are hinted at more strongly within the text. It is possible, for example, to interpret the mother's resistance to her daughter's normalization as a sign that she wishes to maintain an exclusive hold on the privileged civic status motherhood affords. This reading is justified up to a point by an exchange which occurs in part one:

"Sais-tu d'où vient ta peur? dis-je.
– D'où vient-elle? dit ma mère.
– Tu as la frousse que j'en devienne une!
– Je ne comprends pas. Achève, dit-elle. Que tu deviennes quoi?"
Elle avait compris mais elle se faisait humble.
"Une mère! Que je devienne comme les autres, que je sois comme les autres . . .
– Je n'ai pas changé d'avis. Je ne changerai jamais d'avis, dit-elle. Tu n'en auras pas. Je te prie de ne pas donner des coups de pieds au lit.
– Tu as voulu ressembler aux autres et tu y es parvenue, dis-je. A moi, tu l'interdis.
– Je te prie de ne pas élever la voix. Je ne veux pas de scandale", dit–elle. (p. 53)

Less conscious motives may be attributed to the mother in order to explain her behaviour. Our awareness of the identificatory aspect of her bond with Thérèse helps us to find a further (negative) way of accounting for her 'malédiction'. As my analysis of the 'berger d'Arcadie' episode indicated, one consequence of the specular nature of the mother/daughter relationship depicted in *Ravages* is that Thérèse functions as a maternal reflection. Arguably, therefore, she constitutes for her mother a means of access to a second, confirmatory mirror-image of her own self. In the light of this, Thérèse's mother's resistance to her daughter's defection can be read as a sign that she fears the narcissistic (mortal?) wound to which the loss of her daughter/mirror may expose her. The 'matricidal' effect of a daughter's movement away from her mother has been analysed by Jane Flax, who contends that 'if [the daughter] takes the male route of escape, it will, literally, kill her mother [. . .] because she cannot be a mother without her reciprocal partner',[35] and is articulated forcefully by Irigaray in *Et l'une ne bouge pas sans l'autre* ('Avec ton lait, ma mère, tu m'as donné la glace. Et si je pars, tu perds l'image de la vie, de ta vie').[36] In her discussion of *La Princesse de Clèves*, Marianne Hirsch locates matricide as a key motif within modern accounts of daughterly individuation, suggesting that in a whole range of female-authored texts 'the mother is painfully murdered so that the daughter should not need to take her place, so that she can separate'.[37] In part one of *Ravages*, the possibility of Thérèse's mother's death is evoked on a number of occasions. This validates, to a degree, the argument that if she strives to prevent her child's (œdipal) movement towards Marc/individuation, it is because she instinctively senses that it will bring about her own 'obliteration'.

The entangled character of the bond between Thérèse and her mother does not simply transform the younger woman into her mother's confirming reflection. It also leads both women to behave on occasion as if Thérèse were her mother's *mother*, thereby highlighting the unconscious boundary/identity confusion to which mothers and daughters are prone to succumb. The ease with which Thérèse and her mother assume each other's roles is apparent when Thérèse enters the mother's bedroom in part one. As she does so, the older woman sulkily refuses to embrace her errant daughter and hides beneath the bedclothes, provoking Thérèse into pretending to abandon her mother 'comme si elle était [son] bébé' (p. 47). The way in which the two women oscillate between maternal and filial positions is also suggested in part three when Thérèse reflects 'Ma mère est mon enfant que je réchauffe sous mon jupon' (p. 315). Thérèse's 'maternal' stance *vis-à-vis* her mother is most noticeable in those parts of *Ravages* in which her mother's marriage provides the focus. In these sections, it is the mother who is presented as a defecting, œdipal daughter, bent on substituting father-love for mother-love, whilst Thérèse is transformed into an abandoned, resentful mother-figure. Given that Thérèse and her mother appear to lack a definitive sense of the position each occupies, or is supposed to occupy, within the maternal/filial relation, it is conceivable that the mother's hostile reaction to Thérèse's defection stems from an unwillingness to be deprived of the 'maternal' care her daughter's presence affords. The way in which the mother solicits Thérèse's protection and reassurance in parts one and three of *Ravages* lends support to this particular reading, which confirms Flax's argument that women often become mothers 'to regain a sense of being mothered themselves' and pressurize daughters 'to provide the care [they] themselves had lacked in their child-hood'.[38] None the less, this and the other explanations of the maternal embargo outlined above must ultimately, and for two reasons, be deemed incomplete.

Firstly, the interpretations of Thérèse's mother's conduct discussed so far are insufficient because they remain implicit. It is certainly possible to find hints that the mother resists Thérèse's pursuit of normality because she dreads losing sociosexual privilege, or fears the narcissistic wounding to which the dis-appearance of her daughter/mirror might expose her, or wishes to preserve the care of a daughter who is somehow her 'mother' too. However, there is nothing in the text which encourages us to opt definitively for any of these readings. Secondly, and more importantly, they ignore the 'reading' the mother herself makes of her own interdictory behaviour. Since it is Thérèse who narrates *Ravages*, we have little chance of discovering, objectively, the mother's perspective on the events the work describes. Because the novel is a first-person narrative woven by her daughter, the desires which dictated Thérèse's mother's behaviour at the time these events occurred inevitably remain obscure. However, the inclusion in *Ravages* of passages in which words spoken to Thérèse by her mother are reported *directly* does enable us, if we take them at face value, to gain a less intangible, and arguably more accurate, under-standing of maternal motivation than we might otherwise have. In one such passage, Thérèse's mother justifies her prohibitions to her daughter in a way which helps the reader to perceive another possible explanation of her embargo against feminine normality, and to view it in a more positive light.

The passage in question begins when Thérèse angrily accuses her mother of denying her the social and sexual status conferred upon the older woman by the fact that she is married and has produced a child. Thérèse's overriding desire at this point is to emulate her mother, embrace heterosexuality and motherhood, and become 'comme les autres' (p. 53); her mother, however, is adamant that she should not do so. Her motives seem purely repressive, until she explains to Thérèse that if she is denying her access to a femininity which she herself has adopted, it is because she is seeking to protect her daughter from what she knows to be a form of 'esclavage': 'Je te portais et je me disais: "Si c'est une fille, ce ne sera pas une esclave!"' (p. 54).

This remark may be treated as further evidence of an egotistical reluctance on the mother's part to relive, through Thérèse, distressing aspects of her own life — particularly since she states that she has experienced motherhood as a 'calvaire' (p. 49). However, given the way in which feminine sexual 'normality' and female enslavement are presented as synonymous in part three of *Ravages*, it is more productive to read it positively, and to view Thérèse's mother's interdiction as a sign that she is attempting to shield her child from harm. An element of the 'bébé-de-la-ruelle' phantasm reinforces our impression that her intentions are actually quite laudable. It occurs as Thérèse, having returned to the 'ruelle' to wait for the reappearance of the baby, considers what her mother would do if she found her with it (i.e. discovered that her daughter had not after all renounced her pursuit of 'normal', œdipal femininity). Thérèse's reflections, although potentially ironic, indicate that her mother's actions, for all their violence, are designed to protect her ('Maman me l'a pris mon bébé. Si maman savait que je suis ici elle me battrait. Elle me battrait pour ma santé', p. 60). Since it is primarily the existence, within *Ravages*, of an association between (œdipal) femininity and 'esclavage' that encourages us to accept Thérèse's mother's own explanation of her prohibition and to read it as largely (if not exclusively) altruistic, we need to explore the ways in which this association is established, and to investigate the nature of the enslavement within which Thérèse's search for 'normal' femininity gradually entraps her.

Womanhood and Slavery

Ironically, it is Marc who draws Thérèse's attention to the fact that she has been transformed into an 'esclave' by the femininity she has assumed as a result of his phallic intervention and her desire for the penis he possesses and she lacks. He does so after her attempts to prevent him from working and force him to make love to her have exasperated him. His words ominously echo the reference to 'esclavage' made by Thérèse's mother in part one of *Ravages*, and are obviously intended to remind us of it:

Je couvris de baisers le bas de son pantalon.
"De l'espace, du large! Va dans ton coin! Mes clichés viennent trop vite.
– Tes clichés viennent trop vite. C'est ma faute. Veux-tu que je les remue? Je ne prendrai aucune initiative. Tu commanderas. Je ferai de mon mieux."
Marc se pencha encore sur les cuves: il sortit les plaques noires et blanches, il les plongea dans la cuvette au-dessous de l'eau courante.
"Les esclaves, ça m'a toujours répugné, dit-il. (p. 245)

The enslavement to which Thérèse is made subject by her entry into a sexual order governed by the phallic sign takes two forms. The first involves her in a servile dependency upon the penis/'sceptre' she venerates. If Thérèse is prepared to prostrate herself before Marc, it is because he alone can offer her the valorizing, phallic 'recognition' that she, clearly alive to her status as female 'castrate', requires. This is made apparent by her quasi-religious adoration of his sexual organ ('Le voir jusqu'à ce que j'en meure, jusqu'à ce que je descende tout droit dans le fond de la terre en le voyant toujours. Le voir [. . .] Tant besoin de le voir prisonnier délivré. Tant besoin de voir sa douce folie d'orgueil. [. . .] Je le vois, je l'aime et c'est pour lui que je me traîne aux pieds de Marc', p. 201). Thérèse's dependence on Marc's penis is exacerbated by the fact that he, obsessively protective of his narcissistically overvalued member, is increasingly eager to deny her access to it. In part one of *Ravages*, when she has not yet embraced a feminine normality predicated upon castration and penis envy, he is evidently gratified by the interest it arouses in Thérèse. Indeed, the text implies that her manifestations of nascent desire in his hotel room transform her, in his eyes, into a confirming mirror that is no less reassuring than the real mirror his room contains and assuages his abiding castration anxiety — which reinforces the point made by Virginia Woolf that women serve the male sex 'as looking-glasses possessing the magic and delicious power of reflecting the figure of man at twice its natural size':[39]

Il regarda dans la glace:
"Quelle barbe!"
Il la flattait avec le revers de la main.
Marc . . .
– Vous voulez que je me rase?
– Non, ne vous rasez pas. J'ai triché tout à l'heure. Je vous ai vu.
– Nu?
Il monta sur le lit avec son châle enroulé autour du corps.
"Oui: nu."
Il se laissa tomber.
"Que voulez-vous qu'on y fasse? Un homme c'est un homme." (p. 43)

However, once they are married and her 'normalization' appears complete, the situation changes. Marc comes to perceive Thérèse's feminine 'otherness' as a threat to his masculinity, and to view her need of him as castratory instead of gratifying. Her sexual overtures, whose emasculatory aspect seems clear even to Thérèse herself ('Je le prends par les cheveux, je l'embrasse avec tant de brutalité qu'il me semble que je le décapite', p. 205),[40] begin to terrify him, and lead him to react to his wife in a way which makes the extent of his fear of castration very obvious ('Tu me posséderais si je ne me défendais pas. Combien de fois t'ai-je répété que je voulais mes coudées franches?', p. 226). Confronted with the threat of emasculation, Marc turns from Thérèse to a more comforting human mirror/double, his friend Paul, with whom he enjoys a relationship that is deeply, if undeclaredly, homoerotic. Paul, as Thérèse realizes when she observes the pleasure the two men find in each other's company, provides her husband with the narcissistic reassurance he requires, and which she is no longer able to offer ('Paul rit et Marc noyé dans la béatitude sourit distraitement [. . .]. Marc baissa la tête. Le rayon dirigé sur la fente de son pantalon, c'est la fumée de la cigarette d'un homme qui se sent homme', p. 218–19). Marc's gradual withdrawal of the sexual interest for which she hungers leaves Thérèse in a state of humiliating subjugation, which she articulates after he disingenuously accuses her of losing the strength of character she possessed when they first met:

–J'étais détachée de toi. Je ne peux plus me détacher de toi. Si tu voulais comprendre, si tu essayais de comprendre . . . Je ne peux pas me détacher de toi. Je ne peux pas. Toi, quand c'est fini, tu te lèves, tu t'habilles, tu siffles, tu pars, tu disparais. Pour moi c'est la nostalgie qui commence. Je ne cesse jamais de te vouloir, toi, avec ta chair, avec tes plaintes. (p. 226)

The 'esclavage' to which Thérèse is exposed in part three of *Ravages* is not simply sexual. The second aspect of the servitude which emerges as an integral part of the œdipal femininity she assumes is revealed once she discovers that she is pregnant. Thérèse learns that she is carrying Marc's child after they have separated and his departure has led her to attempt suicide. When she tells him the news, he reacts with joy, even though their relationship has deteriorated and she is reluctant to keep the baby. The way in which he expresses his desire for paternity illuminates the real function, within a 'phallocentric' sexual order, of the motherhood awaiting Thérèse — and reveals the enslaving nature of the maternal state which, Freud suggests, should make her 'complete'.

Marc makes two significant observations to Thérèse regarding the consequences of her conception. The first concerns the baby in her womb, of which he says 'Ce serait gentil un petit garçon qui me ressemblerait' (p. 304). This comment suggests that Thérèse has become for Marc a kind of maternal breeding ground, a means to reproduce and immortalize his own masculinity, and endorses Irigaray's argument that in the sociosexual order as it stands, the mother merely represents a 'matrice — terre, usine, banque — à laquelle sera confiée la semence-capital pour qu'elle y germe, s'y fabrique, y fructifie, sans que la femme puisse en revendiquer la propriété ni même l'usufruit, ne s'étant que "passivement" soumise à la reproduction'.[41] Her pregnancy has transformed Thérèse, in Marc's eyes, into 'matière pour reproduction';[42] something which, if inherently worthless, has 'valeur d'usage'[43] since it permits him to acquire a male child, a second self. His other self-congratulatory remark, 'Après tout je suis un homme' (p. 304) suggests moreover that his pleasure at Thérèse's potential production of a son does not simply stem from the fact that it will enable him to reproduce himself *physically*. As we saw above, Thérèse's post-marital accession to feminine 'otherness' meant that she ceased to function for Marc as a reassuring mirror, in which his 'phallicity' was confirmed. If he is now able, in her presence, to assert his masculinity as he did in part one, this is likely to be because she has become once more a suitable 'miroir pour redoublement'.[44] The metamorphosis he perceives in her is indubitably the consequence of his (unconscious) belief that her acquisition of a child/penis will make of her a 'phallic mother'; that is, a phallic *double* instead of a threatening feminine other, and therefore a source of renewed specular gratification.[45] Furthermore, it is probably also the case, although his remarks confirm this only indirectly, that Thérèse's future maternity delights Marc because it offers him the possibility of (re)gaining a form of (sexual) access to his *own* mother. Marc's mother is dead and therefore lost to him. If Thérèse bears a (male) child 'qui [lui] ressemblerait', then he will find his mother again in his wife and will at last be allowed to satisfy the taboo (because incestuous) desire for the maternal parent which, Freud informs us, remains with the male subject throughout his life.[46]

The above discussion makes apparent how, and why, Thérèse is transformed into an 'esclave' in part three of *Ravages*. Her 'esclavage' is clearly a function of her pursuit of a model of femininity which, even in the 'bébé-de-la-ruelle' episode, emerges as restrictive — because Thérèse equates the 'ruelle' which symbolizes the œdipal identity she embraces inside it, with enclosure and discomfort ('J'ai froid. Je ne peux pas sortir de la ruelle. [. . .] Il fait froid dans une ruelle en été', p. 58). More specifically, her state of subjugation derives from her humiliating need for the penis she venerates, her 'amour [. . .] servile du père-mari [i.e. Marc] susceptible de le lui donner',[47] and her eventual metamorphosis, once she becomes pregnant, into a 'matrice/miroir' whose purpose is to guarantee 'le pouvoir du père de se reproduire et de se représenter, de perpétuer son genre et son espèce'.[48] Fortunately for Thérèse, the servitude to which her (œdipal) defection exposes her does not prove to be enduring. This is because two of the experiences she undergoes permit her gradually to recognize and reject her own 'esclavage', and to evolve towards a different state of being.

THÉRÈSE'S ABORTION: THE PENIS REPUDIATED

The first of these formative experiences occurs before Thérèse's discovery that she is pregnant, when her marriage is disintegrating. Having learnt from Marc that he intends to leave and to deny her further access to the phallic valorization he provides, she responds by trying to commit suicide. Despite the fact that her abortive attempt to asphyxiate herself initially represents a gesture of help-lessness, it ultimately emerges as productive because it seems to enable her to develop a sense of the pernicious character of the femininity she has assumed. Thérèse's nascent perception that her pursuit of normal, heterosexual feminin-ity has resulted in her own enslavement is conveyed implicitly at this stage, in the account we are given of a visit she and Marc make to a market after she has recovered from her unsuccessful attempt at self-destruction. During the visit, Thérèse sees a string of dead rabbits, whose female, martyrized bodies, with their shamelessly open 'cuisses', offer a tableau of feminine sexual subjection which mirrors her own state. The inclusion in the narrative of this spectacle, and the way in which her vision of it is presented, hints that Thérèse is beginning to intimate the 'esclavage' to which she has succumbed:

Il y a la parade militaire et de l'alignement de music-hall dans cette revue des martyrs. Je veux parler de régiments de lapins dépouillés, suspendus à la barre fixe, offrant l'effusion de leurs cuisses ouvertes commes des femelles chavirées. Ces cadavres cuiront à la casserole. (p. 273)

It is not however until Thérèse discovers that she is going to have a child that her awareness of the restrictive character of the sexual order she has entered is consolidated and articulated explicitly. If her prospective maternity is a source of satisfaction to Marc, it clearly causes Thérèse to see that her accession to motherhood will transform her into an 'ouvrière/machine',[49] a cog within a 'procès de spécula(risa)tion du sujet masculin'[50] that allows no place for *her* autonomy and desire. That she is alive to what the production of a child/penis signifies and that she rejects the fate which lies in store is made clear when she inwardly declines the maternal 'mask' of mediatory functionality Marc evidently wishes her to assume, and opts instead to abort:

"Tu l'es de combien?
– Quatre mois et demi", dis-je accablée.
Il me regarda.
Aurais-je le masque? Je n'ai pas le masque, je n'aurai pas le masque.
"Je ferai mon devoir", dit Marc. (p. 303)

Thérèse's abortion may be interpreted in a number of ways. If we choose to read her mother's interdiction as negative and inescapable, and to view Thérèse as her mother's creature, then her decision to abort must be under-stood in terms of her incapacity to ignore (destructive) maternal dictates. Elements of the conclusion of *Ravages* validate this reading, notably Thérèse's observation that she has 'sacrificed' everything to and for her mother, her perception that her miscarriage constitutes a 'cadeau de reine' she must offer the mother (p. 311), and her comment to the latter 'Nous avons fait ce que tu voulais. C'est l'essentiel' (p. 318). None the less, Thérèse's decision to expel her unwanted fœtus may be interpreted in a more positive way. It can be viewed as a transgressive act of liberation, by means of which a noxious model of (phallocentric) femininity is abandoned by Thérèse and her 'esclavage' is finally shattered.

Freud's vision of feminine development suggests that the acquisition of a (male) child enables a woman eventually, and belatedly, to overcome the lack to which she is subject, and to satisfy her abiding desire for the penis. The child a woman bears symbolically stands in for the phallic member which she does not originally possess, and which her discovery, in infancy, of the 'fact' of her castration leads her to envy. In *Ravages*, the Freudian penis/child equivalence[51] is clearly acknowledged and accepted (as much of Freud's theory of femininity *seems* to be accepted). Marc's sexual organ is variously represented as a 'prisonnier qui voulait *naître*' (p. 31), a 'prisonnier *délivré*' (p. 201), and a '*petit* tombé du nid' (p. 231), and the fœtus the abortion eventually detaches from inside Thérèse is likened to two objects which are obviously phallic symbols: a '*lame* barbouillée' and a '*langue* coupée' (p. 238). The full, radical significance of the novel's endorsement of the Freudian baby/penis equation only becomes apparent however once the reader learns of Thérèse's decision to abort. Given the phallic status of the fœtus she is carrying, Thérèse's determination to destroy it cannot simply be understood in terms of a (conscious) desire on her part to bring to an end an unwanted pregnancy. She is clearly also, at a deeper, symbolic/unconscious level, finally rejecting, as she rejects the child/penis, the œdipal trajectory she has followed, a trajectory of which the baby she ejects is both the logical end-product and the phallic emblem. That she becomes able to perform this act of repudiation undoubtedly reflects the insights regarding her sexual subjugation she is afforded after her failed suicide attempt, and her subsequent realization that the maternity she faces will serve only to exacerbate her 'esclavage'.

We are encouraged to interpret Thérèse's abortion as a symbolic expulsion of the phallus and as a step on the road to a different kind of femininity by the fact that on several occasions she declares that she wishes to miscarry in order to 'redevenir une jeune fille' (pp. 304, 306), i.e. to reassume the identity that was hers *before* her œdipal movement towards Marc and 'esclavage'. The inclusion, at the end of *Ravages*, of images of rebirth and renascence intensifies our impression that once she has expelled the baby/penis she becomes free to embrace a new, albeit unspecified, form of womanhood that lies (potentially) outside the phallocentric/œdipal order. These images dominate the account we are given of Thérèse's penultimate conversation with her mother, which occurs in the clinic where she is taken after septicaemia has set in and where she finally loses her child:

> Je sentis la masse de coton et de bandages.
> "Je ne boiterai pas?
> – Tu courras, tu voleras", dit-elle.
> Je soulevai le drap:
> "C'est mon sang?
> – C'est ton sang. Tu seras toute neuve", dit ma mère. (p. 330)

The reference to 'sang' that Thérèse makes here is particularly significant. The reason for this becomes apparent once we return to an earlier stage in her story and read her above remark in conjunction with another section of *Ravages* in which blood is evoked. In part two, Thérèse visits the countryside, in order to sell lace and establish some distance between herself and Cécile, her 'mother/lover'. In the course of her visit, during which she displays her wares to another mother and daughter pair, blood (specifically menstrual blood) emerges as the symbol of woman's capacity to transcend the servitude (phallocentric) femininity and motherhood impose upon her:

> Maintenant, mère et fille, il faut que vous m'achetiez du jour Venise. Je vendrai après leur avoir expliqué leurs rêves: l'eau sale mène aux ennuis, les fleurs seront des pleurs, les enfants sont des présages de tourment, mais le sang, femmes, le sang c'est notre victoire. (p. 160)

The words 'le sang, femmes, le sang c'est notre victoire' convey the powerful message that as long as a woman bleeds every month, her womb remains empty of the penile substitutes ('enfants/présages de tourment') whose production ensures her (definitive) containment within a phallic economy that reduces her to the status of man's 'matière pour reproduction, miroir pour redoublement'. Although the 'sang/victoire' association means little when we encounter it in part two, our recollection of it helps us, after we reach the point in *Ravages* at which Thérèse aborts and bleeds once more, to interpret her freshly-flowing blood as a sign that she has defeated the feminine 'esclavage' which has enclosed her. Her mother's comments 'tu courras, tu voleras' and 'tu seras toute neuve' increase our sense that this is the case, and suggest that both women are aware of the transformation the younger has undergone. The exchange between mother and daughter strongly indicates that Thérèse is extricating herself from a sexual order that has damaged her and is being 'reborn', through the anti-œdipal act of abortion.

All of the above enables us to view Thérèse's termination of her pregnancy as a (victorious) rejection of a phallic/œdipal feminine psychosexual identity rather than as a (weak) gesture of submission to a mother who is selfish and restrictive. It is important none the less to recognize that although it does not constitute a capitulation, the abortion Thérèse undergoes does allow her to effect a kind of 'return to the mother'. That this accompanies her ejection of the baby/penis is suggested by Thérèse's account of the circumstances in which she awakens from the torpor that engulfs her after she aborts: 'Je revenais au monde et, à deux pas de mon lit, ma mère dans leur fauteuil se tournait les pouces. Je n'avais plus mal et je la revoyais' (pp. 329–30).

Thérèse's words indicate that she is reaffirming her relationship with the mother from whom her defection to Marc has distanced her. This may initially appear surprising, since at the very end of *Ravages* the bond between the two women seems irretrievably shattered and Thérèse seems to have reached a 'Mirror Stage'[52] that is indicative of a definitive *separation* from her mother:

> "Viens", dit-elle.
> Elle m'entraîna dans le couloir. Elle me soulevait de terre.
> Je volais, j'étais guérie. Nous dépassâmes les portes des malades. La clinique se reposait. Ma mère me poussa en avant. Je me trouvai devant un miroir.
> "Ta petite taille. Tu as retrouvé ta petite taille", dit-elle.
> Pour la première fois, ses paroles n'avaient pas de résonance en moi. J'étais seule. Enfin seule. (p. 330)

The contradiction which the juxtaposition of the above, almost contiguous extracts apparently reveals is, however, only superficial. That is because the solitude to which Thérèse accedes at the end of *Ravages* is a complex state that does not in reality exclude her mother, or mean that the lost bond between the two women is not recuperated in some form. Earlier sections of the novel's conclusion — notably the account we are given (in yet another of Thérèse's monologues) of the hyperlucid reflections which penetrate her consciousness as she slowly loses the fœtus she has carried — make this clear.

In the monologue in question Thérèse appears initially, as she does at the very end of *Ravages*, to be embracing a state of absolute solitariness and to be refusing future involvement in any kind of relational attachment at all ('J'avale du propydon, je vois clair en arrière. Que de détours, quel marivaudage tragique pour ne pas m'avouer que je veux être seule, dormir seule comme je souffre maintenant', p. 327). However, once Thérèse elaborates upon the nature of the solitude for which she is opting it becomes evident that this is not as straightforward as we might think:

Bébé sanglant, j'étais la promesse de mademoiselle la solitude aux yeux de verglas. Que d'inventions pour me détourner d'elle. "Si je guéris, mademoiselle, nous aurons froid ensemble sur une table d'altitude. C'est là que nous nous allongerons et que nous nous serrerons". (p. 327)

These hermetic lines suggest that in choosing 'solitude', Thérèse may seem simply to be envisaging a state of splendid isolation but is actually turning towards a partner/companion from whom she has been detached by her own (œdipal) 'inventions'. The partner in question is a woman 'aux yeux de verglas', to whom she will regain access once she has been 'guérie' by her abortion. This fact makes it possible to read her remarks as a declaration of her willingness to

turn back to her mother, whom she has previously repudiated and of whom
'mademoiselle la solitude' may be taken as a symbol. Various aspects of the
text enable us to interpret the female figure Thérèse's imagination conjures up
as a maternal double, and to view the phantasmic encounter Thérèse envisages
as a sign that a 'return to the mother' is being instigated. For one thing, an
earlier mention of the 'acier' (p. 318) in Thérèse's mother's eyes means that we
are reminded of her when the frosty orbits of 'mademoiselle la solitude' are
evoked. Secondly, Thérèse's vision of the embraces she and 'mademoiselle'
will exchange after her abortion-cure ('Si je guéris, [. . .] nous nous serrerons')
can be understood in terms of a mother/daughter reunion, since their (curiously) celebratory character calls to mind another celebratory rite, the 'fête'
Thérèse's mother announces that she and her daughter will share once the
termination of Thérèse's pregnancy is assured ('Tu guériras et nous ferons une
de ces fêtes', p. 321). Thirdly, the reference to the coldness which Thérèse
believes she and 'mademoiselle la solitude' will encounter on their 'table
d'altitude' intensifies our sense that her prospective meeting with 'mademoiselle' constitutes a symbolic *renouement* with her abandoned mother. This is
because, almost immediately after she makes this reference, coldness is evoked
again, in connection with the situation she and her mother found themselves in
while Thérèse was still unborn ('Vous me l'avez dit, ma mère, pendant neuf
mois, ensemble nous avons pleuré, ensemble nous avons grelotté', p. 327). The
parallelism of 'nous [Thérèse + Mlle la solitude] aurons froid ensemble' and
'ensemble nous [Thérèse + her mother] avons grelotté' (like that which links
'Si je guéris, [. . .] nous nous serrerons' and 'Tu guériras et nous ferons une de
ces fêtes') strengthens our impression that in addressing personified solitude
and articulating her desire to (re)form an allegiance with her, Thérèse is
expressing a desire to renew the mother/daughter tie.

Thérèse's embrace of solitariness does not then entail a continued refusal of
her mother, even though the last words of *Ravages* ('J'étais seule. Enfin seule')
seemingly hint that it does. However, the sense of solitude which abortion
affords Thérèse can be taken as a sign that its cathartic character has enabled
her to overcome the more *restrictive*, fusional aspects of her bond with the
mother. That this is the case is indicated by the penultimate sentence of
Ravages: 'Pour la première fois, ses paroles n'avaient pas de résonance en moi'.
This suggests not that Thérèse has separated from her mother completely, but
that the two women are less oppressively entangled each with the other than
they have been hitherto. Our impression that Thérèse's abortion-cure affords
them access to a state in which they are neither divided nor bound inextricably
together, but rather coexist 'contiguously', is intensified when we turn to a later
segment of Thérèse's description of her ejection of the baby/penis. Here her
'return to the mother' is suggested poetically, and is presented in a more
evidently positive way than in the 'mademoiselle la solitude' passage:

Si je guéris [. . .], je reviendrai avec un ruban pour ma prison. Avec un ruban simple comme le ciel. Les plaines sont ma prison qui respire à l'aise. J'ai mal. Je suis seule, je suis la statue qui veut se remettre debout dans la plaine. J'ai trop mal. Je guérirai. Je serai le marbre de la plaine. (pp. 327–28)

This extract, like much of the end-section of *Ravages*, is extremely intricate. In it, Thérèse seems to be declaring that once her abortion/*guérison* is complete, she will recuperate the lost mother/daughter tie ('je reviendrai avec un ruban') and will do so joyously because, whereas her bond with her mother had previously represented a 'prison', it will henceforth constitute a much freer space (a 'plaine') in which she will be able to breathe and which will not oppress her ('Les plaines sont ma prison qui respire à l'aise'). The renewal of the maternal/filial tie that she envisages, since it will no longer impose stifling entanglement, will enable her to recover from the ravages of her phallic 'esclavage' (i.e. 'se remettre debout dans la plaine') and is therefore cause for celebration. Her vision of herself as an erect marble statue is suggestive, here, of the strength and vitality she evidently believes *renouement* with her mother will afford her, and not of paralysis or sterility. The statue clearly functions therefore as a positive symbol, which stands in contrast to the negative images of the 'berger d'Arcadie' and the 'mannequin de pureté' that were associated with Thérèse earlier on in *Ravages*, when her relationship with her mother was at its most difficult.

Maternal/filial reunion is a complex and potentially problematic phenomenon. In her analysis of Duras's *Le Vice-Consul*, which she reads as an allegorical quest for the mother, Marcelle Marini argues that mother/daughter reintegration represents, for the daughter, a quasi-suicidal act, because 'retrouver la mère, ce n'est pas (re)trouver enfin son identité, c'est se perdre corps et biens'.[53] Marini's point is that the recuperation of the mother/daughter tie involves the daughter in a return to a primal state of fusion with the mother which denies her access to individual subjectivity. In moving back towards her mother at the end of *Ravages*, Thérèse does not however (in spite of her poignant remark 'Je veux mourir dans ton lit', p. 315) appear to be succumbing to the self-immolation Marini evokes. What she is presented rather as trying to do is to end the 'exile' that the Œdipal Family Romance imposes upon daughters (and mothers). This exile — described by Irigaray as 'une extradition, une expatriation, hors de [. . .] (son) économie désirante'[54] — becomes the lot of the daughter once a break in her primordial relation with her mother is effected by her discovery of castration and her concomitant movement towards father-love. It is an exile to which Thérèse evidently feels she has been exposed, and which, at the end of *Ravages*, she may be considered to be rejecting in favour of an attempted recuperation of her lost (pre-œdipal) bond with her mother.

The primordial phase of Thérèse's relationship with her mother is signalled symbolically in *Ravages* by the period she calls 'Avant'. 'Avant' stands for the time which predated Thérèse's defection to Marc and which also preceded her mother's 'treacherous' marriage to Thérèse's stepfather. 'Avant' signifies an idyllic stage in Thérèse's dealings with her mother when their relationship was completely exclusive and, moreover, verged upon the erotic — as Thérèse's various accounts of the rituals she performed in childhood for her mother (her 'frottage' of the mother's 'steps', for instance) suggest.[55] It constituted a kind of 'all-female pre-œdipal realm',[56] a time during which Thérèse had no thought of defecting to the phallic male and embracing a feminine destiny/identity circumscribed by 'paramètres masculins', and neither, if she is to be believed, did her maternal parent.[57] Thérèse clearly perceives her abortion as the means by which 'Avant' may be resurrected, since after she has visited a second abortionist and begun to miscarry she tells her mother 'C'est comme avant [. . .]. Je laverai les pierres de notre maison pour toi. Tu auras trois pierres bleues. C'est comme avant' (p. 310). Consequently, her decision to abort may be interpreted as an attempt to revive a buried, privileged relation between herself and her mother that was characterized by *total* feminine exclusivity. Since 'Avant' lies deep in the past, since the kind of return to origins Thérèse seeks is generally deemed to be unrealizable, and since, more importantly, her mother never repudiates her own husband (who is none the less curiously absent throughout the novel), Thérèse's efforts to recuperate the exclusivity of the 'pre-œdipal' realm appear unrealistic. However, because her mother seems to discern and even to share her daughter's nostalgic desire to reinstate the past ('"Tu te souviens de ma grippe espagnole? Tu ne quittais pas mon lit. Comme tu m'aimais! Tu avais huit ans"', dit-elle avec nostalgie', p. 312), Thérèse's project is perhaps less fantastic than we might suppose. While the open-ended nature of the conclusion of *Ravages* means that we cannot, ultimately, judge the success of her endeavours, this final part of the novel reads none the less like a contemporary reworking of the Demeter/Kore myth, in which a mother and daughter are restored to each other after an intrusive male has separated them, and the 'essential female tragedy' of mother/daughter exile is reversed.[58]

While *Ravages* appears at first simply to endorse Freud's (descriptive? prescriptive?) account of the evolution of feminine sexual 'normality', the ending of Thérèse's story means that it may also be read as a work of considerable feminist significance, in which a phallocentric model of gender evolution is reversed, and the 'loss of the daughter to the mother, the mother to the daughter' intrinsic to that model is presented as undesirable and (potentially, at least) resolvable.[59] *Ravages* may, moreover, be deemed 'feminist' because its conclusion implies that women — daughters and mothers — need be able to access an intersubjective, differentiated relation *with each other*, as opposed to coexisting in fusional mode, or abandoning each other altogether, or functioning merely as commodities placed in the service of male subjects bent on self-reproduction (a fate Thérèse very nearly embraces). What

Ravages ultimately calls for, arguably, is the advent of a new status quo, in which 'the daughter [might] situate herself in her identity with respect to her mother',[60] and in which the existence/necessity of a 'généalogie féminine' (a recognized order of mother-to-daughter relations) might be acknowledged.[61] In other words, the 'message' of the closing pages of Leduc's novel may be taken to have an instinctively Irigarayan flavour. Irigaray argues that under patriarchy, 'le lien entre mère et fille, fille et mère doit être supprimé, au bénéfice de la relation fils-père, de l'idéalisation du père et du mari comme patriarches',[62] which means that women (daughters) lose the possibility of interrelation/encounter with a female (m)other. She contends moreover, especially in texts published in recent years (notably *Ethique de la différence sexuelle* (1984) and the essay 'La Limite du transfert'),[63] that because women are accorded, in the patriarchal order, no identity or space outside the maternal function, i.e. the place of the mother, they cannot avoid entering into rivalry with each other for possession of it, or achieve (mediated) relationships amongst themselves. The consequence of all of this, for Irigaray, is an unethical state of affairs, in which 'subject-to-subject relations between women',[64] particularly mothers and daughters, are precluded — because women simply interact as competitors (for the maternal place) and/or as non-subjects, deprived of the possibility of individuation and exchange 'entre elles'.[65] The remarkable thing about *Ravages* is that in it, Violette Leduc seems — focusing as she does on issues of mother/daughter division, rivalry and 'exile' — to articulate an intuitive awareness of the kind of problems Irigaray's theoretical work foregrounds, and appears, furthermore, to indicate one (admittedly extreme and individualistic) way of overcoming the loss/competition/fusion which, for Irigaray, currently dog the mother/daughter bond.

A feminist interpretation of *Ravages* of the kind I have offered, sustained as it is by detailed references to the text, is only one of a number of interpretations invited by the novel. That this is so reflects the fact that *Ravages* is an ambiguous work, whose complexities cannot be adequately contained in any single reading. This is less true of *Thérèse et Isabelle*, the text which began life as the prologue to *Ravages* but was subsequently transformed, after Gallimard's censorship, into a separate novella. Of the three works which make up my corpus, it is *Thérèse et Isabelle* which is most likely to appeal to the feminist critic who turns to female-authored texts in order to discover new or liberatory images of womanhood and female-to-female interaction. As we shall see in chapter three, this novella, unlike the two other works I have already discussed, actively and consistently celebrates female bonding, and depicts a 'good' feminine relationship that neither belongs to the realm of infantile fantasy (like the relation between the heroine of *L'Asphyxie* and her 'good' mother/grandmother) nor represents (like the bond between Thérèse and her mother in *Ravages*) a lost and only potentially recuperable idyll. In chapter three, the pertinence of an Irigarayan approach to Violette Leduc's work will be re-examined.

NOTES

1. Jacob Stockinger, *Violette Leduc: The Legitimizations of 'La Bâtarde'* (unpublished Ph.D. thesis, University of Wisconsin–Madison, 1979), pp. 111–12.
2. Ibid., p. 124.
3. This reading is favoured by Dominique Aury, who interprets the end of *Ravages* as a 'retour à la docilité envers sa mère' on the part of its heroine, of whom she comments 'elle se fait avorter purement par soumission à sa mère' ('Les Enfants perdus', *La Nouvelle Revue française* (July 1955), pp. 116–17 (p. 116)). Charles-Merrien takes the same line, suggesting that it is above all Thérèse's abortion which signals her defeat by her mother. According to this critic, the birth of a child would have allowed Thérèse to emerge from a state of dependency *vis-à-vis* her mother and liberate herself, but Thérèse's decision to terminate her pregnancy, to 'rester petite fille' and 'demeurer en fusion avec sa mère' (op. cit., p. 87) indicates her incapacity to place her own welfare above that of her mother. The mother's aim, in Charles-Merrien's view, is to ensure that Thérèse remains 'purifiée de toute souillure masculine' (ibid.) so that she herself is not reminded of the unfortunate experience of men and maternity which she has had in the past. Thérèse aborts, for Charles-Merrien, because she knows that 'pour satisfaire sa mère, il faut donner la mort, car porter la vie entraînerait sa colère, son rejet et son abandon' (ibid., p. 85). While the reading Charles-Merrien offers is coherent, Thérèse's mother's embargo against heterosexuality and maternity can be interpreted differently — as I shall demonstrate.
4. Roland Barthes, *Le Plaisir du texte* (Paris: Editions du Seuil, 1973), p. 75.
5. Marianne Hirsch, 'A Mother's Discourse: Incorporation and Repetition in *La Princesse de Clèves*', *Yale French Studies*, 62 (1981), 67–87 (p. 73).
6. Cécile's identification with Thérèse's mother is suggested in various ways. Remarks addressed to Thérèse by both women are strikingly similar. After Thérèse comes home in part 1 of *Ravages*, after spending the night with Marc, her mother comments 'Ce que tu as pu me tourmenter!' (p. 49) and when Thérèse has provoked a miscarriage in part 3, she tells her daughter 'Tu me feras toujours peur' (p. 311). At the start of part 2, Cécile, finding Thérèse outside their 'pavillon' with her eyes bandaged, cries 'Ne me fais pas peur', and comments 'Tu me feras toujours peur' (p. 75). Later in part 2, Cécile tells Thérèse 'Tu veux me faire peur, tu veux me tourmenter' (p. 156). The parallel between the mother and Cécile, Thérèse's 'mother/lover', works on a vestimentary level too. Before their final conversation, at the end of part 2, Thérèse buys Cécile a sea-blue headscarf, decorated with 'des ancres, des gouvernails, une étoile, des points cardinaux' (p. 165). When Thérèse's mother visits her after her miscarriage, her headgear closely resembles that offered Cécile by Thérèse, since she wears 'un fichu bleu décoré de poissons blancs' (p. 318). Furthermore, both women are associated by Thérèse with a stage in her life described as 'Avant'. At the start of part 2, when Thérèse and Cécile discuss the fleas that have infested their home, Thérèse observes to Cécile 'Nous allons tuer ces puces, je dormirai et tu me retrouveras comme avant', to which her 'mother/lover' replies 'Avant quoi?' (p. 79). At the end of part 3, as she prepares to abort, Thérèse informs her mother 'C'est comme avant [. . .]. Je laverai les pierres de notre maison pour toi. Tu auras trois pierres bleues. C'est comme avant' and the latter, echoing Cécile, asks 'Avant quoi, mon petit gueux?' (p. 310). On two occasions, Thérèse finds herself with her mother, before a mirror. When Thérèse stands in front of another mirror with Cécile, in part 2, she reflects that 'tous nos amours sont un même prolongement' (p. 180). This indicates that, on a symbolic level at least, her relationship with Cécile and her bond with her real, biological mother, are indissociable, and that Cécile and the real mother, like the mothers of *L'Asphyxie*, are facets of a single maternal entity.
7. Jane Flax, 'The Conflict between Nurturance and Autonomy in Mother-Daughter Relationships and within Feminism', *Feminist Studies*, 4 (February 1978), 171–89 (p. 173).
8. Marianne Hirsch, 'Review Essay: Mothers and Daughters', *Signs*, 7 (1981), 200–22 (p. 206).
9. Nancy Chodorow, 'Family Structures and Feminine Personality' in Michelle Rosaldo and Louise Lamphere (eds), *Women, Culture and Society* (Stanford: Stanford University Press, 1974), pp. 42–66 (p. 48).
10. See Chodorow, op. cit., and Flax, op. cit. See also Chodorow, 'Gender, Relation and Difference in Psychoanalytic Perspective', in Alice Jardine and Hester Eisenstein (eds), *The Future of Difference* (New Brunswick and London: Rutgers University Press, 1987), pp. 3–19, and Flax, 'Mother-Daughter Relationships: Psychodynamics, Politics and

Philosophy' in ibid., pp. 20–40. See also Chodorow, *The Reproduction of Mothering: Psychoanalysis and the Sociology of Gender* (Berkeley and Los Angeles: University of California Press, 1978) and Luce Irigaray, *Et l'une ne bouge pas sans l'autre* (Paris: Editions de Minuit, 1979).

11. Chodorow (who belongs to the (non-Kleinian) object–relations school of psychoanalysis, and relies only indirectly on Freud) focuses on the influence upon gender-identity evolution and mother/daughter interaction of social and cultural factors. Luce Irigaray's analysis of the mother/daughter relation reflects the more philosophical approach to psychoanalysis which has been adopted in France, and owes more to the Freudian account of sexual identity as an *unconscious* — and unstable — construct. Irigaray also relates women's lack of intersubjective individuation/boundaries to the (non)place allotted the female 'subject' within the symbolic order under patriarchy — a polemical stance absent from Chodorow's work. Both women, however, foreground the importance of a girl's pre-œdipal bond with her mother and come to similar conclusions regarding the undifferentiated character of the mother/daughter relation. For a helpful account of the differences between Irigaray and Chodorow, see Margaret Whitford, 'Rereading Irigaray', in Teresa Brennan (ed.), *Between Feminism and Psychoanalysis* (London and New York: Routledge, 1989), pp. 106–26 (pp. 110–13).

12. Chodorow, 'Family Structure and Feminine Personality', p. 58.

13. 'Mothers tend to identify more strongly with their girl babies. They do not seem to have as clear a sense of physical boundaries between themelves and their girl children as do mothers of boys. Women in therapy have frequently said that they have no sense where they end and their mothers begin, even in a literal, physical way.' (Flax, 'The Conflict between Nurturance and Autonomy', p. 174.)

14. Irigaray, op. cit., p. 7.

15. In part 1, when Thérèse is trying to decide whether to make love with Marc, she senses the presence within herself of a watchful, statue-like figure, a 'vierge en ébène' (p. 44), which evidently symbolizes her mother and her interdiction against sex. The mother/statue association is reinforced by words the mother herself utters, during her row with Thérèse:
   Ma mere tourna la tête du côté de sa pendule Directoire:
   "Je n'ai pas fermé l'œil.
   – C'est que tu l'as voulu.
   – Une mère, en quoi crois-tu que c'est fait? En marbre?".". (p. 49)

16. For Flax, the 'painful bind' Thérèse finds herself in is the direct consequence of the symbiotic mother/daughter bond and is the lot of all daughters. 'The Conflict between Nurturance and Autonomy', p. 178.

17. This expression is taken from Jane Gallop's *Feminism and Psychoanalysis: the Daughter's Seduction* (Basingstoke and London: Macmillan, 1982), p. 56. Gallop employs it, in her discussion of Irigaray's *Speculum, de l'autre femme* (1974), in order to evoke the appeal of the phallic father for the œdipal daughter once she discovers castration, her (taboo) desire to seduce the father, and the seduction exercised by Freud, the 'Father' of psychoanalysis, over even his most recalcitrant daughter, Irigaray. Its relevance to Thérèse's story will become apparent in the following pages.

18. Leduc underwent psychiatric treatment and was certainly familiar with Freud. She had read the 'Destin' section of *Le Deuxième Sexe 1*, in which Beauvoir analyses Freud's views on femininity, and describes this essay in glowing terms in a letter to Beauvoir dated 30 May 1949 (reprinted in *Les Temps modernes*, October 1987, p. 13).

19. Thérèse actually sees his penis earlier, when Marc forces her to have oral sex in a taxi. The description of this scene was removed by Gallimard editors, however, and replaced by lines of dots (p. 34). Those elements of it that remain indicate none the less the extreme significance of Thérèse's very first sight of Marc's sex: 'J'étouffai mon cri. "C'est la première fois", dis-je' (p. 34). Beauvoir, shocked by Gallimard's censorship, wrote to Sartre: 'Dure journée avec Violette Leduc. Elle sortait du lit où elle s'était jetée avec 39 de fièvre après l'entretien avec Lemarchand. [...] La scène du taxi scandalise littéralement les gens: Queneau, Lemarchand, Y. Lévy, j'ai l'impression que ça les blesse en tant que mâles' (Simone de Beauvoir, *Lettres à Sartre* (Paris: Gallimard, 1990), p. 424).

20. 'The castration complex of girls is [...] started by the sight of the genitals of the other sex. They at once notice the difference and [...] its significance too. They feel seriously wronged, often declare that they want 'to have something like it too', and fall victim to 'envy for the penis', which will leave ineradicable traces on their development and the formation of their character and which will not be surmounted in even the most favourable cases without a severe expenditure of psychical energy. [...] The discovery that she is castrated is a turning point in a girl's growth. Three possible lines of development start from it; one leads to sexual

inhibition or to neurosis, the second to a change of character in the sense of a masculinity complex, the third, finally, to normal femininity.' (Freud, 'Femininity', *SE*, 22, pp. 125–26.) For Freud, line three develops as follows. The girl who has recognized her 'castration' extends it to other females and finally to her mother as well (ibid., p. 126), is 'driven out of her attachment to her mother through the influence of her envy for the penis' (p. 129), turns to her father 'with the wish for the penis which her mother has refused her and which she now expects from her father' (p. 128) and 'enters the Œdipus situation as though into a haven of refuge' (p. 129).

21.   In the conversation between Thérèse and her mother in part 1, the mother appears inanimate and prostrate, despite her anger. Her passivity, which arguably hints at Thérèse's new sense of her mother's castrated state, is illuminated by her last words to Thérèse in this part of *Ravages*: 'Maintenant va te reposer et éteins. Que je me repose aussi' (p. 58). Thérèse twice becomes aware of physical defects in her 'mother/lover' which also convey her awareness of maternal castration:

> Sa robe de toile remontée au-dessus des genoux ne cachait plus ses jambes taillées dans le bloc. Je lui pardonnais ma cruauté lorsque je regardais ses mollets. Oui, ses imperfections me bouleversaient.' (pp. 87–88)

> Cécile revint dans la chambre. Ses escarpins neufs enlaidissaient ses pieds, ses jambes gaînées de soie étaient trop grosses. Les défauts physiques de Cécile étaient si généreux qu'ils m'inspiraient de la générosité. (p. 144)

Significantly, perhaps, Freud treats feet and shoes as fetish objects that function, for men, as 'substitutes for the absent female phallus' (Freud, 'Fetishism', *SE*, 21, pp. 147–57 (p. 155)).

22.   Voyeurism and erotic possession are linked by numerous psychoanalytic critics, because of the eye/penis parallel Freud establishes in 'The Uncanny', Lacan's reference to the 'privilège du regard dans la fonction du désir', and his assertion that 'le domaine de la vision [est] intégré au champ du désir' (Lacan, *Les Quatre Concepts fondamentaux de la psychanalyse* (Paris: Seuil, 1973), p. 80). The theme of voyeurism is central to Lacan's *œuvre* and will be re-examined.

23.   Reading Marc's actions in terms of the voyeuristic gratification M. de Nemours derives may seem far-fetched. However, other parallels between *Ravages* and *La Princesse de Clèves* — a text which Leduc admired — justify doing so. I shall allude to these later on.

24.   'Le fantasme se distingue du rêve par son degré bien supérieur de logique et de cohérence. S'il prend sa source dans les pulsions inconscientes, il a subi une élaboration secondaire plus poussée que celle du rêve, qui lui permet de s'intégrer à la vie diurne et d'accéder à la conscience sans avoir besoin de l'état de moindre vigilance offert par le sommeil.' (Madeleine Borgomano, *Duras: une lecture des fantasmes* (Paris: Astre, 1988), pp. 114–15.)

25.   'La différence capitale entre monologue immédiat et style indirect libre, que l'on a parfois le tort de confondre, ou de rapprocher indûment [est que]: dans le discours indirect libre, le narrateur assume le discours du personnage, ou si l'on préfère le personnage parle par la voix du narrateur, et les deux instances sont alors *confondues*; dans le discours immédiat, le narrateur s'efface et le personnage se *substitue* à lui'. (Genette, *Figures III* (Paris: Seuil, 1972), pp. 193–94.)

26.   See *Ravages*, pp. 31–32, 43–44 and 221–24.

27.   See Pierre Guiraud, *Dictionnaire historique, stylistique, rhétorique, étymologique de la littérature érotique* (Paris: Payot, 1978), p. 157.

28.   See ibid., p. 385. Guiraud's sources are Alfred Delvau, *Dictionnaire érotique par un professeur de langue verte* (1864); and J.-P. Leroux, *Dictionnaire comique, satyrique, burlesque, libre et proverbial* (1752).

29.   'By [masculinity complex] we mean that the girl refuses, as it were, to recognize the unwelcome fact [of her castration] and, defiantly rebellious, even exaggerates her previous masculinity [sic], clings to her clitoridal activity and takes refuge in an identification with her phallic mother or her father.' (Freud, 'Femininity', *SE*, 22, pp. 129–30.)

30.   'The wish with which the girl turns to her father is no doubt originally the wish for the penis which her mother has refused her and which she now expects from her father. The feminine situation is only established, however, if the wish for a penis is replaced by one for a baby, if, that is, the baby takes the place of a penis in accordance with an ancient symbolic equivalence.' Ibid., p. 128.

31.   See note 3.

32.   According to Irigaray, in the patriarchal sociosexual order of which Freud's discourse is an exemplary product, feminine sexuality is represented in terms of, and circumscribed by, an androcentric norm — which means that women are denied knowledge of/access to their

identity and desires: 'La sexualité féminine a toujours été pensée à partir de paramètres masculins. [. . .] Les zones érogènes de la femme ne seraient jamais qu'un sexe clitoris qui ne soutient pas la comparaison avec l'organe phallique valeureux, ou un trou-enveloppe qui fait gaine et frottement autour du pénis dans le coït, ou un sexe masculin retourné autour de lui même pour s'auto-affecter. De la femme et de son plaisir, rien ne se dit dans une telle conception du rapport sexuel. Son lot serait celui du "manque", de l'"atrophie" (du sexe), et de l'"envie du pénis" comme seul sexe reconnu valeureux' (Luce Irigaray, *Ce Sexe qui n'en est pas un* (Paris: Editions de Minuit, 1977), p. 23).

33. Hirsch, 'A Mother's Discourse', p. 78.
34. Bachelard explores the symbolic association of the sea and the mother in detail — see *L'Eau et les rêves* (Paris: José Corti, 1947).
35. Jane Flax, 'Mother-Daughter Relationships: Psychodynamics, Politics and Philosophy', p. 37.
36. Irigaray, *Et l'une ne bouge pas sans l'autre*, p. 20.
37. Hirsch, 'A Mother's Discourse', p. 77.
38. Flax, 'The Conflict between Nurturance and Autonomy', p. 174.
39. Virginia Woolf, *A Room of One's Own* (London: Grafton Books, 1977), p. 35.
40. Thérèse's sense of the castratory nature of her behaviour emerges from her reference to her 'decapitating' embraces — Freud equates decapitation with emasculation in 'The Taboo of Virginity', *SE*, 11, pp. 191–208 (p. 207).
41. Irigaray, *Speculum, de l'autre femme* (Paris: Minuit, 1974), p. 16.
42. Irigaray, *Ce Sexe qui n'en est pas un*, p. 147.
43. Ibid., p. 30.
44. Ibid, p. 147.
45. As Irigaray argues in the opening section of *Speculum, de l'autre femme*, 'La Tache aveugle d'un vieux rêve de symétrie' (pp. 8–162), the Freudian model of psychosexual development constructs femininity in such a way that at several phases of her evolution the female subject is not theorized as feminine at all, but rather as a pseudo-male. In the Freudian system, the pre-œdipal little girl, as yet unaware of her 'castration', is 'really' a little man (a 'fact' which helps us understand perhaps why the latently homosexual Marc does not initially feel threatened by Thérèse), and the mother who has acquired a child-penis is a 'phallic mother' — for her pre-œdipal offspring at least. Thus, according to Irigaray, the Freudian system, and the economy of which it is a symptom, are predicated upon a 'vieux rêve du "même"' (p. 27) and are fundamentally 'hom(m)osexual'. This helps the reader to grasp why Marc, clearly a 'Freudian' *par excellence*, stops dreading castration and feels able to assert his phallic masculinity once Thérèse becomes pregnant. The point is that by entering a state that will furnish her with a penile substitute, she ceases (in Freudian terms, as Irigaray reads them) to incarnate threatening female otherness and is reabsorbed into phallic 'sameness'.
46. 'A boy's mother is the first object of his love, and she remains so too during the formation of his Œdipus complex and, in essence, all through his life.' (Freud, 'Femininity', p. 118.) According to Irigaray, the (taboo) desire for the mother which continues to drive the male subject can find satisfaction once his wife has a son because he becomes (as Marc clearly hopes to become) a 'père qui reconnaît en ce garçon, son fils, un même que lui' and, in consequence, a 'père [. . .] re-produit, re-présenté, re-mis au monde, re-materné, re-désiré, par sa femme plus que jamais devenue, redevenue sa mère' (*Speculum*, p. 94).
47. Irigaray, *Ce Sexe qui n'en est pas un*, p. 23.
48. Irigaray, *Speculum, de l'autre femme*, p. 89.
49. 'La femme, dont il est impossible de suspecter l'intervention dans le travail d'engendrement de l'enfant, [devient] l'ouvrière anonyme, la machine, au service d'un maître-propriétaire qui estampillera le produit fini.' Ibid., p. 21.
50. Ibid., p. 20.
51. See 'On the Transformation of Instincts with Special Reference to Anal Eroticism', *SE* 17, pp. 125–33.
52. The 'Mirror Stage' denotes for Lacan that moment of self-recognition experienced by a young child as it perceives and identifies with its own image in a mirror for the first time. Although the 'stade du miroir' does not give the infant a true image of itself, since its totalizing effect obscures the 'impuissance motrice' in which the baby still finds itself, this phase of human development is vital because it affords the subject a first (if illusory) sense of coherent, individuated identity. In other words, the Mirror Stage represents a 'situation exemplaire [. . .] où le *je* se précipite en une forme primordiale' (Lacan, 'Le Stade du miroir comme formateur de la fonction du Je telle qu'elle nous est révélée dans l'expérience psychanalytique', *Ecrits* (Paris: Seuil, 1966), pp. 93–100 (p. 94)).

53. Marcelle Marini, *Territoires du féminin* (Paris: Editions de Minuit, 1977), p. 128.
54. Irigaray, *Speculum, de l'autre femme*, p. 47. Irigaray argues that whereas men 'remain in continuous relation with [their] first object, with [their] first love', i.e. with their mother, women, who are obliged by the œdipal process to break their libidinal attachment to the mother and can retrieve it via displacement far less easily than men, are exiled from the mother's body and consequently from themselves (Luce Irigaray, 'Women's Exile' (interview with Couze Venn), *Ideology and Consciousness*, 1 (1977), 62–76 (p. 76)).
55. Pièr Girard locates in Leduc's *L'Affamée* a primordial mother/daughter erotic idyll which resembles that evoked in *Ravages*, a 'relation privilégiée entre la mère et la fille, relation qui fut très vite désavouée, reniée par Berthe et de ce fait non seulement inavouable pour l'auteur mais aussi mise au secret dans les ténèbres et les cadavres qui jonchent le récit' ('L'Affamée de Violette Leduc', *Topique* (January 1985), pp. 113–28 (p. 121)).
56. Hirsch uses this phrase to describe the country retreat in which Mme de Clèves lives with her mother before going to court — which, for Hirsch, symbolizes 'the œdipal realm the Princess must enter if she is to grow up' ('A Mother's Discourse', p. 76). Hirsch's association of the pre-œdipal with the pastoral is illuminating, since in *Ravages* 'Avant' is also linked with (idyllic) rurality. Thérèse tells her mother in part 3, 'Je peux gratter la terre. Je peux voler pour toi dans les champs. C'est comme avant' (p. 310) and reflects in part 2, as she observes the mother and daughter pair to whom she sells lace: 'Gérer une ferme avec ma mère . . . Mon paradis perdu' (p. 160).
57. The 'fidelity' Thérèse imputes to her mother during 'Avant' is evoked in the 'bébe-de-la-ruelle' episode, even (ironically) as the mother is about to marry ('Elle dit que nous vivrons toujours ensemble, que nous ne nous quitterons jamais' (p. 61) and is articulated in another flashback to the past in part 3, in which the voyeuristic activities of a suitor, Aimé, are the focus: 'Ma mère entrait dans sa vingt-neuvième année, ma mère ne voulait pas voir le jeune homme debout dans les branches. Que le visage de ce gamin était grave et féminin . . . "Ta mère est-elle chez elle? — Oui, Aimé. — Que fait-elle ta mère? — Elle se lave les dents, Aimé. — Elle est seule? — Elle est seule parce que je suis venue sous l'arbre, Aimé. — Tu crois qu'elle m'entend, tu crois qu'elle me voit? — Elle ne vous voit pas, elle ne vous entend pas, Aimé. Elle n'aime que moi"' (p. 325). The fact that Aimé spies on the mother in the same way that Marc spies on Thérèse in part 2 reinforces our impression of the boundary/ identity confusion between the two women, and intensifies our sense that the female characters in *Ravages* are never entirely disentangled and separable from each other.
58. Adrienne Rich, op. cit., p. 237.
59. Ibid.
60. Margaret Whitford, 'Introduction to section III', in Whitford (ed.), *The Irigaray Reader* (Oxford: Blackwell, 1991), pp. 157–64 (p. 159).
61. The concept of a feminine genealogy is central to Irigaray's recent work. She contends that it is currently unrecognized and nonfunctional, because the 'official' genealogical basis of patriarchy is the father/son relation, which always supersedes and renders invalid that binding women.
62. Irigaray, *Ethique de la différence sexuelle* (Paris: Editions de minuit, 1984), p. 106.
63. First published in 1982, 'La Limite du transfert' is reprinted in *Parler n'est jamais neutre* (Paris: Editions de minuit, 1985), pp. 293–305.
64. Margaret Whitford, *Luce Irigaray: Philosophy in the Feminine* (London and New York: Routledge, 1991), p. 182.
65. For a comprehensive account of why Irigaray argues that women's lack of a space/identity outside the maternal function precludes intersubjective relations between them, see Whitford, 'Rereading Irigaray'. The Irigarayan link between woman's confinement within the place/identity of the mother and her status as non-subject works as follows. As Diana Fuss explains, for Irigaray, the consigning of woman to the maternal function transforms her into 'the ground of essence, its precondition in man [. . .] the ground of [his] subjecthood'. This in turn means that woman is 'not herself a subject' — precisely because her role is to enable man's access to/possession of subjectivity. (Diana Fuss, *Essentially Speaking* (Routledge: New York and London, 1989), p. 71.)

CHAPTER 3

THÉRÈSE ET ISABELLE:
AN IDYLL ABANDONED

Constituting as it does a revised version of what was originally the opening section of *Ravages*, *Thérèse et Isabelle* contains themes and images which are also present in that novel; however, the account of female-to-female bonding which Leduc's 1966 novella offers is undoubtedly more radical, and more visionary, than that which emerges from *Ravages*. In *Thérèse et Isabelle*, whose focus is the electrically homoerotic relationship that exists between its eponymous, adolescent heroines, Leduc is writing in a pioneering mode. Her radicalism turns upon her representation of a sexual bond which is (largely) devoid of the problems the heroine of *Ravages* encounters in her dealings with her mother and her 'mother/lover', and which, arguably, anticipates that order of 'femmes-entre-elles' which Irigaray, in her writings of the 1980s, posits as both culturally unacknowledged and very necessary. Irigaray calls for the coming into being of such an order as early as 1974, in *Speculum, de l'autre femme*, yet presents it as currently inadmissible. Its inadmissibility, she claims, stems from the fact that the conditions of its possibility are problematized by the non-recognition, and inadequate symbolization, in a culture that is 'monosexual' and androcentric, of 'le désir de la femme pour elle-même [. . .] pour une même, la même'.[1] In this chapter, I intend to explore the nature of the sexual relation Leduc envisions in *Thérèse et Isabelle*, and to argue that while it proves to be transitory, it is characterized by a harmony which distinguishes it from the feminine familial/sexual bonds depicted in *Ravages*. My aim is also to demonstrate that in creating an account of what might be termed 'love of the same in the feminine', Leduc looks forward, instinctively, to Irigaray's vision of a female homosexual economy, based upon subject-to-subject relations of pleasure and desire between women.

'A HOMOSEXUALITY WHICH IS ENTIRELY FEMININE . . .'[2]

The Thérèse/Isabelle relation is not the only lesbian union to be scrutinized in the three texts under examination in this study. Although Cécile functions primarily as a maternal substitute in *Ravages*, she is also, obviously, Thérèse's sexual companion. However, the homoerotic tie that binds the two women in the novel differs considerably from that portrayed in *Thérèse et Isabelle*. This is because in *Ravages* Cécile adopts *vis-à-vis* her lover a mode of behaviour which may be deemed 'masculine', which transforms her into a kind of pseudo-husband, and which metamorphoses her lesbian bond with Thérèse into a mime of a heterosexual marriage.[3] Ironically, it is Cécile's refusal of the 'esclavage' that the novel shows to be an integral part of heterosexual femininity which is the source of her pursuit of 'masculinity'. This refusal is suggested in the following extract from *Ravages*, in which she addresses her rival, Marc, and declares her relief at not being a man:

– Se raser chaque matin . . . Quelle corvée. Je ne voudrais pas être un homme, dit Cécile.
– Et même si vous le vouliez . . .
Il reprit:
– Le calendrier que vous regardez douze fois par an . . . "Nous ne le regardons jamais", dit Cécile. (p. 104)

Cécile's last words in the above passage convey her rejection of the model of femininity which emerges in *Ravages* as woman's lot within the heterosexual relation (i.e. a femininity that leads ineluctably towards maternity, and entails restriction and enslavement). However, her unwillingness to accept feminine subordination paradoxically causes her to usurp the place of the resented male, and to assume a masculine gender role. Cécile turns herself, in other words, into a profoundly inauthentic personage, almost becoming 'that figure referred to, in various times and circumstances, as the "mannish lesbian", the "true invert", the "bull dagger", or the "butch"'.[4]

Cécile's quest for 'mannishness', which is particularly apparent in the early part of the middle section of *Ravages*, is suggested in a number of ways. A conversation she has with Thérèse after Marc's disruptive arrival in their 'pavillon' reveals that on occasion she indulges in a form of transvestism in order to evade the 'normal' femininity she despises:

Je secouai Cécile:
"Où est la chemise d'homme que tu avais achetée à Riva-Bella? Eveille-toi!
– Dans le carton vert . . .
– Lève-toi, cherche avec moi. Ne te rendors pas!"
Cécile se leva. Elle arriva la première dans le cagibi, elle trouva la chemise d'homme, elle vérifia le col, les manchettes, les boutons, les boutonnières.
"Crois-tu qu'il aura suffisamment chaud? C'est un frileux, dit-elle.
– Comment le sais-tu?
– Je sais que c'est un frileux", redit Cécile.
Elle tâtait le tissu:
"C'est rêche, c'est sec. Un homme . . . et dans la chemise d'homme que je m'étais achetée!" dit-elle. (p. 121)

This exchange does more than reveal Cécile's readiness to employ the time-honoured strategy of vestimentary disguise as a means to modify her gender identity. Since her insistence that Marc is a delicate 'frileux' suggests an attempt on her part to 'feminize' him, her remarks also indicate her need to undermine the masculinity of the males with whom she comes into contact. Her desire to appropriate the role and the authority of the men whose sexual attentions she shuns is also made apparent by the way in which she behaves towards Thérèse. On various occasions in the central section of *Ravages*, it becomes obvious that she seeks to transform her lesbian partner into a 'wife' and to impose upon her the passive femininity she herself has rejected. When, for example, Marc intrudes into their home, she instructs Thérèse 'Fais la maîtresse de maison' (p. 89), a comment that serves only to elicit an ironic smirk from their unwelcome visitor. Cécile seeks also to keep her lover within the protective/restrictive confines of their 'maison', and consistently adopts a 'ton protecteur' (p. 85) which irks Thérèse. Her efforts to enlist Marc's support in order to persuade Thérèse to stop working as a saleswoman confirm the reader's impression of the pseudo-marital nature of the relationship she seeks to share with her lover, and of her own assumption within that relationship of the position and function of a 'husband':

–[. . .] Vous ne pourriez pas, vous, la persuader de changer de métier? Elle s'use. C'est trop dur pour elle. Colporteur, ce n'est pas un métier de femme! Je ne cesse pas de le lui répéter. Elle ne veut pas que je travaille pour deux. (p. 110)

The homoerotic bond between the 'mannish' Cécile[5] and Thérèse corresponds to a conventional vision of female homosexuality, inspired by Freud's 1920 essay 'The Psychogenesis of a Case of Homosexuality in a Woman'.[6] Since it is based to a considerable degree upon 'foreign', heterosexual gender positions, and implicitly involves a master/slave model of interaction too (because Leduc clearly equates heterosexuality with the master/slave dynamic in *Ravages*), it embodies what Cixous chooses to term 'Lesbianism'. A 'Lesbian' bond, according to Cixous, is a relationship which remains firmly within the phallic/patriarchal order, 'gives way to the latent "man-within", a man who is reproduced, who reappears in a power situation', and constitutes a union in which 'the phallus is still present'.[7] Since the Thérèse/Cécile sexual union is evidently 'Lesbian' in the Cixousian sense, the reader never has the feeling of being invited to admire it, or to perceive it as in any way ideal. It is simply a counterfeit marriage, characterized, like Thérèse's relationship with Marc, by 'les ravages du jeu "maître-esclave"'.[8] Indeed, it confirms the argument offered by Kristeva in her essay 'Eros maniaque, éros sublime' that even in a homoerotic encounter with another woman, 'une femme est entraînée dans la même dialectique d'affrontement au Phallus, avec tout le cortège [. . .] d'épreuves de domination-soumission qu'il suppose'.[9] In the closing section of her essay, Kristeva includes an extremely pessimistic account of the possibilities intrinsic to lesbian interaction. She suggests that female homosexuality, while it excludes men, cannot preclude a 'confrontation au pouvoir', because the construction of human (psycho)sexuality and the masculine nature of the libido mean that the erotic domain is irredeemably 'phallic' and that there can be no 'érotique du féminin pur'.[10] If lesbianism seeks to avoid the 'affrontement au Phallus' that Kristeva posits as ineluctable, then, she claims, it simply ends up by reproducing the relation of fusion which exists between a mother and her child in the pre-natal period, and generates a 'mort de n'être qu'un *on*: identité perdue, dissolution léthale de la psychose, angoisse des frontières perdues'.[11] For the reader familiar only with *Ravages*, it would seem that Leduc echoes the Kristevan exegesis of lesbian interaction. Once we begin to explore the homoerotic bond she envisages in *Thérèse et Isabelle*, however, it becomes clear that this is not in fact the case. Unlike Thérèse and Cécile, the heroines of Leduc's later text enjoy a sexual relationship which, for much if not all of the time, 'functions [. . .] on the level of nonpower'[12] and which, moreover, does not lead to identity and boundary loss of the kind Kristeva evokes. Consequently, what Leduc offers, arguably, in *Thérèse et Isabelle* is a kind of utopian counterpoint to the vision of lesbianism Kristeva constructs in 'Eros maniaque, éros sublime'.

So how does Leduc represent feminine homoeroticism in her novella? The reader is given an account of only three of the days and two of the nights Thérèse and Isabella spend together. During this brief period, the lovers create a carnivalesque erotic idyll which, although it fails to endure, affords them a degree of fulfilment and pleasure which eludes the female protagonists of the other works explored in this study. That they achieve this is a consequence of the unique character of the bond they forge. Superficially, their relationship seems not to be entirely dissimilar to that which exists between Thérèse and Cécile. Isabelle frequently appears (to an even greater extent than Cécile, in fact) to be a dominant and domineering 'femme phallique',[13] whose treatment of Thérèse is, on occasion, sadistic in the extreme. Her 'phallicity' is conveyed by the descriptions we are given, of which the following are the most striking, of her severity and her authoritarian behaviour towards her partner:

Elle était nue, sévère, très droite au milieu de la chambre. (p. 75)

Isabelle est prête à me poignarder. Cette idée me traversa pendant que je rangeais aussi les serviettes et les gants éponge sur la porte-serviette. J'attendis un coup de couteau.
[. . .]
Soudain, elle me tira par les cheveux. Elle enfonça son dard dans ma nuque. (pp. 36–37)

Son angoisse, son autorité, ses ordres, ses contre-ordres m'égaraient. (p. 51)

Elle arrivait. Je comptais ses pas dans la grande allée. Quinze roulements de tambour ont passé sur mon cœur. Que de fois j'ai été exécutée pendant qu'elle venait. (p. 87)

The violently penetrative nature of certain of the sexual advances Isabelle makes to Thérèse intensifies our (initial) impression that she, like Cécile, is a 'mannish' lesbian, and that the bond she shares with her lover is consequently predicated once more upon a masculine/feminine, master/slave model:

La cordelière de ma robe de chambre tomba sur la descente de lit. Isabelle regardait ma chemise de nuit.
– Oh, dit-elle, que c'est blanc...
Elle me jeta sur son lit, elle entra mais elle dégaina tout de suite. Une petite fille avait soulevé le rideau, une petite fille nous regardait. Elle s'enfuit, elle hurla:
– Du sang, j'ai vu du sang.
– Rentre chez toi! commanda Isabelle.
Isabelle regarda ses trois doigts sanglants.
[...]
Je me glissai dans mon lit, je regardai la tache rouge sur ma chemise de nuit.
[...]
Je sortis de mon lit, je réparai les dégâts de ma guerrière. (p. 90)

In reality, however, the relationship between Thérèse and Isabelle is more complex and infinitely more ideal(ized) than the 'marriage' that unites Cécile and Thérèse in *Ravages*. The (phallic) violence which Isabelle directs at Thérèse does not in fact, for most of the novella, denote an authentic and damaging attempt on her part to accede to mastery. This is because, as the hyperbolic image of the 'guerrière' contained in the above extract hints, her sadism represents one element within a highly ritualized sexual game the lovers invent quite deliberately, a game based upon mutuality and assent, in which conventional master/slave, subject/object erotic positions are provisionally exploited, rather than being seriously and definitively adopted by either adolescent. Isabelle's assumption of a penetrative, violent mode of conduct *vis-à-vis* her partner is, in other words, primarily 'formal' and 'ludic', a fact that is signalled by her refusal to take her sadism beyond certain limits, or to manifest it outside the exclusive erotic space she and Thérèse create within the dormitory of their *collège* ('– Je veux t'étrangler. Je le veux, dit-elle. Mais elle ne serait pas', p. 60). More importantly, she does not cling doggedly to the position of control and authority she manifestly occupies in the above passage. On a number of occasions, she surrenders her 'phallicity' to Thérèse, who takes on the dominant/ sadistic role her lover has abandoned, so that their erotic stances are reversed:

J'entrais dans sa bouche comme on entre dans la guerre: j'espérais que je saccagerais ses entrailles et les miennes. (p. 30)

– Je voudrais vous manger.
Je l'ai poussée contre le mur, j'ai cloué ses mains avec la paume de mes mains. (p. 11)

J'étais sadique. Attendre et faire attendre est une délicieuse perdition. (p. 50)

J'avais déclaré la guerre dans sa bouche [...]. (p. 98)

The erotic flexibility which characterizes the relationship between the lesbian adolescents and frees it from the threat of ossification is in evidence throughout *Thérèse et Isabelle*. It is most apparent in an episode that occurs towards the end of the tale, in which the lovers play with, exchange, and finally cast aside an imaginary penis and the oppositional, hierarchized gender positions phallocentric (hetero)eroticism imposes. As the scene begins, Thérèse is in the *dortoir*, in bed, in a state of semi-consciousness. By her are two roses she has earlier bought as a gift for Isabelle, which, like the 'mauvaises herbes' in *Ravages*, may be interpreted as phallic substitutes — Charles-Merrien comments, for instance, that in Leduc's writing, 'la rose est bien le symbole de la verge' and cites passages from *L'Affamée* where the link is made explicit.[14] In a dream, Thérèse imagines how Isabelle begins to 'penetrate' her, with her own hand and with the rose-phallus:

Je rêvai: Isabelle tenait mon poignet, promenait ma main et les fleurs sur mon sexe. Je m'éveillai labourée, affamée. (p. 92)

However, when Isabelle actually arrives, she immediately renounces the 'virility' which Thérèse has dreamt she will manifest, and which is consolidated by her possession of the phallic roses Thérèse has offered her. She does so by returning the flowers to Thérèse and by inviting her lover to subject her to a mock decapitation, which, in Freudian terms, symbolizes 'castration' (as we saw in chapter two, Leduc exploits the decapitation/castration link in *Ravages* also). Isabelle's readiness to succumb to castration/decapitation is signalled here by the reference to her 'col Danton', by her baring of her neck, and by Leduc's narrator's reference, later on in the same episode, to her lover's 'tête décapitée' (p. 98):

Elle mit le verre et les roses dans mes mains, elle rejeta ses cheveux, elle me montra son col Danton, son cou. Ma lampe de poche et le verre à dents s'entre-choquaient. (p. 93)

Once Isabelle submits to 'castration', Thérèse assumes the phallic position her partner has cast off — this is suggested by the way in which her action with the flowers repeats that which she has earlier attributed to Isabelle, and by the fact that her behaviour is described as 'severe' — and takes charge of the intensely stylized sexual 'fête' the lovers share. By doing so, she transforms their sexual encounter from one which simply perpetuates the master/slave dynamic into one that overturns it:

Je promenais des guirlandes de bronze, je traînais des roses en fer forgé autour de son cou.
– La fête, la fête, dis-je sévèrement.
Isabelle protégeait son cou. Elle recula. (pp. 93–94)

The way in which Thérèse and Isabelle oscillate joyously between active and passive, phallic and non-phallic sexual roles suggests the richness of the homoerotic 'fête' they create. Nevertheless, the facility with which they exchange these roles clearly cannot be taken as conclusive proof that their relationship represents an authentic *alternative* to what Cixous terms 'phallocracy'.[15] The fact that neither girl is locked *permanently* into a position of (masculine) mastery or one of (feminine) passivity does not mean that they completely escape the 'affrontement au Phallus' which Kristeva regards as the essence of all erotic encounters. Other aspects of the end part of *Thérèse et Isabelle* hint however that the lovers do manage on occasion entirely to transcend the phallic master/slave dynamic Kristeva evokes. In the section of the text that follows the above extracts, Thérèse and Isabelle invent a homoerotic game in which the (imaginary) penis and the hierarchized roles associated with phallocentric sexuality play no part at all. This suggests that they succeed after all, at this point at least, in transgressing the heterosexual, 'maître/esclave' erotic norm in a way that does not occur within the Cécile/ Thérèse relationship and manage, moreover, to break out of a phallic sociosexual order which, according to Irigaray, suppresses 'la spécificité du désir *entre femmes*' — in part because it cannot conceptualize it:[16]

Le trouble grandissait, le ciel en un seul nuage demeurait en moi. Nous nous appelions dans le blanc des yeux. Il fallait mourir ou bien se décider. Je suis venue:
– Ouvre ton col.
Je fermais les yeux, j'écoutais si elle ouvrait sa chemise de nuit.
– Je t'attends, dit Isabelle.
L'œil rose me regardait, la rose dans le verre à dents se penchait de leur côté. Mes bras sont tombés; je voulais bien devenir leur martyr. Ils m'envoyaient leurs rayons de tiédeur et déjà leur soie pesait dans mes mains vides. Je suis partie vers eux et, comme les fruits, ils ont mûri. Ils gonflaient: je leur confiais le soleil. Isabelle, adossée à la cloison, les regardait comme je les regardais.
– Ferme ton col, dis-je.
Le chuchotement d'une élève, comme les autres soirs, a rajeuni la nuit.
Isabelle souriait à sa gorge. Je sais où je l'aimerais si je l'avais encore: je l'aimerais sous le ventre des brebis.
Isabelle ouvrait ma chemise de nuit, Isabelle hésitait, Isabelle était avide. Je ne l'aidais pas: je jouissais de la convoitise d'une reine débraillée. Le soupir tomba de l'arbre du silence, deux gorges s'élancèrent, quatre foyers de douceur irradièrent. De l'absinthe coula dans mes veines. (pp. 94–95)

In this passage, an active/passive model of erotic interchange is replaced by one that is brought into being by the contact of four aroused female breasts ('deux gorges s'élancèrent, quatre foyers de douceur irradièrent'). In consequence, the hierarchization that inevitably arises when erotic communion is achieved via the invasion of one partner's body by the other's is diminished, making way for a much greater degree of sexual equality. The images of fecundity and nurturance which the extract contains suggest, moreover, that what we witness here is the generation of a kind of homoerotic pleasure which Cixous describes in her 1976 interview 'Rethinking Differences' as 'a sort of composite affection, a maternal, sisterly, filial diffusion', and which seems to elude phallic erotic models and laws.[17] Cixous's equation of lesbian eroticism and 'maternal' affection is sweeping and more than somewhat problematic. As Marianne Hirsch observes, the mother/daughter tie, belonging as it does to the patriarchal family unit, may be considered to be 'fraught with potential dangers' that are unlikely to inhere in intragenerational, sexual bonds between women of the same age, since such bonds stand a better chance of constituting 'a space of relations carefully situated [...] outside the structures of patriarchal institutions'.[18] However, Cixous's comments regarding the pleasurable 'diffusion' feminine homoeroticism can/should engender help us to see that in the section of her novella where Leduc evokes the fruitful caresses of her lovers' 'foyers de douceur', an erotic encounter of an unusual — and arguably more 'feminine' — nature is being imagined.

Our impression that Thérèse and Isabelle create a sexual union which escapes (total) enclosure within the phallic libidinal order is intensified by the fact that the pleasure the adolescents experience is disseminated and all-embracing, and goes beyond the purely genital to take in the whole body. Leduc's lovers seem in fact to enjoy the 'jouissance différente',[19] the pluralistic pleasure, which Irigaray presents in her controversial essay 'Ce sexe qui n'en est pas un' as being unique to women: 'La femme n'a pas un sexe. Elle en a au moins deux, mais non identifiables en uns. Elle en a d'ailleurs bien davantage. Sa sexualité, toujours au moins double, est encore *plurielle* [...] Or, la femme a des sexes un peu partout. [...] La géographie de son plaisir est bien plus diversifiée, multiple dans ses différences, complexe, subtile, qu'on ne l'imagine . . . . dans un imaginaire un peu trop centré sur le même'.[20] Irigaray's argument is that women's sexual pleasure is basically multi-faceted and diffuse, but is both restricted and rendered unrepresentable within a patriarchal/phallocentric order in which the erotic 'space' is circumscribed by the dictates of male sexuality and especially by man's need to find a receptive vaginal 'trou-enveloppe' to take in and stimulate his penis.[21] Since the erotic satisfaction Thérèse and Isabelle achieve is, as the following extract shows, highly pluralistic and conforms to Irigaray's contention that woman's pleasure (unlike man's 'monolithic', penile *jouissance*) comes from her entire anatomy, the reader gains the sense that such satisfaction — and the relation which engenders it — have, as Cixous puts it, effectively 'entered into the feminine':[22]

Nous apprenions, nous retenions que les fesses sont des sensitives. Nos mains étaient si légères que je suivais la courbe du duvet d'Isabelle sur mon bras, la courbe de mon duvet sur son bras. Nous descendions, nous remontions avec nos ongles effacés la rainure de nos cuisses refermées, nous provoquions, nous supprimions les frissons. Notre peau entraînait notre main et son double. Nous emmenions les pluies de velours, les flots de mousseline depuis l'aine jusqu'au cou-de-pied, nous revenions en arrière, nous prolongions un grondement de douceur de l'épaule jusqu'au talon. Nous cessâmes.

– Je t'attends, dit Isabelle.
La chair me proposait des perles partout. (p. 105)

The intensity of the erotic pleasure Thérèse and Isabelle discover together
enables each to commune with her partner in a privileged way. This is
suggested by the references to their joined hands which recur throughout the
novella (see pp. 63, 75, 99, 104, and 106). In *Ravages*, Thérèse's heterosexual
relationship with Marc and her pseudo-marriage with Cécile both excluded this
particular form of human communication. In *Thérèse et Isabelle*, however, the
lovers' hands (and bodies) are so constantly in contact that the two girls appear
on occasion to attain a state of almost total intersubjective connection:

Je plongeai ma main dans l'eau, je remis l'épingle dans ses cheveux.
– Je veux cette main, dit-elle.
Elle me glaçait en me choyant. J'étais séparée de ma main que je ne reconnaissais
pas. (p. 14)

– Plus souple, dit-elle, à la main qui n'était plus la mienne, qu'elle guidait. (p. 22)

La main d'Isabelle qui me troublait autour de ma hanche c'était la mienne, ma main
sur le flanc d'Isabelle, c'était la sienne. (p. 105)

Other passages within the novella reinforce our awareness of the intermingling
of self and other which the adolescents' homoerotic activities allow them to
achieve:

Nous nous accordions tant que nous disparaissions. (p. 23)

Elle venait, elle respirait par mes poumons. (p. 48)

Je recevais ce qu'elle recevait, j'étais Isabelle. (p. 52)

Je voyais ce qu'elle voyait et ce qu'elle écoutait avec la vue et l'ouïe de notre sexe,
j'attendais ce qu'elle attendait. (p. 78)

The interpersonal mingling which is suggested in the above extracts constitutes, according to Bataille, the very essence of the erotic experience, and
explains why erotic pleasure is so often likened to death — his point being that
eros and thanatos, in their different ways, both engender a 'sens de la
continuité de l'être', with the result that 'de l'érotisme il est possible de dire
qu'il est l'approbation de la vie jusque dans la mort'.[23] Bataille argues
moreover than for a relation of erotic continuity to come into being, a form of
violation has to occur, by means of which the boundaries between normally
discontinuous human individuals are temporarily and violently shattered ('Essentiellement, le domaine de l'érotisme est le domaine de la violence, le
domaine de la violation. [...] Que signifie l'érotisme des corps sinon une
violation de l'être des partenaires?').[24] Within heterosexual sex, Bataille
suggests, it is the male partner who functions as the 'boundary breaker', who
perpetuates the act of violation, while the woman merely submits to it.[25] In

Thérèse et Isabelle, however, the erotic intermingling which Bataille evokes and which the adolescents certainly enjoy does not (as much of the above discussion indicates) appear to depend on the lovers' adoption of the unequal roles of 'boundary-breaker' and 'partie féminine dissoute'. It is not, in other words, the product of a violent violation of subjective isolation, but rather the result of total, harmonious, self/other communion. More importantly, although self and other are shown to intermingle in the novella, what we do not see is a concomitant *loss* of autonomy and subjectivity. It is this fact which distinguishes the lesbian relation Leduc constructs in *Thérèse et Isabelle* from the other fundamental female bond on which her writing focuses — i.e. that which exists between mothers and daughters. In *Ravages*, Leduc stresses the problems of non-individuation and identity loss that the mother/daughter relation can impose. As the next section of my chapter will demonstrate, a key feature of *Thérèse et Isabelle* is her emphasis on the *absence*, in the homoerotic relationship she chronicles in her novella, of these problematic phenomena.

LESBIAN MIRROR-BONDING

In *Ravages*, the difficulties engendered by the entangled, unmediated nature of the mother/daughter relation are made very apparent. That the same difficulties do not characterize the lesbian bond Leduc depicts in *Thérèse et Isabelle*, even though it too involves identification and self/other commingling, is (paradoxically) suggested in the novella by references to mirrors and to asphyxiation. In *Ravages*, suffocation and self/other mirroring are evoked in order to highlight the negative aspect of the mother/daughter dynamic. By contrast, in *Thérèse et Isabelle* they suggest the non-conflictual, privileged character of the feminine homoerotic bond portrayed in the work.

In *Thérèse et Isabelle*, as in *Ravages*, mirror-imagery is employed in order to convey the identificatory nature of the relationship between its two principal female protagonists. Throughout the text, the lovers' capacity for mutual 'reflection' is stressed repeatedly.[26] It is very clear however that lesbian reflective identification differs from that which prevails within the mother/daughter relationship. In part one of *Ravages*, the specular nature of her bond with her mother is shown to transform Thérèse into a paralysed reflection of her maternal parent and, therefore, to deprive her of her own individual, subjective identity. In *Thérèse et Isabelle*, on the other hand, the mirroring process is a much more equal one, and seems in consequence to allow both lovers to gain a heightened sense of self, as well as of interpersonal communion. When the lesbian adolescents 'reflect' each other, the reader senses that each girl becomes a subject in her own right and that mutual mirroring does not engender a hierarchized subject/object, self/reflection encounter, in which one partner loses her autonomy. Consequently, *Thérèse et Isabelle* anticipates the vision of 'ideal' lesbian mirroring Irigaray evokes in her poetic essay 'Quand nos lèvres se parlent', whose narrator informs her lover: 'Entre nous, l'une n'est pas la "vraie", l'autre sa copie, l'une l'original(e), l'autre son reflet'.[27] The positive qualities imputed in Leduc's novella to lesbian specularity are particularly evident in the following extract:

La main d'Isabelle qui me troublait autour de ma hanche c'était la mienne, ma main sur le flanc d'Isabelle, c'était la sienne. Elle me reflétait, je la reflétais: deux miroirs s'aimaient. Notre promenade à l'unisson ne changea pas quand elle rejeta sa chevelure, quand je repoussai le drap. (p. 105)

The risk of identity loss and of enclosure within the maternal orbit that daughters can face is suggested in *Ravages* by references not only to mirrors but also to asphyxiation. In *Thérèse et Isabelle*, however, 'étouffement' is presented positively, as a privileged state which both partners appreciate, because it permits them to consolidate their erotic union:

Nous nous serrions jusqu'à l'étouffement. (p. 9)

– Plus fort, plus fort . . . Serrez à m'étouffer, dit-elle. (p. 10)

J'ouvris la bouche, [son sein] entra. Je croquais dans les veines précieuses, je me souvenais du bleuté: il m'étouffait. (p. 95)

The fact that Thérèse's identificatory relationship with her lover does not undermine her sense of her own individual subjectivity but rather enhances it is conveyed by two key fragments of the novella. In the first, in which she silently addresses Isabelle, Thérèse indicates how their union has meant that she has emerged from the state of non-being in which she previously felt herself to be enclosed: 'J'ai trouvé en te rencontrant un sens à mon néant' (p. 100). In the second, Thérèse suggests that far from precluding selfhood, her interpenetrative bond with Isabelle has made it accessible to her. Self/other commingling has, in other words, engendered identity instead of obliterating it: 'Enfin j'étais moi-même en cessant de l'être, enfin' (pp. 106–07).

Clearly, if the homoerotic relationship described in *Thérèse et Isabelle* is a 'relation duelle, spéculaire, d'indistinction, de confusion de soi et de l'autre',[28] i.e. a kind of 'imaginary' union, it is not one which involves its participants in an alienating loss of subjectivity.[29] In this respect, the lesbian relation portrayed in the novella evidently remains distinct from the mother/daughter bond, notably as it is depicted in *Ravages*. Elements of *Thérèse et Isabelle* do however suggest that the relationship between the adolescents is not entirely dissimilar to a mother/daughter relationship. On two occasions, Thérèse likens the almost palpable tie between herself and her lover to a kind of umbilical cord, a 'fil de l'attente' (p. 99), and a 'maillon' (p. 105). More importantly, images that are employed to suggest the nature of her erotic union with Isabelle are also used in the account the reader is given of the blissful relationship Thérèse shared with her mother before the latter's cataclysmic marriage (*Thérèse et Isabelle*, like *Ravages*, contains evocations of a lost mother/daughter idyll, that preceded the mother's marital 'defection'). This increases our impression that the two bonds are not completely unalike.

In *Thérèse et Isabelle*, as in *Ravages*, Thérèse's past, exclusive (pre-œdipal?) relation with her mother is associated both with the pastoral realm (pp. 19, 20) and with the notion of a 'fête'. This is made apparent in a passage which describes how sensations provoked by the pressure of Isabelle's head on Thérèse's breasts arouse in Thérèse memories of happiness shared in the past with her mother, and which therefore encourages us to look for similarities between the lesbian and mother/daughter relationships evoked within the text:

– Étouffe-moi, dit Isabelle.
Elle se reposait pendant que je l'étouffais et que je m'efforçais de la changer en grain de beauté sur mon sein gauche. Je la serrais, j'avais le frisson à la pointe de l'herbe en hiver.
– Oui, tu m'aimes, dit Isabelle.
Je me soulevais, j'avais les diamants du froid sur mes épaules.
Je me souvenais, je me retrouvais sous le pommier: ma mère m'emmenait dans une prairie pour une fête très personnelle quand le vent d'hiver bousculait avril, quand le vent d'été engourdissait novembre. Nous nous installions deux fois l'an sous le même pommier, nous déballions notre goûter tandis que le vent entrait dans notre bouche, sifflait dans notre chevelure. Nous étendions le foie gras sur du gros pain, nous buvions le champagne dans le même verre à bière, nous fumions une Camel, nous regardions les frissons de jeunesse du blé en herbe, les frissons de vieillesse du chaume sur les toits. Le vent, manège d'éperviers, tournait au-dessus de notre amour et de notre goûter. (p. 103)

Three aspects of the above extract suggest parallels between the lost maternal/ filial idyll it describes and the homoerotic tie between Thérèse and Isabelle which is the main focus of Leduc's narrative. Firstly, the fact that Thérèse's defunct idyllic relation with her mother is likened to a 'fête très personnelle' reminds us of the lesbian union between the adolescent lovers, because that relationship is also presented on several occasions as a 'fête', of a nocturnal, erotic nature ('Nous avions créé la fête de l'oubli du temps', p. 30; 'Je braquai ma lampe de poche, j'éclairai les fleurs que j'avais achetées, je goûtai à l'atmosphère de gala', p. 89). Secondly, the setting in which the mother/ daughter 'fête' occurs, the 'prairie', recalls images employed elsewhere in the novella in connection with the secret space of desire and *jouissance* Thérèse and Isabelle generate within the confines of their *collège*.[30] Early on in the novel, this is compared by Thérèse to a 'jardin' (p. 13), access to which she senses she must eventually lose. Later on, the lovers' sexual space, or rather the trace of it that remains as dawn interrupts their embraces, is likened to '[d]es prés laiteux et mouillés' (p. 33). Later still, when Thérèse is overwhelmed by a vision of a natural domain outside the *collège* in which she might love Isabelle more freely than she is able to inside it, her evocation of the imaginary 'blés' (p. 44) where she will undress her partner looks forward once more to the mother/daughter 'prairie' described in the 'fête' passage reproduced above. Thirdly, the account of the mother/daughter idyll contained in the extract establishes an association between love and eating ('Le vent, manège d'éperviers, tournait au-dessus de notre amour et de notre goûter'). Significantly, a similar association is in evidence in the descriptions we are given of certain of the caresses Thérèse and Isabelle exchange, caresses which suggest that the lesbian lovers transform ingestion into an extreme expression of homoerotic desire:[31]

Je creusais dans son cou avec mes dents, j'aspirais la nuit sous le col de sa robe: les racines d'un arbre frissonnèrent. (p. 10)

Soudain, elle me tira par les cheveux. Elle enfonçait son dard dans ma nuque. (p. 37)

J'ouvris la bouche, il entra. Je croquais dans les veines précieuses [. . .]. (p. 95)

Isabelle se soulevait, lente, lente, ses lèvres intimes se refermaient sur ma hanche. (p. 100)

Isabelle se souleva, elle mordilla une mèche de mes cheveux:
    Ensemble, dit-elle. (p. 106)

Clearly, then, there are various elements of the homoerotic bond Thérèse shares with Isabelle which link it to her (earliest) relationship with her mother, as well as aspects of her union with Isabelle which make it apparent to the reader (particularly a reader familiar with *Ravages*) that the erotic dynamic between the lovers does not merely *reproduce* a mother/daughter relation. Critics who have studied *Thérèse et Isabelle* hitherto have tended to focus uniquely on the parallels which exist between the two relationships, and to imply that these reveal that Thérèse, driven by bitterness at her mother's 'betrayal', is simply endeavouring to establish with Isabelle a *substitute* maternal/filial relation. This particular reading, although valid up to a point,[32] overlooks the key fact that what Thérèse and her lover are actually shown to achieve in the novella is the creation of a bond which recuperates the more positive aspects of the mother/daughter relation but which distances those elements of it that generate conflict. Thérèse and Isabelle form a union which allows the resurrection of the privileged, mutual communion Thérèse enjoyed with her mother in the past, but which does not involve the problems of non-individuation and self/other enclosure that the mother/daughter connection can engender. In view of this, the relations between Leduc's lovers may be likened once again to those depicted in Irigaray's 'Quand nos lèvres se parlent', which, according to Carolyn Burke, 'partake of the pre-œdipal relations between mothers and daughters without, however, recreating their roles.

Resurrected in the present this [...] paradise of mutual affection does not resemble the psychoanalysts' description of [...] crises over the need for individuation. There is no need to seal off the self from the other'.[33]

In the final analysis, what kind of bond is Leduc charting for much — if not all — of her novella? As the latter section of my discussion has indicated, it is clearly the sort of union which Marianne Hirsch describes as 'offering only the benefits and not the pitfalls of same-sex bonding'.[34] It makes accessible a unique — and perhaps uniquely *female* — type of erotic pleasure. It stimulates an idyllic mode of self/other, female-to-female exchange, without imposing a loss of individuality and subjective status. Arguably, it represents a relationship whose essence is predicated upon a contiguity which maintains differentiation and subjectivity (hence the insistently *singular* pronouns present in the key account we are offered of lesbian mirroring: 'Je la reflétais, elle me reflétait, *deux* miroirs s'aimaient', p. 105), rather than upon that continuity which is so characteristic of the mother/daughter tie, and which engenders a fusion that destroys subjectivity. It is in part Leduc's signalling, in *Thérèse et Isabelle*, of the absence of damaging fusion in the sexual bond she creates which suggests that her novella may productively be read as a forerunner of Irigaray's accounts of what a 'female homosexual economy' might involve. In the following pages, the significance of this concept, and the kind of thinking which led Irigaray to privilege it, will be explored in further — if inevitably over-schematic — detail.[35] This will enable us, *inter alia*, to understand why Leduc may be considered to have produced, in *Thérèse et Isabelle*, an innovative and pioneering text.

As the introduction to this chapter and the concluding section of chapter two indicated, Irigaray is much exercised by the problems attendant upon female subject-to-subject relations, and upon (the emergence of an order of) 'l'amour du même entre femmes ou au féminin', i.e. love of the same in the feminine.[36] One of the explanations she offers for the difficulties which she perceives to exist within female (intersubjective) relationships connects to the fact that patriarchal culture is constructed, in her view, upon an 'échange des femmes'[37] between men. This, she argues, means that woman has the status of object, which obviously problematizes the notion of feminine intersubjectivity. More importantly, she relates the unworkability of all of those bonds which may be subsumed under the 'umbrella' title of *entre-femmes* to the absence, in the symbolic order in its current form, of words, images and codes which symbolize female relationships adequately, and thereby somehow mediate them, allowing them space to exist and function. In *Ethique de la différence sexuelle* and 'Misère de la psychanalyse', for instance, she argues that because relations between women, love and desire between women, are still without any real possibility of signification within language, and can barely even be imagined in the ruling, 'hom(m)osexual/centric' system of representation, they are virtually doomed to dysfunctionality.[38] The symbolic inadequacy which Irigaray foregrounds stems, in her opinion, from the prototypical occlusion of the bond between mothers and daughters. The non-symbolization of the mother/daughter relation is, in other words, paradigmatic — and generative — of the dearth of symbolic and imaginary territory accorded to 'love of self on the side of women'.[39]

Irigaray's essential point (if so complex a body of argumentation can be reduced to an 'essence') is that because feminine interrelation — whether 'vertical' (fille → mère, mère → fille) or 'horizontal' ('l'entre-femmes, ou entre "sœurs"')[40] — cannot be properly articulated/conceptualized in the symbolic as it stands, relationships between women are impelled into unmediated proximity/fusion, competition, or unworkability. As long as women have insufficient access to a 'maison de langue'[41] which might allow them to speak, and speak of, their 'amour du/de la même', there can be no possibility of individuation, interaction or encounter between them. The way to remedy this situation is to provoke a change in the symbolic order, a change in discourse. The symbolic needs, Irigaray argues, to be modified in such a way as to admit symbolic forms which would allow women to signify, appropriately, their distinct identity from, and desire for, other women — notably their mothers.[42] A precondition of such change is the recognition not only of the existence and validity of a 'généalogie féminine' — the genealogical order of mothers and daughters referred to at the end of chapter two of this study — but also of an order of 'entre-femmes', a feminine homosexual economy. This latter concept sums up what Irigaray perceives to be still fundamentally lacking. It suggests a recognized social and discursive space allotted to loving, mediated and symbolized subject-to-subject relations between women. It would, amongst other things, be generative of culturally embodied representations of female-to-female bonds, which would 'correct' the deforming versions of these bonds that the masculine imaginary has engendered to date.

So how does all of this relate to *Thérèse et Isabelle*? In her novella, Leduc is clearly imagining a relation of feminine differentiation, desire and specificity (love of the same), which is not modelled on phallocentric (hetero)sexuality, and which does not, more importantly, succumb to the various instances of dysfunctionality — fusion, rivalry etc. — that are imposed upon women, according to Irigaray, by a 'pathological' symbolic-social order. This alone makes it tempting to read Leduc's text as containing an account of lesbian love which looks forward to Irigaray's vision of what an economy of 'entre-femmes' might ideally entail. There is, moreover, another reason for perceiving Leduc as a kind of Irigarayan *avant la lettre*, and for treating *Thérèse et Isabelle* as a proto-Irigarayan production. This derives from the potential impact of Leduc's novella. One of the suggestions Irigaray makes in *Le Corps-à-corps avec la mère* is that, in spite of the lack of suitable representational precedents, it is possible — and indeed imperative — to produce positive conceptualizations of feminine bonds, of the kind that the women's movement and women writers have evolved in recent times. The creation of such conceptualizations, she infers, has the subversive effect of modifying the misrepresentational images of 'l'entre-femmes' which the patriarchal imagination offers us, and may therefore help to provoke the change in the symbolic she deems so necessary. Taking the mother/daughter tie as her example, she contends that 'la relation mère/ fille, fille/mère constitue un noyau extrêmement explosif dans nos sociétés. La penser, la changer revient à ébranler l'ordre patriarcal'.[43] In *Thérèse et Isabelle*, Violette Leduc is envisaging the currently unacknowledged, the buried — i.e. the possibility of feminine intersubjectivity and female-to-female love. In so doing, she is undermining the coherence of a sociocultural and discursive order that offers women too few figurations of love of the same in the feminine — and may consequently be considered to be anticipating, and responding to, the 'call to arms' Irigaray articulates in *Le Corps-à-corps*. For this reason, and despite its apparently 'apolitical' colour (compared, say, to Wittig's 'aggressive' *Le Corps lesbien*), we can read *Thérèse et Isabelle* as a profoundly disruptive text. It is also a utopian text. It does not, however, suggest that the bringing into being of subject-to-subject relations between women is an easy option. It is with an analysis of this final dimension of Leduc's novella that I shall bring this chapter to a close.

ARCADIA ABANDONED

The relationship of self/other desire and 'contiguity' — it is worth noting, in parenthesis, that Margaret Whitford locates contiguity as the symbol *par excellence* of Irigaray's vision of a female homosexual economy[44] — which obtains between Thérèse and Isabelle, for all its perfection, ultimately comes to grief. This is because it can only exist within the cocooned, all-female world of the *collège* Thérèse and Isabelle inhabit. Once Leduc's lovers encounter the public, heterosexual sphere that lies beyond the walls of their gynaeceum, their privileged union starts to disintegrate.

The *collège* functions as a 'maison de rendez-vous' (p. 55), inside which Thérèse and Isabelle are able to create their own 'private space of desire'.[45] While the lovers remain within its confines, it acts as a rampart separating them from the world of social and sexual normality which exists outside it and proves hostile to the adolescents' lesbian union. Clearly, the school is not a completely friendly and protective environment, since although it shields Thérèse and Isabelle from the hostility of the public, external domain, its institutional character means that it also belongs to that domain. When Thérèse simulates a fainting fit after Isabelle has caressed her indiscreetly in the presence of other pupils, it is because the social, public, and consequently inimical aspect of the *collège* milieu has come to the fore, and has become oppressively apparent to her: 'Je m'étais fait disparaître parce que je ne pouvais pas l'aimer en public: le scandale que je nous avais épargné retombait sur moi seule' (p. 40).

Even within the *collège*, the relationship between Thérèse and Isabelle is subjected to intangible forces of division. The assaults upon their homoerotic unity which the lovers face inside it are primarily aural and scopic. The sounds made by their classmates are particularly intrusive, and constantly threaten to disrupt Thérèse's communion with Isabelle:

Les cris, les rugissements, le bruit des conversations dans la cour venaient par rafales.
– Plus fort, plus fort . . . Serrez à m'étouffer, dit-elle.
Je la serrais mais je ne supprimais pas les cris, la cour, le boulevard et ses platanes. (pp. 9–10)

Les cris de la cour nous transperçaient. (p. 12)

Des petites filles nous disloquaient avec leurs cris. (p. 39)

The curious gaze of a fellow pupil also damages their unity on one occasion, bringing their embraces to an abrupt end:

Elle me jeta sur son lit, elle entra mais elle dégaina tout de suite. Une petite fille avait soulevé le rideau, une petite fille nous regardait. Elle s'enfuit, elle hurla:
– Du sang, j'ai vu du sang.
– Rentre chez toi! commanda Isabelle. (p. 90)

In spite of the intrusions to which Thérèse and Isabelle are exposed within the *collège*, it none the less affords them shelter and protection. It is only when they go beyond its boundaries and enter the town that their union is seriously undermined. This is because, by abandoning the feminine enclave which is the *collège* and the 'private space of desire' it encircles, Thérèse and Isabelle render themselves vulnerable, unwittingly, to an order of sociosexual conventionality and of lack and disjunction within which their relationship becomes anomalous. The unease and reluctance Thérèse manifests when Isabelle informs her that the two of them are to visit the local doctor suggests that she unconsciously intuits what lies in store for them once they pass through the 'sortie interdite' (p. 46) of the school ('– On était bien ici, dis-je dans le brouhaha. [. . .] Nos rapports se défaisaient, mon cœur n'avait plus de forces. Sortir avec elle, c'était incroyable', p. 59). Isabelle, however, is determined that their excursion should take place, since she believes that it will provide them with an opportunity to love each other less inhibitedly than they can in the *collège*. It is for this reason that she takes Thérèse, once they have left the school, to Mme Algazine's brothel.

Like the *collège*, Mme Algazine's establishment is a 'maison de rendez-vous'; however, its effect upon the lovers' homoerotic unity, unlike that of the *collège*, is wholly injurious. Because it is a public place, a site of 'normal', heterosexual, and commercial love, it represents the very antithesis of the 'private space of desire' to which the school affords Thérèse and Isabelle access. That it will impose division and disharmony upon the lovers is suggested even before they enter it. As they hesitate before the door of the 'maison' and Isabelle endeavours to convince her partner that they should go in, the images of separation and amputation contained in the description of their surroundings intimate to the reader the fate that awaits them:

> Nous arrivions sur une place avec une ronde d'arbres tout en moignons.
> – Tu te décides?
> – Je n'ose pas, dis-je.
> Nous tournions, furieusement autour des arbres amputés.
> – Alors? C'est oui ou c'est non?
> – Nous étions bien dans le collège . . .
> – On sera bien mieux que dans le collège, dit Isabelle. (p. 65)

The hostility of the brothel environment, and its status as part of a dominant heterosexual order that will damage the lovers' homoerotic, identificatory bond, are further implied by the account we are given of the interior of the 'maison' and of the individuals Thérèse and Isabelle encounter once they enter it. The brothel represents a grotesque travesty of the secret erotic universe they create at night, in the *dortoir* of their *collège*. This universe and the *jouissance* it affords the adolescents are consistently associated in the novella with the pastoral, the natural, and the wild.[46] The absurdly genteel, vulgar décor of Mme Algazine's 'dress shop' seems to parody, ironically, the savage, verdant imaginary world which is the arena for their nocturnal embraces:

> [Il y avait] une courette agréablement encombrée de bégonias tubéreux, de lierres, de géraniums-lierres, de vignes en pot, de fougères, d'arrosoirs, d'étagères pour les plantes.
> [. . .]
> Isabelle regardait un tableau avec des rochers orange, des vagues de confiture bleue. Les oiseaux qui chantaient dans les cages commentaient ce tableau. (p. 67)

The inhabitants of the 'maison', its proprietress and her bearded client, appear as (covertly) antagonistic to the lesbian lovers as the milieu in which Thérèse and Isabelle come across them. Both are superficially welcoming and even protective, but seek in their different ways to exploit the adolescents. The exaggerated politeness the 'barbu' displays when they first encounter him ('– Vous permettez, dit un barbu, vous permettez à moins que vous n'ayez sonné. Dans ce cas . . .', p. 66) barely conceals a voyeuristic curiosity regarding their 'aberrant' sexuality ('– Vous connaissez sans doute le chemin, insinua-t-il d'une voix gourmande qui ne ressemblait pas à sa voix de dehors', p. 66). The 'maternal' kindliness Mme Algazine manifests ('– Entrez, mais entrez donc . . . La voix venait d'une montagne de bienveillance', p. 67) masks a desire to profit financially from the lovers' need for privacy (– L'électricité coûte cher, le pétrôle aussi, l'huile aussi, les allumettes aussi. Tout coûte cher, dit Mme Algazine avec la voix de sa vraie nature', p. 70). Moreover, Mme Algazine and the 'barbu' seem the very embodiment of a heterosexual *état civil* in which the ineffable union Thérèse and Isabelle have forged inside the *collège* is metamorphosed into something that is freakish and asocial. They form a legislative, quasi-parental couple, whose reactions convey to the lovers that the bond they share is 'abnormal'. Mme Algazine's dismissive treatment of the adolescents makes this particularly apparent:

Isabelle se leva:
  – Nous sommes ici pour une chambre.
Mme Algazine nous considérait et jouait avec son collier.
  – Nous désirons la louer pour une heure environ, dit Isabelle.
La cage accrochée à l'anneau de la suspension se balançait, l'oiseau pépiait sous la coupole de porcelaine.
  – Je vois, dit Mme Algazine.
Elle rejeta son collier de perles dans son dos.
  – Vous êtes mineures, dit-elle. (p. 68)

  – Nous voulons vous louer une chambre, vous dis-je.
Mme Algazine ouvrit ses yeux:
  – Pourquoi ne m'avez-vous dit cela en arrivant, mes petites filles?
  – On vous l'a dit.
Les ailes, parfois, se meurtrissaient aux barreaux des cages, la blessure dans notre esprit était grise.
  – Vous êtes mineures? . . . Évidemment. (p. 69)

It is when Thérèse and Isabelle reach the room Mme Algazine rents them that the inimical character of the public/heterosexual space manifests itself most clearly, and it becomes obvious that by entering the brothel the lovers have entered a world governed by lack and disunity. The accelerated, feverish nature of the caresses Isabelle and Thérèse exchange inside the room indicates to the reader that they are reacting unconsciously to the hostility of their environment and are attempting to combat it by racing through as many of their habitual erotic rituals as possible. Their failure to 'recognize' each other as they do so hints that their efforts are likely to be in vain:

Ma bouche rencontra sa bouche comme la feuille morte la terre. Nous nous sommes baignées dans ce long baiser, nous avons récité nos litanies sans paroles, nous avons été gourmandes, nous avons barbouillé notre visage avec la salive que nous échangions, nous nous sommes regardées sans nous reconnaître. (p. 71)

In the brothel bedroom, the forces of disjunction the lovers encounter even in the *collège* gain significantly in intensity. As in the school, these forces manifest themselves aurally and visually. Whereas Thérèse and Isabelle were able however, while they remained inside the *collège*, to transcend them, they find it increasingly difficult to do so in Mme Algazine's 'maison'. The sounds which damage and undermine their unity and their erotic communion are those made by a heterosexual couple in an adjoining room. Thérèse's growing preoccupation with these noises (whose 'regular' rhythm makes the heterosexuality of the couple quite apparent) inhibits the pleasure to which the lovers' erotic exchanges have accustomed them:

> – On remue dans la chambre à côté, dis-je.
> Elle se dressa. Je la dévastais lorsque je la faisais attendre.
> [. . .]
> – Je veux que tu viennes, dit Isabelle.
> – Le bruit de notre lit la nuit . . .
> – Ce n'est pas le bruit de notre lit la nuit, dit Isabelle.
> Je prêtai l'oreille. Le rythme régulier ne ressemblait pas au rythme saccadé dans la cellule d'Isabelle.
> – Qui est-ce?
> – Un couple. (pp. 71–73)

The scopic assaults to which the adolescents are subjected in their rented bedroom are the work of a faceless (and possibly imaginary) voyeur, whose diaphanous but intrusive presence Thérèse strongly intuits. The voyeurism episode chronicled in this part of *Thérèse et Isabelle* inevitably reminds us of the section of *Ravages* in which Marc spies on Thérèse and Cécile; however, in contrast to that scene, we — like Leduc's lovers — do not know the identity of the voyeur hiding in Mme Algazine's 'maison de rendez-vous', and are not even sure that he/she exists. The existence in *Ravages* as well as in *Thérèse et Isabelle* of 'scenes of spying' makes plain the thematic centrality, in Leduc's writing, of 'le regard'. Interestingly, *La Bâtarde* contains a further scene of voyeurism, which also takes place in a 'maison de rendez-vous', in the Rue Godot de Mauroy in Paris (see *La Bâtarde*, pp. 225–30). In this third episode, Leduc's protagonist Violette makes love to her lesbian partner Hermine in front of a male voyeur, who is paying for the privilege of watching them, in order to buy a green lacquer table she covets, and, arguably, to 'usurp' the virility of the male observer.[47] Violette's behaviour and responses here differ considerably from those of the heroine/narrator of *Thérèse et Isabelle*, who feels nothing but fear once she senses that she and her partner are being scrutinized by a third party. The terror Thérèse experiences, which Isabelle does not share, increases the disharmony between the adolescent lovers, and prevents them from attaining the state of mutual satisfaction they normally achieve:

> – Il y quelqu'un. Je l'ai vu.
> – Tu me tortures!, dit Isabelle. (p. 79)

> – Tu es infernale. Je finirai par te maudire, dit Isabelle, qui se crispait.
> – On nous voit, on nous regarde, me suis-je plainte.
> – Où cela?
> Isabelle s'était remise sur le ventre: elle secouait les barreaux du lit.
> – Il y a un œil. Je le vois.

– Tais-toi, tais-toi! Presque . . . Presque . . . Cela monte, cela monte, dit Isabelle. Elle se tourna sur le dos, elle plia ses jambes qu'elle ramena au creux de son estomac. Elle se consumait.
– C'est ma faute si tu n'as rien, dis-je.
– Je n'aurai rien et c'est ta faute, dit Isabelle.
– Sur la vitre . . . L'œil . . . (p. 80)

The forces of division to which Thérèse and Isabelle are exposed in Mme Algazine's establishment have a profoundly destabilizing effect upon their relationship. Each girl reacts to them in a very different fashion. Thérèse seems to feel compelled, particularly by the aural intrusions she and Isabelle encounter, to distance herself from her lover and from the homoerotic union which has hitherto satisfied her entirely. This is suggested by the description we are given of the mesmeric effect the sounds made by the heterosexual couple in the next room exert upon her:

– Le bruit recommence.
Je ne pouvais pas m'arracher à cette cadence régulière.
– Écoute!
– Je n'entends rien, dit Isabelle.
J'étais captive du rythme, j'étais condamnée à le suivre, à le souhaiter, à le redouter, à me rapprocher de lui. (p. 74)

This passage indicates that at this stage Thérèse is being powerfully, if unconsciously, drawn to the sexual 'normality' embodied by the couple whose activities she overhears. Her perception of their rhythm as captivating, regular, and somehow *souhaitable* implies this strongly, and suggests that she is succumbing here not to the influence of an intrusive, phallic/paternal male, as the (œdipal) heroine of *Ravages* does, but rather to the less palpable, insidious imperatives of the order of heterosexual and social conventionality to which she and Isabelle have ill-advisedly exposed themselves. Our sense that this is the case is strengthened by the fact that whereas Isabelle is able to ignore and dismiss their aroused neighbours, Thérèse becomes increasingly willing to accord them importance:

On ouvrit, on referma une porte.
– C'est *le* couple!
Isabelle étouffa un bâillement:
– Oui, *un* couple. (p. 77, my emphasis)

The reader's impression that Thérèse is being pulled in the brothel towards sexual 'normality' is further reinforced by the account the episode contains of her uncharacteristically negative reaction to the sight of Isabelle's vagina. Normally, she idolizes its complex and convoluted form; here, however, she appears to long for contact with a more simple, and different, sex organ, the penis her lesbian partner lacks. Indeed, Thérèse may be considered to manifest at this point the contempt for the female 'sexe qui n'en est pas un' that Irigaray suggests to be the norm in a patriarchal cultural order in which the phallus and the 'phallomorphic' — the single, the stable and the unified — are privileged:[48]

> Elle ōuvrait ses cuisses.
> – Si tu ne veux pas, dis-le.
> Je plongeai dans le sexe. J'aurais mieux aimé qu'il fût plus simple. J'avais presque envie de le recoudre partout. (p. 77)

Another, apparently innocent reflection of Thérèse's strengthens still further our sense that in the 'maison de rendez-vous' she becomes increasingly alienated from the homoerotic rites which, in the collège, satisfied her completely:

> – Longtemps, longtemps, psalmodiait Isabelle.
> Je donnais comme un disque détraqué qui se répète. Son plaisir commençait chez moi. Je revins à l'air libre. (p. 78)

The image of the 'disque détraqué' contained in the above extract suggests to the reader that Thérèse feels that in loving Isabelle she has somehow followed the wrong course, or gone astray, and that her lesbian eroticism constitutes a sexual aberration — particularly since the notion of 'détraquement' is also associated with lesbianism (as aberration) in Ravages, by Marc ('[Marc] me lâcha: "Toi, les femmes t'ont détraquée"', p. 244). The repetitive licking of her lover's genitals in which their homoerotic exchange involves her, even though it assures not only Isabelle's pleasure but also her own, seems at this point almost to be a source of irritation to Thérèse, which she is keen to abandon ('Je revins à l'air libre'). This, along with the other elements of the brothel episode I have outlined, leaves the reader with a growing conviction that Thérèse submits in the 'maison' to the lure of 'normality', and that her submission is the consequence of the disruptions to which her union with Isabelle is made susceptible within the malevolent confines of Mme Algazine's establishment.

Isabelle's reaction to the forces of division she encounters in the brothel differs from Thérèse's. Faced with these forces and with their alienating effect upon her lover, her response is to assume a more dominant, 'phallic' stance vis-à-vis Thérèse than she has previously sought to do. As Thérèse becomes increasingly uneasy and distant, Isabelle manifests more strongly her capacity for (phallic, objectifying) violence, with the result that this ceases to seem merely ludic or ritualized, as it does in the collège, and instead becomes genuinely menacing. The reader senses that whereas, in their 'private space of desire', Isabelle's violence contributes positively to the carnivalesque sexual games in which she and Thérèse indulge, it becomes potentially destructive in the brothel, and consequently exposes the relation between the adolescents to the 'ravages du jeu "maître-esclave"' Kristeva associates with (phallic) eroticism. This becomes particularly apparent at the point in the brothel episode at which Thérèse's obsession with the heterosexual couple reaches its climax:

– Moins de bruit. On se plaint, dis-je.

Quelqu'un était emmuré dans la chambre à côté de la nôtre, quelqu'un qui essayait de s'enfuir et qui n'y arrivait pas.

Isabelle limait ses ongles.

– Empêche-moi d'entendre! dis-je. Tiens, tu as une nouvelle lime . . .   – J'en ai plusieurs, dit Isabelle.

Isabelle continuait de limer l'ongle du pouce.

La dernière plainte monta jusqu'à l'étoile polaire. La lime d'Isabelle grignotait le silence.

Isabelle remit sa lime dans son sac à main:

– Nous perdons notre temps. Pourquoi avons-nous loué cette chambre?

– Je ne sais plus, dis-je.

Isabelle me gifla.

– Je ne sais plus, je ne sais plus . . .

Isabelle me donna une autre gifle.

– C'est un couple. Il y a un couple près de nous, dis-je.

Elle prit le guéridon, elle le lança contre le marbre de la cheminée. La fureur d'Isabelle m'enchantait. (pp. 74–75)

Two of Isabelle's actions in the above extract highlight the extent to which she modifies her behaviour towards Thérèse inside the antagonistic universe of the brothel, and hint at the further disequilibrium this provokes within the adolescents' relationship. Firstly, the account the passage contains of her activities with her nail file suggests that in the rented bedroom she feels compelled seriously to seek out a position of mastery, instead of simply playing with 'phallicity' as she has done before. In the *collège*, she stops using her 'lime' (a power symbol) in Thérèse's presence and throws it away, because she perceives that her possession of it reveals her capacity to be a dominant 'femme phallique', and threatens the harmony of her ('feminine') union with her lover:

– Ne limez pas vos ongles. Cessez.

Isabelle ouvrit la fenêtre de ma cellule.

– Vous avez jeté votre lime?

– Elle vous déplaisait, dit Isabelle. (p. 36)

In the brothel, however, Isabelle is driven to flaunt her 'lime' before Thérèse and, implicitly, to indulge in the kind of symbolic phallic power-play she has hitherto avoided. Secondly, the blows she inflicts upon Thérèse in the latter part of the extract also indicate that the nature of her response to her lover is undergoing a metamorphosis. The desire to strike Thérèse which Isabelle manifests in the brothel bedroom, since she has earlier suppressed it within the *collège*, confirms the reader's impression that in Mme Algazine's 'maison' she succumbs to a new determination to accede definitively to a position of domination. If, in other words, Thérèse feels tempted in the 'normal' space of the brothel simply to turn away from her 'aberrant' homoerotic union with her lover, Isabelle's reaction is to try to transform that union into a power relation in which it is she who has the upper hand, and to erode the intersubjective equality that previously characterized it. The reader senses that her attempt to assume a position of mastery partly reflects her belief that this will aid her to reawaken Thérèse's flagging sexual attention. That she succeeds in doing so is indicated by the reference at the end of the passage to the perverse satisfaction her violence arouses in Thérèse ('La fureur d'Isabelle m'enchantait'). In spite of this, however, it is clear that the blissful self/other communion the lovers' embraces habitually allow them to achieve inside the *collège* is shattered within the 'maison de rendez-vous'.

The privileged nature of the intersubjective union Thérèse and Isabelle enjoy inside their secret erotic universe is suggested, as we saw earlier, by evocations of their capacity for mutual, non-hierarchized reflection. The disintegration, in the public/heterosexual space of the brothel, of the communion the lovers usually share is also conveyed through references to mirroring. The brothel bedroom contains a real mirror, in which Thérèse focuses first upon the ghostly reflection of the (heterosexual) couples who have used the room in the past and who now fascinate her, then upon that of the couple she and Isabelle form, and lastly upon her own, individual reflection, with which she becomes increasingly preoccupied. The description we are given of her activities before the glass strongly suggests that she is ceasing here to rely on her mirror/lover Isabelle and on their specular bond in order to derive a sense of identity, and is instead beginning to pursue a new state of subjective isolation, from which Isabelle is excluded. This, more than any other aspect of the brothel episode, is indicative of the depredations inflicted upon the lovers' homoerotic union by and within the order of 'normality' they encounter inside the 'maison':

Je tombai sur Isabelle, je déshabillai la forme des jambes, du cou-de-pied, je me vis dans la glace. La chambre était vieille, la glace me renvoyait les croupes et les caresses des couples. Je mis sa jambe dans mes bras, je la frôlai avec mon menton, ma joue, mes lèvres. Je flattais un archet, le miroir me montrait ce que je faisais, les gifles qu'elle m'avait données m'excitaient.

– Tu me fuis, dit-elle.

Je regardais dans la glace ses mains jointes sur sa toison, j'avais un plaisir de solitaire.

– Tu ne te déshabilles pas comme moi? dit Isabelle.

J'embrassais son genou, je me regardais dans le miroir, je m'aimais dans mon regard.

– Tu me négliges, dit Isabelle.

Je me séparai du miroir: le sexe des douces profondeurs. Mais le miroir m'attirait, le miroir me redemandait pour d'autres caresses solitaires. Je caressai les lèvres et la toison d'Isabelle avec son doigt. J'avais le poids du plaisir sur ma nuque.

– Qu'est-ce que tu fais?

– Dors une minute.

– Je me demande si tu m'aimes, dit Isabelle.

Je ne voulais pas lui répondre oui. (pp. 75–76)

At this stage in her tale, Thérèse, who is more obviously at a (metaphorical) 'stade du miroir' here than her counterpart in *Ravages* is at the end of that work, is abandoning identification with Isabelle in favour of an identification with her own, individual reflected image. Thérèse's embrace of isolation, which her confrontation with the mirror facilitates (the glass clearly acts in the scene as an intrusive third party, and even as a rival to Isabelle),[49] radically dislocates the relation of contiguity/intermingling she and her lover establish in their *collège*. This leads Isabelle to articulate a bitter litany of loss ('Tu me fuis [. . .] Tu me négliges [. . .] Je me demande si tu m'aimes'), which makes it evident that the privileged union she shares with Thérèse has indeed been profoundly damaged in the brothel.

The breakdown in the lovers' ability to communicate and commune with each other that is apparent in the above passage, like Thérèse's growing fascination with the 'normal' heterosexuality embodied by the couple in the next room, and Isabelle's tacit efforts to transform her bond with her lover into a (genuine) master/slave relation, derives from the fact that in the brothel the adolescents come up against, and succumb to, a set of impalpable but powerful taboos which render their lesbian relationship unworkable. These taboos, to whose overarching influence they respond intuitively rather than consciously, clearly preclude relationships which involve self/other interpenetration, departure from the social/sexual 'norm', and feminine erotic intersubjectivity. In the light of this, they may be taken to incarnate the guiding principles of the 'hom(m)osexual/social' order currently in place, in which — as Irigaray reads things, at least — the only mode of love of the same/self is that which exists in the masculine, and there is no real possibility of an (unproblematic) 'amour du même au féminin'.[50]

Evidently, it is by entering the world of the social/heterosexual, through their excursion to the brothel, that Thérèse and Isabelle provoke the disintegration of the lesbian bond they create inside their *collège*. Surprisingly, once they return to their school, the lovers are able to rediscover, briefly, their damaged idyll. As the following account of their exchange of gazes in the *dortoir* implies, re-entry into their gynaeceum permits them to recuperate the self/other communion and the flow of mutual desire which eluded them in Mme Algazine's establishment:

> Je cherchai sans franchise la rigole entre les seins et c'est à cause de mon regard hypocrite qu'elle croisa les revers de sa robe de chambre. Le portail entre ses yeux et les miens s'ouvrit: nous avions retrouvé la liberté d'aimer et de regarder. Mon regard me revenait comme la vague qui s'est fait mal. Je domptais les miroirs dans ses yeux, elle domptait les miroirs dans mes yeux. (p. 96)

In this brief extract, there are two kinds of 'regard' at stake. The first, the 'regard hypocrite' which Thérèse directs at Isabelle's breasts, is merely objectifying, and is rapidly banished. The second, evoked in the latter stages of the passage, expresses desire and demand, and is transmitted by both lovers. The description we are given of this other 'regard' — which confirms Lacan's point that 'le domaine de la vision [est] intégré au champ du désir'[51] — suggests that by this stage in their story, Thérèse and Isabelle have succeeded in reactivating the relation of mutuality they were forced in the brothel to abandon. Each adolescent, as Thérèse's 'Je domptais les miroirs dans ses yeux, elle domptait les miroirs dans mes yeux' indicates, is now once again in a position to send a desiring look towards her partner, to win recognition and acceptance of her desire instead of meeting blank refusal, and to re-establish lost self/other commingling ('Le portail entre ses yeux et les miens s'ouvrit: nous avions retrouvé la liberté d'aimer et de regarder'). Neither girl blocks off the desire/ gaze transmitted by her lover, but appears rather to acknowledge and return it, by directing at her partner a loving look which resembles and complements that which she has previously received — hence Thérèse's observation 'Mon regard me revenait comme la vague qui s'est fait mal'. This remark of Thérèse's implies that in the 'scopic' field created by her exchange of gazes with her lover, she gains from Isabelle a desiring look which is identical to, and therefore completes, her own. This in turn suggests that she and Isabelle achieve the kind of scopic encounter which, for Lacan, can never be more than a fantasy. In the Lacanian schema, desire (of which the gaze is a vehicle) is never and can never be satisfied — which explains why he states in *Séminaire XI* that 'quand, dans l'amour, je demande un regard, ce qu'il y a de foncièrement insatisfaisant et de toujours manqué, c'est que — *jamais tu ne me regardes là où je te vois*'.[52] However, in the realm of 'le regard' as it is imagined by Leduc, scopic complementarity clearly is possible — and contributes to the disappearance of the barriers which their visit to Mme Algazine's 'maison' erects between Thérèse and Isabelle.

In spite of the fact that Thérèse and Isabelle manage to reconstitute their homoerotic unity upon their return to the *collège*, it nevertheless collapses by the time their tale draws to a close. The ostensible cause of the demise of their union is Thérèse's mother's decision to withdraw her daughter from the school ('Le mois suivant ma mère me reprit. Je ne revis jamais Isabelle', p. 112). However, the reader senses that the disintegration of the lovers' idyllic relationship is due at a more profound level to the damage inflicted upon it by the hostile world of social and sexual 'normality' they encounter in the 'maison de rendez-vous'. Various aspects of the conclusion of *Thérèse et Isabelle* indicate that this is the case. The section of the novella following the account of the adolescents' escapade is punctuated by images conveying loss, division and death. Their inclusion suggests that the separation Thérèse and Isabelle have always dreaded is now much more likely to be realized, and has become so as a result of their trip to the brothel.[53] Moreover, the concluding part of the text contains a dense, lyrical passage which hints that if the lesbian bond between the lovers deteriorates, it is because the perfect mode of self/other interaction to which it has fleetingly afforded them access cannot survive exposure to the (taints of the) 'real' world outside the protective environs of the *collège*:

> Je vois le demi-deuil du nouveau jour, je vois les haillons de la nuit, je leur souris. Je souris à Isabelle et, front contre front, je joue au bélier avec elle pour oublier ce qui meurt. Le lyrisme de l'oiseau qui chante et précipite la beauté de la matinée nous épuise: la perfection n'est pas de ce monde même quand nous la rencontrons. (pp. 111–12)

It is important to recognize too that after the lovers' divisive visit to the brothel has taken place, something of the sublime aspect of their bond is indubitably adulterated, at least as far as Thérèse is concerned. She starts to experience in Isabelle's presence a sense of enclosure and restriction to which she has not previously been susceptible, and which resembles that felt by her namesake in parts one and two of *Ravages* when she is with her mother(s):

> Isabelle agenouillée sur l'oreiller tremblait comme je tremblais. Que mon visage en feu, que ma bouche étaient séparés de son visage, de sa bouche! Ma sœur, ma salive, le manque d'espace, ma condition de galérienne condamnée à jouir sans trêve depuis que je l'aimais m'envoûtaient. (p. 111)

Thérèse also manifests a nascent desire, which she never articulates explicitly, to 'kill off' Isabelle even as she somehow preserves and fetichizes her, a desire that is suggested by her telling observation 'J'embaumai Isabelle avec mes lèvres, avec mes mains' (pp. 108–09). That Thérèse comes in the concluding section of the text to perceive herself as a 'galérienne' and to wish, however unconsciously, to bring her bond with her lover to a close through a symbolic act of immolation is highly significant. This indicates that, in her eyes at least, her formerly ideal relationship with Isabelle is beginning to admit the kind of defects that characterize the (imperfect) maternal/filial bond portrayed in *Ravages*, and further confirms the reader's impression that even though the adolescents' idyll is revived once they re-enter the *collège*, the brothel episode inflicts profound and irremediable damage upon it.

The relationship between *Thérèse et Isabelle* and *Ravages* is one of contrast. The basic focus of each work is more or less identical, since both deal with a powerful feminine tie and with the equally powerful forces that undermine it. In *Ravages*, the union between the novel's heroine and her mother(s) is shown to be so fraught with conflict that Marc's 'œdipal' destruction of it appears, at least initially, to be beneficial to Thérèse. On the other hand, certain, apparently defunct aspects of the mother/daughter bond portrayed in the novel seem to be revived at its conclusion, and the *renouement* between Thérèse and her mother is presented positively, so that the work finishes on a note of optimism. In *Thérèse et Isabelle*, the homoerotic relation between the adolescent heroines of the novella, since it escapes the problems inherent in the mother/daughter bond, is idealized in a way that the mother/daughter union depicted in *Ravages* is not — yet, unlike that union, it succumbs to the abstract but profoundly noxious forces which are unleashed against it and which detach Thérèse from Isabelle. In other words, even though it celebrates feminine same-sex bonding much more forcefully and consistently than *Ravages* does, *Thérèse et Isabelle* must in the last analysis be viewed as a less buoyant work than its predecessor. If *Ravages* tells the tale of the (unexpected) recuperation of a (pre-œdipal) mother/daughter idyll, *Thérèse et Isabelle* chronicles, in part, the process through which a feminine union that borders on the paradisiacal deteriorates and comes to grief. Our sense of the quasi-tragic dimension of the novella is intensified by the fact that the breakdown of Thérèse's idyll with Isabelle, the inevitability of which she articulates to herself during an early encounter with her lover, is tacitly likened to the Fall:

> – Parlez.
> – Non.
> La statue entrera dans le mur, elle sera absorbée par le mur.
> – Vous me quittez?
> – Moi aussi j'attends, dit-elle.
> Plénitude ronde du "non" dit à voix basse, beauté serrée de la boule de neige au mois de mai que je négligerai quand je commencerai de mourir loin des jardins. (p. 13)

At various points throughout this chapter, I have described *Thérèse et Isabelle* as a 'utopian' text, and the pessimism of its conclusion does not detract from the utopian quality of the account of female intersubjectivity it offers. What are we to make of the visionary character of Leduc's novella? As Margaret Whitford argues, the weaving of utopian visions does not necessarily signify an effort on the part of their author to offer blueprints for an ideal future. The creation of such visions can represent, more realistically, an attempt at the production of a shift in consciousness, a shift which might, for instance, engender a reconsideration of what women's status is, and should be, *vis-à-vis* each other (and the other sex).[54] It would be absurd to suggest that, in writing *Thérèse et Isabelle*, Violette Leduc consciously sought to provoke a change in thinking about the possibilities and difficulties pertaining to female intersubjective interaction. The historical moment at which she was writing and her inevitable lack of familiarity with the complex issues addressed by contemporary feminist theorists such as Irigaray mean that she could not possibly have been pursuing such a goal. However, her imagining of a lesbian utopia and her account of the disintegration of that utopia in the world of the 'normal' cannot fail to cause today's readers to reflect upon what Irigaray suggests to be a key issue of our time — the current lack of a 'space' in which the female subject might situate herself healthily in relation to other women.

Until now, my discussion has focused exclusively on the account the reader is given in *L'Asphyxie*, *Ravages* and *Thérèse et Isabelle* of the complexities of feminine bonding and interaction. In the next and final chapter of this study, the nature, and 'gender', of the language contained in *Thérèse et Isabelle* will be explored, in an attempt to establish whether Leduc wrote about the (almost) perfect feminine relationship which exists between the adolescent lesbian heroines of her text in a discourse that was also 'feminine'.

NOTES

1. Luce Irigaray, *Speculum, de l'autre femme*, p. 125.
2. Cixous thus describes an 'ideal' form of lesbianism, which 'has nothing to do with hetero-sexuality, and which leaves no room for man such as he is' (Cixous, 'Rethinking Differences', in George Stambolian and Elaine Marks (eds), *Homosexualities and French Literature* (Ithaca and London: Cornell University Press, 1979), pp. 70–86 (p. 75)).
3. Our sense of the 'marital' character of Thérèse's bond with Cécile is reinforced by the parallels set up in *Ravages* between the Thérèse/Cécile and Thérèse/Marc relationships. Each lover rejects Thérèse's hand, Marc on p. 140 ('"Faut pas me découvrir ainsi, p'tit." Il m'avait refusé sa main'), and Cécile on p. 145 ('Cécile voulait bien de ma main, mais elle ne la serrait pas entre les siennes') and p. 148 ('Cécile bâilla sur son poignet. "Lâche ma main", dit-elle'). Both repudiate the possessive gazes Thérèse directs at them ('Cécile voyait comment je la regardais. [. . .] Cécile soupira; elle baissa les yeux', p. 153, '[Le] visage [de Marc) redevenait méchant. "Tu t'accuseras à un autre moment. Et ces yeux suppliants, et ce regard mal-heureux que je rencontre partout!"', p. 240). Both refuse the gifts she offers when they are abandoning her (pp. 180, 255), and try to oblige her to give up the 'valises' in which she carries the goods she sells and which denote her professional and, on a symbolic level, her sexual independence (pp. 62, 110, 111).
4. Esther Newton, 'The Mythic Mannish Lesbian: Radclyffe Hall and the New Woman', *Signs*, 9 (1984), 557–75 (p. 558). Newton argues that during the period when women like Hall were writing, the association of lesbianism and masculinity (which Hall upheld) was not only unavoidable but also politically expedient, and should not be condemned out of hand, even though it endorses patriarchal gender categories.
5. The reader's awareness of Cécile's mannishness is reinforced by her rather obviously 'male' use of various symbolic objects associated elsewhere in *Ravages* with Marc, masculinity and the penis/phallus:

   Cécile emmaillota le morceau de glace dans le fichu:
   "Cigarette?"
   Elle avait l'air de me faire des avances. (p. 78)

   – Son gâteau va brûler!
   Cécile partit. Elle ouvrait le four, elle enfonçait, elle ressortait, intact, le couteau dans mon cœur. (p. 145)

   Maintenant Cécile palpait le briquet à l'intérieur de sa poche. (p. 178)

6. Sigmund Freud, 'The Psychogenesis of a Case of Homosexuality in a Woman', *SE*, 18, pp. 147–72. In this essay he suggests that the object choice of a female homosexual is determined by masculine/virile drives, and that the (active) lesbian is therefore a man manqué. His description of the psychosexual development of the young lesbian whose analysis forms the basis of his essay contains the remarkable observation that, after an unconscious sexual disappointment during puberty, his patient 'changed into a man and took her mother in place of her father as the object of her love' (p. 158). Freud's account of this case of feminine homosexuality is at least partially responsible for the widely held belief that in lesbian relationships, one partner is always a pseudo-male, while the other is womanly, a passive 'wife'. This vision of lesbian relations also derives from the writings of nineteenth-century sexologists, notably Krafft-Ebing.
7. Cixous, op. cit., pp. 74–75.
8. Kristeva, *Histoires d'amour* (Paris: Denoël, 1983), p. 81.
9. Ibid., p. 80.
10. Ibid.

11. Ibid., p. 81.
12. Cixous, op. cit., p. 75.
13. Charles-Merrien, op. cit., p. 197.
14. 'La rose est bien le symbole de la verge, comme en témoigne cette comparaison prise dans *L'Affamée* à propos de deux trapézistes au music-hall: "Je suis un dénicheur et un redresseur de sexe. Je commence mon numéro. Ma main s'envole. Elle monte jusqu'aux cintres, elle redescend. Elle va au but. Elle est entre les jambes de l'acrobate. Elle réfute des accessoires minables en pleine lumière. Elle les veut plus apparents que la rose des liseuses en cuir repoussé." (*L'Affamée*, Edition Folio, p. 173) [Leduc] adoptera également cette image à propos de Marc qui se refuse et s'éloigne d'elle "sans lui laisser la rose dont la fraîcheur se serait déroulée jusqu'à ses pieds." (*Ravages*, Folio, p. 329).' Ibid., p. 217.
15. Cixous, op. cit., p. 74.
16. Irigaray, *Speculum, de l'autre femme*, p. 125. According to Irigaray, in the phallocentric/patriarchal cultural order, as articulated by Freud, it is extremely hard to 'think' (as Leduc seems to do in *Thérèse et Isabelle*), and therefore to practise, a feminine homosexuality which does not mime heterosexuality. This is not to say that such a homosexuality — i.e. one which engenders a genuinely feminine geography of female relations and consequently permits the realization of women's desire for other women — cannot exist:

> Que la femme puisse désirer une "même" qu'elle, quelqu'une du "même" sexe, qu'elle puisse elle aussi avoir des appétits d'auto– ou d'homosexualité, cela ne peut se comprendre, et semble d'ailleurs inadmissible. Cela, en fait, se rencontre rarement dans cette histoire, phallocentrique, où la valeur est réservée au pénis ou à ses équivalents. Et où il n'est pas facile d'être hors système, hors "commerce". La revendication d'homosexualité féminine ne suffisant évidemment pas à mettre en cause le privilège du phallus.
> Ce qui ne signifie pas que le désir de la femme pour elle-même, pour le même — pour la même, une même — ne soit pas à reconnaître. N'ait pas à trouver, ou retrouver, une économie possible (*Speculum*, pp. 125–26).

17. Cixous, op. cit., p. 75.
18. Marianne Hirsch, *The Mother/Daughter Plot: Narrative, Psychoanalysis, Feminism* (Bloomington and Indianapolis: Indiana University Press, 1989), pp. 133, 136.
19. Irigaray, *Speculum, de l'autre femme*, p. 127. The 'other' *jouissance*, or sexual pleasure, to which Irigaray refers is one which she posits as specific to women who succeed in eluding enclosure within a heterosexual model of eroticism. It is a 'plaisir sexuel spécifique', a 'jouissance différente, complémentaire ou supplémentaire, de celle recherchée dans l'hétérosexualité' (Ibid.).
20. Irigaray, *Ce Sexe qui n'en est pas un*, pp. 27–28. It is as a result of comments like this that Irigaray has been accused, by materialist feminists, of adopting an 'essentialist' position, which reduces women to a set of anatomical, and worse still, natural characteristics and fails (apparently) to take on board the key argument proffered by the materialist camp, which is 'that "nature" is always a product of social relations and that sex is always a construction of oppression' (Fuss, op. cit., p. 57). It is certainly possible to read Irigaray's observations regarding the female body/pleasure as essentialist, but we must bear in mind that Irigarayan essentialism is strategic rather than naïve or apolitical. In her essay 'Luce Irigaray's Language of Essence', Diana Fuss explains this argument as follows: 'The point, for Irigaray, of defining women from an essentialist standpoint is not to imprison women in their bodies but to rescue them from enculturating definitions by men. An essentialist definition of "woman" implies that there will always be some part of "woman" which resists masculine imprinting and socialization' (Ibid., p. 61).
21. *Ce Sexe qui n'en est pas un*, p. 23.
22. Cixous, op. cit., p. 74.
23. Georges Bataille, 'L'Erotisme', in *Œuvres complètes* X (Paris: Gallimard, 1987), pp. 11–270 (pp. 17–19).
24. Ibid., pp. 22–23.
25. 'Dans le mouvement de dissolution des êtres, le partenaire masculin a en principe un rôle actif, la partie féminine est passive. C'est essentiellement la partie passive féminine qui est dissoute en tant qu'être constitué' (Ibid., p. 23).
26. This capacity is suggested by the way in which each lover is shown to be a double/mirror-self of the other:

> Je me perdais dans le doigt d'Isabelle comme elle se perdait dans le mien. (p. 32)
>
> Elle s'arrêtait quand je m'arrêtais, elle repartait quand je repartais. (p. 41)

J'accourus dans ses bras comme elle accourut dans les miens. (p. 48)

Our impression that each adolescent functions as her lover's mirror/reflection is intensified by the fact that the words they utter are frequently identical:

– C'est vrai?
– C'est vrai, dit Isabelle. (p. 11)

– Je ne peux plus.
– Je ne peux plus. (p. 17)

– Besoin de toi, dis-je.
– Besoin de toi, dit Isabelle. (p. 25)

– Ne te tais pas, dit Isabelle.
– Je ne me tais pas. Je te porte. (p. 108)

27. Irigaray, *Ce Sexe qui n'en est pas un*, p. 215.
28. Anika Rifflet-Lemaire, *Jacques Lacan* (Brussels: Dessart, 1970), p. 145. An imaginary relationship, for Lacan, is a dyadic bond based upon an identification of the self and another being/image. The first imaginary union exists in the pre-œdipal period, between a child and its mother. Even after this is shattered by the father's intervention, the human individual's desire to form imaginary bonds is not banished. The bond between the infant and its reflection, during the Mirror Stage, belongs also to the domain of the Imaginary.
29. In Lacanian terms, imaginary relations preclude subjectivity and individuality because they are predicated upon a 'rapport érotique où l'individu humain se fixe à une image qui l'aliène à lui-même' (Lacan, *Ecrits*, p. 113). Imaginary bonds expose the subject to 'a capture of the moi by another, in an aggressive or erotic relationship' (Anthony Wilden, *Speech and Language in Psychoanalysis* (Baltimore and London: Johns Hopkins University Press, 1968), p. 175). The relationship between Thérèse and Isabelle, however, even though it is a specular 'relation duelle immédiate' (Lemaire, op. cit., p. 145) and may be deemed imaginary, does not, in the account Thérèse gives of it, impose alienation and loss of subjectivity.
30. Significantly, in French erotic discourse fields are commonly associated with the female genitals, and, more generally, with woman's body: 'L'assimilation du vagin à un champ [. . .] labouré, ensemencé, etc., constitue une image fondamentale et qui revient sous mille formes' (Guiraud, op. cit., p. 213).
31. According to C. J. Rawson, the cannibalistic nature of erotic activity, which is suggested strongly in *Thérèse et Isabelle*, is frequently a theme in literary works depicting same-sex relationships: 'Some of the most intensely elaborated treatments of sexual cannibalism occur, as it happens, in homosexual literature: in Genet's *Pompes funèbres* and Monique Wittig's *Le Corps lesbien*. Connections suggested by psychoanalytic writings between homosexuality and the "cannibal" or oral phase may have something to do with this, whether because they are true or because post-Freudian writers have believed them to be' ('Cannibalism and Fiction', *Genre*, 2 (1978), 227–313 (p. 270)).
32. It is partially validated, as Colette Hall points out, by the fact that when Thérèse reflects upon her mother's marital defection, she implies (but only implies) that the union she has formed with Isabelle constitutes an attempt to 'combler le vide laissé par la désertion de sa mère' by establishing a rival 'mother/daughter' bond with her lesbian partner (*Les Mères chez les romancières du XXe siècle*, p. 230): 'Sur terre il n'y a que toi, sur terre je n'aime que toi, me dit [ma mère], mais elle a quelqu'un. J'ai rencontré Isabelle, j'ai quelqu'un. Je suis à Isabelle, je n'appartiens plus à ma mère' (*Thérèse et Isabelle*, p. 21).
33. Carolyn Burke, 'Irigaray through the Looking Glass', *Feminist Studies*, 7 (1981), 288–306 (p. 299).
34. Hirsch, *The Mother/Daughter Plot: Narrative, Psychoanalysis, Feminism*, p. 133.
35. My understanding of the Irigarayan 'female homosexual economy' is indebted to Margaret Whitford's *The Irigaray Reader* (Oxford: Blackwell, 1991) and *Luce Irigaray: Philosophy in the Feminine* (London and New York: Routledge, 1991). Whitford consistently relates the idea of such an economy to an order of 'women-among-themselves, love of the self on the side of women' (Whitford, *Philosophy in the Feminine*, p. 104).
36. Irigaray, *Ethique de la différence sexuelle*, p. 100.
37. Irigaray, *Ce Sexe qui n'en est pas un*, p. 167.
38. 'Il faut qu'un symbolisme soit créé entre femmes pour que l'amour entre elles puisse avoir lieu. Cet amour n'est d'ailleurs possible dès maintenant qu'entre femmes qui peuvent se parler. Sans cet intervalle *d'échange* ou de paroles, ou de gestes, les passions entre femmes s'exercent sur un mode [. . .] assez cruel.' (*Ethique*, p. 103).

'Women cannot speak to each other of their affects in the existing verbal code, and they cannot even imagine them in the ruling systems of representation. Love and desire between women and in women are still without signifiers that can be articulated in language. The result is paralysis, somatization, non-differentiation between one woman and another, enforced rejection or hatred [. . .].' ('The Poverty of Psychoanalysis', in *The Irigaray Reader*, p. 101).

39.   Margaret Whitford, *The Irigaray Reader*, p. 72.
40.   *Ethique*, p. 106.
41.   Ibid., p. 105.
42.   For a helpful account of why and how Irigaray feels the Symbolic (and the imaginary subtending it) must be changed, see Whitford, *Philosophy in the Feminine*, chapter 4 ('Maternal Genealogy and the Symbolic').
43.   Irigaray, *Le Corps-à-corps avec la mère* (Montreal: Editions de la pleine lune, 1981), p. 86.
44.   See Whitford, *Philosophy in the Feminine*, chapter 8 ('Women and/in the Social Contract').
45.   Stockinger, op. cit., p. 193.
46.   This association is apparent, for example, in an early account of the intense pleasure their embraces allow the lovers to enjoy:

> Nous avions effleuré et survolé nos épaules avec les doigts fauves de l'automne, nous avons lancé à grands traits la lumière dans les nids, nous avons éventé les caresses, nous avons créé des motifs avec de la brise marine, nous avons enveloppé de zéphyrs nos jambes [. . .] Quels mariages de mouvements! Des nuages nous aidèrent. Nous étions ruisselantes de lumière.
> La vague vint en éclaireur, elle grisa nos pieds, elle se reprit. Des lianes se détendirent, une clarté se propagea dans nos chevilles. (Ibid., pp. 31–32).

47.   Charles-Merrien points out that in the brothel/voyeurism scene in *La Bâtarde*, there is a hint that the voyeur is impotent, and that '[la] présence du voyeur stimule le désir de Violette, sans doute parce que sa relation avec Hermine est en partie fondée sur le sado-masochisme, mais surtout parce qu'elle détient une virilité dont cet homme est dépourvu' (op. cit., p. 114).
48.   Irigaray, *Ce Sexe qui n'en est pas un*, p. 26. I shall return to the notion of the phallomorphic in chapter 4.
49.   Charles-Merrien also comments on this aspect of the scene, but interprets the role played by the mirror somewhat differently. In her version of the Thérèse/Isabelle/mirror incident, the glass represents not only a 'tierce personne assistant au rite amoureux des deux amantes' but also a 'témoin impérieux' whose presence Thérèse actively welcomes because it enables her to display her 'capacité de faire jouir une femme' and sets up a 'jeu triangulaire [qui] décuple son plaisir' (op. cit., p. 112). Charles-Merrien, in other words, perceives the mirror as a kind of benign voyeur, placed in a relationship of contrast to the (real? imaginary?) voyeur Thérèse intuits behind the *œil de bœuf*.
50.   Irigaray's theorization of why, as things stand, love of the same/self can exist in the masculine but not in the feminine may be summarized as follows. As Whitford explains, patriarchy — as defined by Irigaray — is 'hom(m)osexual', because it represents 'the realm of the same, i.e. of one sex' and 'does not recognize sexual difference' (*The Irigaray Reader*, p. 18). Under the patriarchal system (of which Leduc's brothel is an exemplary element) only the father/son genealogy is recognized, and only the male subject has therefore the means to accede to love of the same — the whole point about a genealogy being that it allows relations of the same/self to obtain, because it mediates them. Irigaray argues, moreover, that 'l'amour du même entre hommes [. . .] ne peut se poser comme tel sans le maternel–naturel–matériel' (*Ethique*, p. 100). What she means here is that love of the same in the masculine is defined against, and constructed upon, the maternal–feminine — which represents a mere substratum or 'sous-sol' (ibid., p. 101) that enables male self/same love and the paternal genealogy to exist. In Irigarayan terms therefore, it is because women a) are excluded from the domain of 'love of the same' by its (inevitable) androcentrism and b) constitute the very foundations of that domain that they cannot themselves achieve an 'amour du même au féminin'.
51.   Lacan, *Les Quatre Concepts fondamentaux de la psychanalyse: Le Séminaire XI*, p. 80. According to Elizabeth Wright, 'Lacan identifies a "scopic drive" for this lodging of desire in looking [. . .]. Freud was aware of such a drive, but stressed mainly its perverse aspects, whereas Lacan extends it to every act of seeing. The eyes, as one of the modes of access for libido to explore the world, become the instruments of this drive' (Wright, op. cit., p. 117).
52.   Lacan, *Les Quatre Concepts*, pp. 94–95.
53.   'La nuit refroidissait nos lèvres jointes. [. . .] Le temps venait et passait avec ses foulards de crêpe.' (p. 96)

'Nous avons entendu le claquement du vent dans le suaire d'un arbre.' (p. 97)

'Nous nous sommes séparées, nous nous sommes attendues, nous avons eu la crevasse de l'effroi entre nous.' (p. 99)

'J'embaumai Isabelle avec mes lèvres, avec mes mains.' (pp. 108–09)

'Le jour prenait la nuit, le jour effaçait nos mariages [. . .].' (p. 110)

54.   See Whitford, *Philosophy in the Feminine*, chapter 1 ('Feminism and Utopia').

CHAPTER 4

WRITING THE FEMININE?

Since the last war, linguistic matters have been of major concern to intellectuals on both sides of the Atlantic; so much so, in fact, that 'it is as though the mid-twentieth-century awareness projects onto language issues which previously were theorised around God'.[1] Given the overarching importance which has been accorded to language in the post-war period, it is unsurprising that it should have become an area of feminist debate. The issue of woman's relationship to language has come under increasing scrutiny, particularly in recent years, and has led feminist writers and scholars to suggest that the words we speak and write are tainted by the patriarchal order which predominates within Western culture and, in consequence, alienate or 'exclude' the female subject who uses them.

In this final chapter, my aim is to investigate the ways in which Violette Leduc views and uses language. Any such investigation clearly necessitates some initial exploration of contemporary analyses of the nature and significance of the linguistic order, and of feminist accounts of the problems of language women encounter. My introductory discussion will focus on the work of French feminist theorists, who have been trained in the speculative disciplines of philosophy and psychoanalysis, rather than on that of Anglo–American women scholars. The theoretical discourses of the former group were published in the decade following Leduc's death and clearly came into being within a conceptual/political/cultural context she would have found quite alien. None the less, because they focus on concerns which are also in evidence in comments Leduc made regarding the nature of writing and in her own texts, it is productive to use them as a point of departure from which to explore her work.

Since the 1970s, French feminists have vigorously denounced what Irigaray has termed 'la sexuation du discours'[2] and have suggested that language is a patriarchal preserve which does not allow for the articulation of sexual difference. Radical French feminist theorists have argued that the linguistic sphere is not neutral but rather 'gendered', that its apparent universality masks a masculine bias, and that it constitutes a domain of masculine privilege in which woman cannot easily find a place or voice. That they should claim this to be the case highlights the debt they owe, however grudgingly, to the psychoanalytic writings of Jacques Lacan.

According to Lacan, the function of the symbolic order — the order of language — is a deterministic one. Lacan writes that each of us is a 'sujet dans le verbe', an individual who is subject *to* language as much as the subject of it, who enters, and is 'produced' by, the linguistic sphere.[3] There is moreover, in the Lacanian schema, an indissoluble bond between language and the phallus. This is because, for Lacan, our transition into the symbolic only occurs once we submit unconsciously to 'castration', which, in Lacanian terms, entails acceptance of the Father's Law and of a resultant rupture of our primordial bond with our maternal parent. As Jacqueline Rose explains, 'in Lacan's account, the phallus stands for that moment of rupture. It refers mother and child to the dimension of the symbolic which is figured by the father's place'.[4] What Lacan suggests, then, is that accession to language is dependent upon a repression of the original relation of desire that binds us to the mother, that this repression is imposed by the Father (here a function or 'code', incarnating an interdictory law, rather than a real and specific individual), and that the symbolic, linguistic system we enter when we effect it has as its central signifier the phallus, which is the symbol both of lack (i.e. of the mother) and of paternal omnipotence.[5]

Lacan's positioning of the phallus not only as the spur to language acquisition but also as the (transcendental) signifier which dominates the symbolic leads him to make telling observation about the relationship between women (who, unlike men, do not possess the fleshly or imaginary equivalent of the phallus, the penis) and language. In a characteristically hermetic passage, he comments:

Il n'y a de femme qu'exclue par la nature des choses qui est la nature des mots, et il faut bien dire que s'il y a quelque chose dont elles-mêmes se plaignent assez pour l'instant, c'est bien de ça — simplement, elles ne savent pas ce qu'elles disent, c'est toute la différence entre elles et moi.[6]

What Lacan seems to be saying is that women and men do not have the same relationship to the realm of words (which, for Lacan, is that of all reality) and that language is uniquely problematic for women. His argument — which we are of course by no means obliged to accept — has been taken to suggest that in a signifying system in which woman is 'cast in the position of other', the female subject 'is both excluded from and elevated *beyond* language'.[7] A different way of putting the same point is that feminine difference cannot be adequately defined (or represented) within an all-embracing linguistic order that is intrinsically phallocentric, i.e. within a 'Discours qui rejette comme irrecevable — inconcevable — toute articulation d'un "je" avec un corps-sexe féminin'.[8] Lacan's remarks about feminine exclusion suggest that, as far as he is concerned, the feminine is — and will remain — unconceptualizable and unspoken in language, and that there is nothing to be done about this sorry state of affairs. It is for this reason, conceivably, that he describes the 'la' of 'la femme' as 'un signifiant dont le propre est qu'il ne peut rien signifier'.[9] French feminists who have worked on the relationship between femininity and language follow Lacan up to a point, in that they too believe that the discursive realm (as it stands, at least) privileges the phallus as transcendental signifier, and precludes symbolic self-definition by/for women. Unlike Lacan, however, neither Luce Irigaray nor Hélène Cixous considers the obfuscation of the feminine by the symbolic order to be irremediable, and each has produced texts which indicate that there may be (specifically feminine) linguistic practices that might allow its articulation.

For Irigaray, transforming the symbolic in such a way that the inscription of feminine difference might be made possible is imperative. She points out that her own *œuvre* derives directly from her need to achieve this goal: 'Je suis une femme. Je suis un être sexué féminin. Le motif de mon travail se trouve dans l'impossibilité d'articuler un tel énoncé; dans le fait que sa production est de quelque façon insensée, inconvenante, indécente'.[10] The change she envisages can only come into being through a radical, transformational 'travail du langage', whose function would be to '*désancrer le phallocentrisme, le phallo-cratisme*, pour rendre le masculin à son langage, laissant la possibilité d'un langage autre'.[11] The linguistic subversion she has in mind works on two levels. It involves not only an assault upon existing codes of representation but also a modification of the structural/stylistic features of discourse which, in her view, are symptomatic of its phallocentrism. As far as representation is concerned, Irigaray suggests that women should, in order to reveal and even remedy the occlusion of the feminine within language, play with those images of femininity it commonly offers us in such a way that their demeaning, 'masculine' character is highlighted. She describes the ludic activity she recommends as 'mimetic':

Jouer de la mimésis, c'est [. . .], pour une femme, tenter de retrouver le lieu de son exploitation par le discours, sans s'y laisser simplement réduire. C'est se resoumettre — en tant que du côté du "sensible", de la "matière" . . . — à des "idées", notamment d'elle, élaborées dans/par une logique masculine, mais pour faire "apparaître", par un effet de répétition ludique, ce qui devait rester occulté: le recouvrement d'une opération du féminin dans le langage.[12]

The parodic strategy to which Irigaray refers permits, in her view, the demolition of representations of womanhood which are accepted as universally true but which are projections of the male imagination, representations that constitute '[des] images d'Epinal — versions déformées, mutilées de notre histoire individuelle et collective [. . .] qui sont inscrites partout à l'extérieur sous nos yeux'.[13] She does not suggest, however, that mimesis constitutes the only means by which the phallocentrism of the symbolic can be illuminated and (perhaps) undermined. In various texts and interviews, she argues that it is primarily the creation of a new kind of writing *practice* that enables women to undo the masculinization of discourse. For Irigaray, it is above all the fact that the language of Western culture, particularly philosophico–rational language, privileges stable, single, unambivalent significations and is intrinsically teleological which makes it 'phallomorphic', i.e. (symbolically) marked by a masculine 'logic' or 'imaginary'. Irigaray's point here, as Diana Fuss explains, rests upon her 'strategic misreading of male genitalia' as always and inflexibly unified/'monolithic'/singular, a misreading which is destined to expose the erection, by Lacan amongst others, of 'the phallus as a single transcendental signifier'.[14] What Irigaray is suggesting is that all forms of discourse which valorize 'le *un* de la forme, de l'individu, du sexe, du nom propre, du sens propre'[15] and foreground principles 'based upon the possibility of individuating or distinguishing one thing from another' (e.g. those of identity, non-contradiction and binarism)[16] present 'a certain isomorphism with the masculine sex'.[17] A 'langage autre', which would not efface sexual difference and might admit/symbolize the feminine, must therefore, in Irigaray's opinion, be one whose style allows fixed, single meanings to be subverted, i.e. one that is characterized by ambivalence and indeterminacy:

Ce "style" ou "écriture" de la femme met plutôt feu aux mots fétiches, aux termes propres, aux formes bien construites. [...] Son style résiste à, et fait exploser, toute forme, figure, idée, concept solidement établis. Ce qui n'est pas dire que son style n'est rien, comme le laisse croire une discursivité qui ne peut le penser. Mais son "style" ne peut se soutenir comme thèse, ne peut faire l'objet d'une position.[18]

There will always [...] be a plurality in feminine language. And it will not even be the Freudian 'pun' i.e., a superimposed hierarchy of meaning, but the fact that at each moment there is always for women, 'at least two' meanings, without one being able to decide which meaning prevails, which is 'on top' or 'underneath', which 'conscious' or 'repressed'. [...] A feminine language would undo the unique meaning of words, of nouns: which still regulates all discourse.[19]

[A feminine language] has nothing to do with the syntax which we have used for centuries, namely, that constructed according to the following organization: subject, predicate, or; subject, verb, object. For female sexuality is not unifiable, it cannot be subsumed under the concept of subject. Which brings into question all the syntactical norms ...[20]

The plurivocal language Irigaray envisions is obviously the antithesis of the 'monolithic'/rational, and can justifiably be described as poetic. In addition, such language is, for Irigaray, 'vulvomorphic', because its plurality and fluidity stand in (a metaphorical) relation to the non-unified form of woman's genitalia, to the decentred nature of her pleasure, and to the process of endless touching and separation which Irigaray associates with the two lips of the vagina ('La femme "se touche" tout le temps, sans qu'on puisse d'ailleurs le lui interdire, car son sexe est fait de deux lèvres qui s'embrassent continûment').[21] The 'parler femme'[22] she envisages might be taken, then, to constitute 'an unalienated language transparently expressing the real, a *parole* analogous to the female body, that would speak the female body directly'[23] — were it not for the fact that, as Jane Gallop points out, 'Irigaray's vulvomorphic logic is not predestined by anatomy but is already a *symbolic* interpretation of that anatomy',[24] and forms part of her 'attempt to define the characteristics of what a differently sexualized language would be':[25]

C'est que dans ses dires aussi — du moins quand elle l'ose — la femme se re-touche tout le temps. Elle s'écarte à peine d'elle-même d'un babillage, d'une exclamation, d'une demi-confidence, d'une phrase laissée en suspens . . . Quand elle y revient, c'est pour repartir ailleurs. D'un autre point de plaisir, ou de douleur. Il faudrait l'écouter d'une autre oreille comme *un "autre sens" toujours en train de se tisser, de s'embrasser avec les mots, mais aussi de s'en défaire pour ne pas s'y fixer. S'y figer.*[26]

In her explorations of language, Cixous too suggests that it is the creation of multivalent discourse which permits the articulation of the feminine within the symbolic. On the one hand, she argues that the kind of language she has in mind — an excessive, disruptive language that no longer represses feminine otherness and is consequently 'bisexual' — need not be equated with women or female writers.[27] Yet she also contends that it is in fact women who are more likely to produce the form of discourse in question ('Je dirai: aujourd'hui l'écriture est aux femmes. Cela n'est pas une provocation, cela signifie que la femme admet qu'il y ait de l'autre. Elle n'a pas effacé, dans son devenir-femme la bisexualité latente chez la fille comme chez le garçon. Féminité et bisexualité vont ensemble')[28] and implies, more overtly than Irigaray, that it represents a language of the female body/libido:

Il faut que la femme écrive son corps, qu'elle invente la langue imprenable qui crève les cloisonnements, classes et rhétoriques, ordonnances et codes, qu'elle submerge, transperce, franchisse le discours [. . .].[29]

Le corps de la femme aux mille et un foyers d'ardeurs, quand elle le laissera — fracassant les jougs et censures — articuler le foisonnement des significations qui en tous sens le parcourt, c'est de bien plus d'une langue qu'il va faire retentir la vieille langue maternelle à un seul sillon.[30]

Both Irigaray and Cixous privilege forms of language which are characterized by polyvalence, indeterminacy and ambiguity and, furthermore, relate these forms (however metaphorically) to the polymorphous nature of the female body and woman's libidinal organization. Although compelling, the theories of these radical feminists present certain difficulties. They invite accusations of essentialism and biologism, because they seem to indicate that 'non-phallic' (i.e. subversive and experimental) language directly echoes female sexuality and anatomy.[31] In addition, they set up an (implicit) association between 'feminine' language and the anti-rational which, given the assumptions mainstream patriarchal culture makes about women and the (irrational) discourses they produce, is clearly problematic. They threaten, moreover, to engender a kind of critical ghetto in which women and their language/texts risk becoming enclosed. None the less, the writings of Cixous and Irigaray are in many respects of enormous use to women authors and feminist critics. Above all, they help us to realize that women may well need to write 'differently' in order to represent their femininity — even if we do not accept the particular accounts they offer us of what 'speaking (as a) woman' involves.

In earlier chapters I have concentrated on an analysis of Leduc's exploration of feminine interaction and bonding. Yet she was also preoccupied by the problem of *language* and by the question of the (woman) writer's relationship with it. In the second volume of her autobiography, *La Folie en tête*, written in 1970, Leduc indicates that she experienced the process of literary creation as a struggle with language, which typically took the form of a dogged but often disappointing search for an ideal *mot juste*:

Mon idéal? L'honnêteté d'un cordonnier. Je serre les dents, je cerne une antenne de télévision, une cheminée chapeautée, ce sont mes profondeurs. Je débloque une sensation, une comparaison. Il fait jour, c'est ma nuit. J'ai une croix, je ne la fuis pas lorsque je cherche le mot juste. Mon espoir d'atteindre le but est aussi mon précipice. (p. 52)

J'écrivais, soudain plus rien. Quarante jours de sécheresse se déclaraient en une seconde dans mon désert. Le vocabulaire se retirait. Quoi faire? Comment définir le bleu, ma couleur préférée, comment définir le bleu des yeux d'un chat siamois? Mon coude sur la table, je fermais les yeux, je serrais mes dents, je distendais mes lèvres, je plissais mes paupières, je me creusais pour être visitée. [. . .] L'adjectif ne répond pas à ma prière, il faut poser le porte-plume sur la table . . . Je me retrouve les yeux fermés, paupières plissées, bras tendus; pitié! J'ai besoin d'un adjectif. (pp. 116–17)

Leduc also indicates in *La Folie en tête* that her perception of language as an obstacle became acute when she was writing the first version of what was to appear, eventually and much modified, as *Thérèse et Isabelle* (i.e. when she was working on the section of text which Gallimard refused to publish with the rest of *Ravages* in 1955). In other words, it was the experience of writing about feminine, and more specifically lesbian, eroticism in the 1950s which, according to her later autobiographical text, seems to have forced her to confront the restrictions inherent in language. In *La Folie en tête*, Leduc re-creates the feelings of despair that assailed her as she grappled with words which seemed to isolate her from the sexual sensations she longed to communicate. These sensations were as much her own as those of the aroused adolescents she depicted, since she resorted to masturbation in an attempt to infuse her writing with the erotic reality she was attempting to re-create:

C'est une fugitive, cette sensation, je ne peux pas l'arrêter au passage. (p. 297)

Je leur suis fidèle, je leur obéis: je m'aime. Mon sexe? Pour ne pas *trahir* Thérèse et Isabelle. Exploitation répugnante. Tu vendrais ton sexe à ton porte-plume? Je vendrais tout pour une plus grande exactitude. Tu te vois d'ici pendant que tu écriras? Je vois le résultat: un mot juste, un seul, et je me foutrai de l'opprobre et du péché. (p. 298, my emphasis)

Comment décrire la sensation? Comment *fixer* la sensation? Je n'y parviendrai pas. Je m'aimerai, je m'aimerai pour plus de sincérité. Je serai Thérèse, je serai Isabelle. Il le faut, je me suis engagée avec mon cahier. (pp. 317–18, my emphasis)

J'écrivais, j'écrivais sous leur dictée. J'écrivais d'une main et de l'autre ... je m'aimais pour les aimer, pour les retrouver, pour les *traduire*, pour ne pas les *trahir*. (p. 321, my emphasis)

The above extracts convey Leduc's sense of creative failure, and also suggest the extent to which she perceived the creation of erotic discourse as a (pleasurably) transgressive act ('un mot juste, un seul, et je me foutrai de l'opprobre et du péché'). More importantly, however, they indicate the degree to which she distrusted language and found it wanting. Leduc's awareness of linguistic inadequacy also emerges, more clearly, in a conversation she creates in an early part of the 1966 version of *Thérèse et Isabelle*:

Nous parlons. C'est dommage. Ce qui a été dit a été assassiné. Nos paroles, qui ne grandiront pas, qui n'embelliront pas, se faneront à l'intérieur de nos os.
    J'ai plongé dans ses yeux.
    – Je vous . . .
    Les paroles flétriront les sentiments.
J'ai mis ma main sur sa bouche. Isabelle voulait me le dire.
    – Je vous . . .
Je l'étouffais pendant qu'elle voulait avouer. (pp. 11–12)

In the light of the above, we can assume that possibly from the mid-fifties and certainly by the mid-sixties, Leduc had come to view language as a problematic medium against which the writer (and speaker) must struggle in order to 'fix' or 'translate' aspects of reality — particularly that of feminine erotic sensation.[32] What concerns me here is the *nature* of the restriction Leduc perceived language to represent, the form taken by her combat against linguistic inadequacy, and the textual solutions she attempted to evolve. Did she, for example, having discerned the 'masculinity' of the linguistic order, seek to write about feminine interaction in a discourse which was itself in some way or other 'feminine'? Or did her problems with language derive from a conviction that the words available to the writer who tries to 'translate' private, individual feelings or experiences are banalizing and deforming, and somehow mutilate that which he/she is trying to evoke? As we shall see, both of these hypotheses are justified by comments regarding the nature of writing/language made by Leduc in her autobiographical texts and interviews. What follows is an attempt to explore them further, through a detailed analysis of *Thérèse et Isabelle*. My choice of this text as a focus reflects the fact that it deals almost exclusively with the (unrepresentable? 'difficult'?) area of female eroticism and, moreover, contains an explicit articulation of Leduc's reservations regarding language.

WRITING AGAINST THE MASCULINE?

Violette Leduc undoubtedly lacked the politicized and above all post-Lacanian perspective regarding the pitfalls language holds for women (and in particular for the *écrivaine*) which informs the theoretical writings of contemporary French feminists. Yet there are indications that she sensed the sexes have a different relationship to the linguistic, and specifically the aesthetic, domain and that this poses problems for women writers. A passage contained in *Trésors à prendre*, for example, in which she addresses 'Madame' (Simone de Beauvoir, to whom the text is dedicated), suggests that this was the case:

Vous m'avez dit, Madame, que les femmes avant deux cents ans créeront ce que les hommes créent. Je vous crois, je veux vous croire, puisque vous, dans notre siècle, avec votre intelligence, avec les livres que vous écrivez, vous nous le prouvez avec beaucoup d'avance sur l'horaire, ce féminisme valeureux. [. . .] Avant deux cents ans . . . Il y a un "mais". Ce "mais" invincible c'est la liqueur de l'homme dans le pinceau du peintre, à la pointe du crayon de l'écrivain. (p. 196)

This is a rich and complex extract. Initially, we might be tempted to believe that Leduc is merely (and pessimistically) saying that literature and art are intrinsically 'virile' activities, access to which, for women, is difficult if not impossible (by virtue, presumably, of woman's 'castrated' state, or because 'culture' has historically belonged to men). The passage also has a more subtle, and more positive, dimension, however. In it, Leduc is examining Beauvoir's (reported) observation that in two hundred years, women will create 'ce que les hommes créent'. Although she seems at first to welcome this notion ('Je vous crois, je veux vous croire'), ultimately she refutes it. Her disagreement with Beauvoir may simply reflect a conviction that feminine creativity is rendered impracticable by woman's non-possession of 'la liqueur de l'homme'. Leduc's remarks may, on the other hand, signify a perception on her part that women's artistic and textual productions cannot, but more importantly *should* not, be identical to 'ce que les hommes créent'. We can interpret her comments to mean that women may have problems using aesthetic forms evolved by men, and that any attempt to do so is likely to be unproductive, but that this fact should not deter them from developing a different — feminine? — mode of creativity. When read in this way, the extract need no longer be taken merely to suggest that the creative process is inherently and irremediably virile, and therefore out of reach of women. It can be interpreted as evidence that Leduc (in contrast to her mentor Beauvoir) sensed that while art and writing, traditionally the preserve of men, have been 'marked' by the masculine, women's development of aesthetic forms and models of their *own* is not impossible and is, moreover, a task which is at once formidable and highly necessary.

Arguably, then, Leduc's awareness of the restrictive nature of language stemmed at least in part from her consciousness of the genderization of literary discourse. Remarks made in later interviews indicate, furthermore, that once she began to write about feminine sexuality, and to discover the degree to which language separated her from her subject matter in this key area of experience, she made considerable efforts to overcome barriers raised by linguistic *sexuation*. It appears that she sought to do so by developing a (different) erotic discourse, which was related to her feminine gender and was intended to facilitate the 'mise à jour nécessaire d'une sexualité trop longtemps maintenue secrète'.[33] Interviewed by Madeleine Chapsal after the publication of *La Bâtarde*, two years before *Thérèse et Isabelle* finally saw the light of day, Leduc intimated that she had attempted (and would continue to attempt) to create a 'daring' form of language which would illuminate feminine pleasure in a new and unique way. She makes it quite clear that such language can only be the province of the woman writer. She also indicates that if it is to exist at all, it must be produced by women who read, as she had read, the erotic writings of their 'foremothers', and who, whilst saluting the efforts of these authors, work to extend the discourses they evolved:

Voyez vous, j'ai beaucoup aimé Colette, qui est un bon écrivain, qui est très savante. Mais en la lisant, j'avais le sentiment qu'elle n'avait pas osé, qu'elle s'était retenue. Elle me donnait une sorte de faim, j'en voulais davantage. C'est cela mon but: approcher un peu la sensation dans l'érotisme, la décrire. Je ne suis pas allée très loin, je ne suis pas réellement arrivée à rendre comme il faut l'impression sensuelle. Mais je me dis: j'essaye de déblayer, d'autres y arriveront mieux que moi. Des femmes plus jeunes me liront et diront: "Cette Violette Leduc, elle n'a pas vraiment osé; moi, je vais oser . . .".[34]

The transgressive character of the feminine erotic discourse Leduc wished to create — which, unlike that produced by Colette, was clearly not predicated upon the premise that direct evocation of female and especially lesbian *jouissance* should be avoided[35] — is also made evident in an interview she gave to Pierre Démeron in 1966. In this interview, which appeared in *Candide* after the publication of *Thérèse et Isabelle*, Leduc demands that women, like men, should try to write freely about their sexuality, regardless of the difficulties they might encounter. She goes on:

Devant une feuille de papier je n'ai pas peur, alors que dans la vie je ne veux pas déranger l'ordre établi.[36]

Leduc's evocation of the *dérangement* of the *ordre établi* provoked by discourse of the kind she envisaged indicates her awareness of the disruptive character of such writing. Significantly, her comments are not totally dissimilar to those Irigaray makes regarding the effect upon the phallocentric symbolic/linguistic order of woman's attempts to articulate her 'other' sexual pleasure. According to Irigaray, this pleasure is a 'jouissance qui doit rester inarticulable dans le langage [. . .], sous peine de mettre en cause ce qui étaye le fonctionnement logique'.[37] Irigaray's sense of the unsettling character of woman's eroticism and its transcription into language explains her belief, which Leduc seems also to have shared, that 'ce qui est aujourd'hui le plus interdit aux femmes est d'essayer de parler leur jouissance'.[38] Both she and Leduc however, in their different ways, stress the need to produce a discourse which overcomes the interdictions surrounding feminine *jouissance* and which attempts to give it expression in new, and startling, words.

In summary, Leduc's remarks in *Trésors à prendre* and in the interviews referred to above hint that she was not only alive to the masculine bias of the literary/linguistic sphere, but also sensed the restrictions this imposes to be *particularly* problematic for the woman writer seeking to depict her experience of sexuality. In this, she may be likened to Marie Cardinal, who expresses in *Autrement dit* her own awareness of the problems attendant upon women's articulation of the sexual ('La meilleure manière de prouver qu'il manque des mots, que le français n'est pas fait pour les femmes, c'est de nous mettre au ras de notre corps, d'exprimer l'inexprimé [. . .] Il deviendra alors évident et clair qu'il y a des choses que nous ne pouvons pas traduire en mots. Comment dire notre sexe, la gestation vécue, le temps, la durée des femmes? Il faudra inventer').[39] Leduc evidently also felt that women writers must evolve their own kind of erotic language in order to 'approcher un peu la sensation dans l'écriture', even if such an enterprise is difficult and disruptive. Her interview with Chapsal indicates, moreover, that she herself endeavoured to do so. It is therefore worth investigating the extent to which Leduc, responding to the problem of linguistic *sexuation* and its effects upon/within erotic discourse, was driven to work on elements of language in *Thérèse et Isabelle* in order to develop either an *écriture féministe* or a (more radical) *écriture féminine*.

These terms clearly require definition. The latter refers to the kind of discourse towards which much of the theoretical writings of Cixous and Irigaray points. It is a language which 'reinscribes' within the phallic symbolic, or writes differently, the repressed feminine, a 'language which would be adequate for the body, sex and the imagination (imaginary) of the woman'.[40] An *écriture féministe*, on the other hand, involves a sustained transgression of existing representational codes and linguistic styles which contribute to the denigration or subjection of women. *Ecriture féminine*, in other words, is a kind of gendered poetics, combining (potentially) a different *style* of writing and a language capable of articulating feminine difference/otherness. *Ecriture féministe* constitutes an attempt on the part of the *écrivaine* to subvert distorting images of femininity and also to avoid linguistic/semantic strategies that reinforce or reflect patriarchal power structures. The following parts of this chapter will be devoted to an exposition of the ways in which Leduc may be said, in her erotic writing, to tackle manifestations of linguistic genderization and to create the kind of feminist/feminine discourse defined above. My discussion will focus on three specific aspects of *Thérèse et Isabelle*; its relationship with texts written by male authors in which feminine homoeroticism is an issue, its depiction of the female body, and its account of woman's sexual pleasure.

LESBIAN INTERTEXTS

As Irigaray suggests in *Ce Sexe qui n'en est pas un*, woman is constantly confronted with deformed and deforming representations of the female subject which are cultural embodiments of the masculine imaginary and which language bequeathes to her. They are so prevalent that, unless she is careful, she may internalize and perpetuate images of herself that bear little relation to the reality of her existence and experiences. My purpose here is to demonstrate that in *Thérèse et Isabelle*, Violette Leduc acknowledges (caricatural) representations of lesbianism inherited from male literary predecessors, and simultaneously undermines them, through a strategy of (ironic) rewriting. Her employment of intertextual parody is reminiscent of the deliberate subversion of existing cultural artefacts Cixous discerns in her own writing practice ('La culture [. . .] était donc là, mais faisant barre, m'interdisant, alors que, bien sûr, au fond de mon corps, j'avais un désir d'objets de culture. Je me suis donc trouvée dans la nécessité de les voler. [. . .] Je m'en suis toujours servie d'une façon complètement ironique').[41] This technique constitutes one way in which Leduc detaches *Thérèse et Isabelle* from a gendered, masculine model of (erotic) discourse that distorts feminine homoerotic reality.[42]

The lesbian relationship has preoccupied French female authors of the modern period, and has engendered texts which are radical and disturbing. Lesbian eroticism has also, however, been the subject of works by men of letters, particularly since the eighteenth century. These have been the focus of criticism by women scholars, who illuminate the stereotypes that have characterized representations of feminine homoeroticism in the past.[43] Before Leduc's mimetic/ironic treatment of such representations can be addressed, the nature of the literary tradition to which they belong must be elucidated.

Although the lesbian figured in French literature before 1700, the first extensive accounts of feminine homoerotic love did not appear until the eighteenth century. The most celebrated literary treatment of lesbianism published during the Enlightenment was offered by Diderot. On one level, *La Religieuse* may be deemed simply to highlight, objectively, the oppressive character of a single-sex environment and to reveal the psychological damage an individual may suffer as a result of enforced celibacy. Arguably, therefore, the novel provides no more than a clinically correct account of one way in which lesbian desire comes into being.[44] Despite their radicalism in most matters, however, the *Philosophes* tended to the reactionary when it came to women, and Diderot may be considered no exception. His presentation of the third Superior as a homosexual corruptress has been taken by Lillian Faderman as evidence that he sought to use his account of lesbianism in order to condemn an institution — the convent — in which women achieved an autonomy denied them elsewhere, and to denigrate women who usurped masculine position and privilege.[45] While Faderman undoubtedly overstates her case and ignores the pleasure Diderot permits his heroine to experience in the company of the lesbian Superior, his depiction of feminine homoerotic 'aberration' in *La Religieuse* can none the less be interpreted as a strategy devised to castigate feminine self-sufficiency and to show such women the error of their ways.

In the nineteenth century, an increasing number of male writers took female homosexuality as their subject. Their treatments of 'sapphism' continued to be largely condemnatory, however. One reason for this may have been an association of lesbianism (woman's sexual independence from man) and feminism (her political rejection of patriarchal structures). Antagonism towards female homosexuality masked, perhaps, an antifeminist reaction on the part of male authors, provoked by the growing refusal of nineteenth-century French women to accept traditional roles and socio-economic subjection.[46] The force of this reaction was fuelled toward the end of the century by sexological works in which feminism and lesbianism were explicitly linked — Havelock Ellis, for example, argues that 'the modern movement of emancipation [. . .] has involved an increase in feminine criminality and in feminine insanity' and comments that 'in connection with these we can hardly be surprised to find an increase in homosexuality, which has always been regarded as belonging to an allied, if not the same, group of phenomena'.[47]

The exotic 'otherness' of the lesbian fascinated various nineteenth-century male authors, regardless of whether they were sympathetic to feminine homosexuality. If Pierre Louÿs's *Chansons de Bilitis* (1894) is semi-positive regarding lesbian relationships (which are none the less depicted stereotypically) and represents a challenge to prejudice against female homoeroticism, Baudelaire's *Les Fleurs du mal* and Balzac's *La Fille aux yeux d'or* associate feminism same-sex love with decadence and violence; all three writers, however, evidently found lesbianism tantalizing and saw it as 'synonymous with a mysterious world of feminine pleasure'.[48] Baudelaire's 'Lesbos' and Balzac's *La Fille aux yeux d'or* both contain accounts of lesbian episodes witnessed by a voyeur, the inclusion of which reflects a common perception that lesbian sex was an erotic performance, designed to arouse the male, rather than evidence of woman's desire for her *semblable(s)*. As Shari Benstock suggests, 'for heterosexual men [of nineteenth-century France], lesbian women were associated with a specialized form of prostitution. These lesbian roles were reinforced by nineteenth-century literature (especially in writings by Balzac, Zola, Louÿs, Gautier, and Baudelaire) and exploited by the more exotic Paris brothels, where the lesbian couple was the pièce de résistance'.[49]

If stylists like Baudelaire were as much fascinated as repelled by the otherness of the lesbian, their realist colleagues were less ambivalent, and their treatments of female homosexuality were openly hostile. Following Diderot, social novelists presented lesbians as corrupt and corrupting, vampire seductresses who lead hapless victims astray. Adolphe Belot's *Mlle Giraud, ma femme* (1879) creates a vision of lesbian evil and condemns sexual segregation (here in a boarding school) as morally dangerous. Belot's assault on sapphism is echoed in Zola's *Nana* and Maupassant's *Le Femme de Paul* (1881); both works associate female homosexuality with prostitution and present lesbians as denizens of a perilous *bas-monde*. While Romantic and Decadent writers combined constrasting visions of lesbian exoticism and lesbian corruption, Belot and his successors created a more consistent image of the lesbian as monster.

Although, therefore, images of women loving women appeared more frequently in the texts of the nineteenth century than in those of the Enlightenment, the lesbian 'heroine' clearly fared no better during the later period. In the twentieth century, Proust's Gomorrah did little to transform the tradition of feminine homoerotic denigration. Although he was not crassly condemnatory, his lesbian creations, particularly Mlle Vinteuil and her friend, are depraved and, worse still, rather foolish. Moreover, as is the case with Baudelaire's lesbians, their function seems to be to tantalize a voyeur who witnesses their embraces, and they therefore reinforce a view of lesbianism as an erotic *pièce de résistance*. As female homosexuals, they are barely more convincing than their caricatured sisters of previous centuries, even though tolerance toward 'inversion' was greater by the time Proust was writing — hence Colette's perception that all he had to offer was a vision of a 'Gomorrhe d'insondables et de vicieuses jeunes filles', a 'collectivité de mauvais anges', devoid of 'la foudroyante vérité qui nous guidait à travers Sodome'.[50]

As she wrote *Thérèse et Isabelle*, Leduc appears to have been alive to the existence of a well-established discourse on the theme of lesbianism produced almost exclusively by male authors. Indeed, the way in which her text echoes the works of some of these authors exemplifies what Barthes describes as 'l'impossibilité de vivre hors du texte infini'.[51] However, *Thérèse et Isabelle* may be read as Leduc's attempt to 'write against', even as she appropriated elements of it, a masculine tradition of lesbian misrepresentation which she evidently scorned.

How can the reader be sure that she sought to do so? For one thing, her descriptions of the way in which the original version of her novella came into being indicate that she was driven by a need to institute a break between her own vision of female homosexuality and that conveyed by male-authored texts dealing with the same subject. A passage in *La Folie en tête* highlights her desire to represent feminine homoeroticism in such a way that the notion that lesbianism is an erotic 'turn', a 'charming' feminine aberration providing the male imagination with a subject for its art and the masculine voyeur with sexual stimulation, might be refuted: 'Le sexe n'est pas charmant, le sexe n'est pas exquis. [. . .] Deux femmes se trouvent: ce ne sont pas des compensations, ce ne sont pas des consolations ou bien des gravures galantes. Je voudrais des funérailles mêlées à des fêtes de jambes' (pp. 297–98).

A further extract, from *La Chasse à l'amour* this time, indicates her wish to dismiss the association of lesbian sex and sin/damnation established by male writers of the past, particularly Diderot, who makes the connection in *La Religieuse*, and Baudelaire, who develops it in *Les Fleurs du mal*.[52] Her own lesbian heroines, Leduc implies, are neither vicious nor doomed, because erotic activity permits them to achieve elevated states which resemble no ordinary human experience:

Thérèse et Isabelle sont trop authentiques pour être vicieuses. Il n'y a pas de vices. Il y a des malades à guérir. Le sexe est leur soleil aveuglant. Elles se caressent. C'est leur religion. Leur enfer, c'est le temps. Leur temps est limité. Ce ne sont pas des femmes damnées. Ce sont des privilégiées. Elles échangent ce qu'elles ont trouvé. Elles découvrent le monde entre deux jambes. (p. 21)

The extent of Leduc's desire to interrogate existing visions of lesbianism is revealed most clearly by the 'corrective' references to the works of Diderot, Baudelaire, and Proust contained in the 1966 version of *Thérèse et Isabelle*. Their inclusion suggests that in her novella Leduc consolidated her (feminist) repudiation of masculinist representations of feminine homosexuality, by employing intertextual mimicry in order to dismantle the (gendered) discourse on lesbianism the most illustrious of her male predecessors offered.[53]

There are evident similarities between *Thérèse et Isabelle* and *La Religieuse*. Both texts place their characters within the 'gynaeceum' setting favoured in works dealing with feminine homoeroticism as a site of lesbian love. If Leduc's *collège* is a secularized version of Diderot's convent, her heroines none the less resemble his *religieuses* in various ways. Each sleeps in a *cellule* in which solitary chastity should prevail, and each must accept a *régime* whose highly regulated, austere character recalls monastic life. Isabelle's hair is compared to a *voile* on several occasions (pp. 59, 60, 92), and Leduc depicts her as she makes love to Thérèse in an attitude of prayer ('Elle [. . .] s'agenouilla . . . une sainte lécha mes souillures', p. 34)). Thérèse's dressing gown becomes a habit when she mentions 'la cordelière de ma robe' (p. 90), and when, overwhelmed by the force of Isabelle's orgasm, she recalls 'J'ai eu des stigmates aux entrailles' (p. 53), her experience echoes some of the more excessive manifestations of religious zeal. The expressions of love each girl articulates are 'litanies sans paroles' (p. 71), while pleasure shared with the loved one is a confusion of 'abnégation' and 'béatitude' (p. 52), both (potential) characteristics of a conventual existence.

The above indicates that Leduc consciously sought to duplicate elements of *La Religieuse* (and of the lesbian/convent topos Diderot's novel exemplifies) in *Thérèse et Isabelle*. The relationship between the two texts is, however, more antagonistic than the preceding paragraph suggests, since the account she provides of the 'cloistered' life led by her heroines differs considerably from Diderot's. For Diderot, the institutionalized world of the convent was the source of the plight of his central character, since it exposed her to the risk of physical and psychological harm. In *Thérèse et Isabelle*, on the other hand, the gynaeceum is a protective sphere within which a unique form of self/other interaction becomes accessible. Furthermore, 'religion', far from denoting the institutional/restrictive, becomes a metaphor for all that is private and delightful. Leduc conjures its rituals and rewards in order to evoke a sensual universe to which her protagonists gain entry by virtue of their love. The religious experience is no longer the cause of lesbian 'vice' but rather represents one manifestation amongst many of feminine homoerotic pleasure, discovered in a domain in which the concept of vice has no significance. Leduc's employment of religious imagery ('J'avais la grâce dans le sang, ma mort se laissait corrompre', p. 98; 'Le corps d'Isabelle gravit seul un calvaire sur mon dos', p. 102; 'Marcher sur les flots . . . Je sais ce que cela veut dire sur le fleuve de mes cuisses', p. 107) does not constitute therefore a (childish) blasphemy against conventional Christian morality and its dictates. It enables her rather to recall, and transform, Diderot's cautionary tale of lesbian aberrance generated by institutionalized religion, a transformation achieved through her presentation of feminine homoerotic ecstasy as a sublime, spiritual experience, rather than as a pathological symptom of the unnatural existence led by the 'religious'.

A particular episode of *Thérèse et Isabelle* connects it more firmly with *La Religieuse*, and indicates strongly that Leduc was attempting to rewrite Diderot's (on one level) hostile representation of lesbianism. Early on in the novella, she depicts Thérèse loving Isabelle as a mother might her child, warming her feet in a gesture of comfort:

J'allongeais mon petit, je lui soulevais la tête, je tapotais l'oreiller, je défroissais, je rajeunissais le lit.
– Tu me soignes, dit Isabelle.

Je réchauffais son pied sur mon sein. Isabelle me donnait un enfant. Tantôt je faisais l'amour avec lui, tantôt je le remettais dans le moïse. (p. 22)

This scene is one of generous emotion, in which each partner gives without thought of return and receives from the other the love she has expended. Communion and reciprocity are thus achieved. It may be contrasted with an episode in *La Religieuse*, whose similarity seems unlikely to be coincidental. In the last section of Diderot's work, as in *Thérèse et Isabelle*, the two female protagonists are alone together at night, in the cell of the younger nun,

Suzanne. The Mother Superior demands of and receives from her subordinate the same form of comfort Thérèse offers Isabelle, warming, 'maternal' caresses ('Aussitôt elle mit une de ses mains sur ma *poitrine* et l'autre autour de ma ceinture; ses *pieds* étaient posés sous les miens, et je les pressais pour les *réchauffer*; et la chère mère me disait: "Ah! chère amie, voyez comme mes *pieds* se sont promptement *réchauffés*, parce qu'il n'y a rien qui les sépare des vôtres"').[54] It is made clear to the reader, however, that the older woman's purpose is exploitative, and that she uses her position and intelligence in order to oblige Suzanne to do what is asked of her. In this episode, Diderot creates an image of lesbian perversity masked as innocence, triumphing over youthful inexperience. In Leduc's reiteration of the scene, on the other hand, a love mutually desired and freely given provides the key, and subverts Diderot's vision.

Leduc also 'writes against' representations of lesbianism offered by Baudelaire in 'Lesbos' and 'Femmes damnées: Delphine et Hippolyte'.[55] Despite the poet's fascination with the unfamiliar world of female homoeroticism, and his apparent reverence for Lesbos, with its 'noir mystère' (p. 135) and its 'vierges en fleurs' (p. 135), his attitude to lesbianism appears condemnatory. He decries, for example, the barren character of the lesbian relation, conjuring the 'stérile volupté' (p. 134) of lesbian caresses and informing his *femmes damnées*, Delphine and Hippolyte, that the 'âpre stérilité' (p. 139) of their *jouissance* will ultimately provoke their moral and physical disintegration. Its sterility, which may be read quite literally as a reference to an absence of procreative potential, seems to render the female homoerotic bond invalid to the poet — although, as Claude Pichois comments, Baudelaire's 'opposition morale et théologique à la nature, à la fécondation' could be said to make Lesbos ('la patrie de la contre-nature et de la stérilité') more rather than less appealing to him.[56] Moreover, while Baudelaire suggests that the relationship between Delphine and Hippolyte resembles a mother/daughter bond, he refuses to recognize that their union might consequently be nurturing and life-affirming, since he has Hippolyte tell her 'mother': 'Je veux m'anéantir dans ta gorge profonde/ Et trouver sur ton sein la fraîcheur des tombeaux' (p. 139). Rather than a fruitful gift, 'maternal' nurturance is transformed, in its lesbian manifestation, into a form of insidious destruction, and the sterility of the lesbian union remains unattenuated.

Leduc takes up the challenge posed by Baudelaire's evocation of lesbian sterility. Her lyrical account of lesbian love presents feminine homoeroticism as infinitely fruitful. The absence of a male lover does not prevent a form of 'procreative' exchange ('Isabelle me donnait un enfant. Tantôt je faisais l'amour avec lui, tantôt je le remettais dans le moïse', p. 22; 'Je portais l'enfant le plus ressemblant qu'elle pût me donner d'elle: je portais l'enfant de sa présence', p. 108) and when her heroines adopt mother and daughter roles in the course of their erotic games, the *anéantissement* evoked by Baudelaire is replaced by generous, fecund nurturance. This is implied early on in the novella, when Thérèse describes how, after she and Isabelle make love, she nestles against her lover ('Je baîllais dans les prés laiteux et mouillés', p. 33), and is also implicit in her later reference to their breasts, which, as arousal draws the adolescents together, provide erotic stimulation and 'nourishment' ('Deux gorges s'élancèrent, quatre foyers de douceur irradièrent. De l'absinthe coula dans mes veines', p. 95).

Baudelaire's Delphine is a descendant of Diderot's Superior, an experienced lesbian bent on manipulating a younger, malleable partner. The poet suggests her 'perverse' nature by transforming her into the ultimate symbol of lesbian evil, the vampire.[57] Delphine is presented as an 'animal fort qui surveille une proie/ Après l'avoir marquée avec les dents' (p. 137), ready, once Hippolyte is subjugated, to absorb 'voluptueusement/ le vin de son triomphe' (p. 137) as if it were the blood of the younger woman, who becomes her lover's 'pâle victime' (p. 137). Traditionally, the image of the vampire has formed part of a discourse of lesbian denigration, but Leduc reclaims the symbol from a canon that subjects feminine homosexuality to mockery and condemnation. As we saw in chapter three, her lesbians each adopt the vampiric role in the course of their erotic games; yet neither, as she 'eats' the other, reduces her lover to a 'proie', humiliated and possessed. Instead of representing a cliché symbolizing lesbian evil, cannibalistic vampirism is transformed by Leduc into one element within a polymorphously erotic universe in which all gestures of love are equally valuable.

More significant than Baudelaire's perception of the lesbian as a vampire is his vision of her as a *femme damnée*, which he also inherited from Diderot. Delphine and Hippolyte are doomed socially ('Loin des peuples vivants, errantes, condamnées/ A travers les déserts courez comme des loups;/ Faites votre destin, âmes désordonnées [. . .]' (p. 139)) and physically ('Jamais un rayon frais n'éclaira vos cavernes/ Par les fentes des murs des miasmes fiévreux/ Filtrent en s'enflammant ainsi que des lanternes/ Et pénètrent vos corps de leurs parfums affreux' (p. 139)); above all, however, their sexuality condemns them to an eternity of spiritual torment:

> – Descendez, descendez, lamantables victimes,
> Descendez le chemin de l'enfer éternel!
> Plongez au plus profond du gouffre, où tous les crimes,
> Flagellés par un vent qui ne vient pas du ciel,
>
> Bouillonnent pêle-mêle avec un bruit d'orage.
> Ombres folles, courez au but de vos désirs;
> Jamais vous ne pourrez assouvir votre rage,
> Et votre châtiment naîtra de vos plaisirs. (p. 139)

Baudelaire's tone here is (on one level, at least) ironic. It reflects a social and moral judgement he did not entirely share, and disguises the solidarity with his sapphic heroines he undoubtedly felt.[58] None the less, the image he created of the lesbian as a damned soul is powerful, and its shadow hangs over *Thérèse et Isabelle*. If Baudelaire depicts an existence 'loin des peuples vivants' as a punishment, however, Leduc's Thérèse envisages social exclusion as the means to achieve a more permanent freedom to love. In one of Thérèse's silent monologues, nature and isolation combine to provide a perfect erotic environment, and Leduc's refutation of Baudelaire's wretched lesbian wastelands is palpable:

Donnez-nous vos haillons, saisons. Soyons les vagabondes aux cheveux laqués par la pluie. Veux-tu, Isabelle, veux-tu te mettre en ménage avec moi sur le bord d'un talus? Nous mangerons nos croûtons avec des mâchoires de lion, nous trouverons le poivre dans la bourrasque, nous aurons une maison, des rideaux de dentelle pendant que les roulottes passeront et s'en iront aux frontières. Je te déshabillerai dans les blés, je t'hébergerai à l'intérieur des meules, je te couvrirai dans l'eau sous les basses branches, je te soignerai sur la mousse des forêts, je te prendrai dans la luzerne, je te hisserai sur les chars à foin, ma Carolingienne. (pp. 43–44)

She also replaces his foul nocturnal caverns with a lesbian nightworld in which darkness offers healthy, maternal protection ('La nuit s'engageait, la nuit: notre couverture de cygne. La nuit: notre baldaquin de mouettes', p. 89) and her lovers' erotic exchanges generate their own illumination ('Nous avons été béantes de lumière, nous avons eu une irruption de félicité. Nos jambes broyées de délices, nos entrailles illuminées', p. 107)). More importantly, as she points out in *La Chasse à l'amour*, her lesbians are clearly *privilégiées* rather than *damnées*. Lesbian eroticism assures access not to the infernal abyss but to a paradise of pleasure:

Isabelle voyait son paradis. (p. 52)

La visite était proche dans mon paradis. (p. 107)

Je me détachais de mon squelette, je flottais sur ma poussière. (p. 107)

Various aspects of Leduc's picture of female homosexuality in *Thérèse et Isabelle* may therefore be read as a rejection of the exotic, febrile vision of lesbian marginality which emerges from Baudelaire's poems. A further intertextual subversion is generated by her treatment of a relationship which Baudelaire evokes in 'Lesbos' but which is also, more famously, depicted by Proust in *A la Recherche du temps perdu*, that of the lesbian couple and the voyeur. In Baudelaire's poem and especially in the scene Proust creates between Mlle Vinteuil and her female lover in *Du Côté de chez Swann*, a male narrator/voyeur appears to be sexually aroused by the spectacle of lesbian activity, illuminating the much exploited potential of the lesbian bond as an erotic 'turn', and echoing the point made by Lucienne Frappier-Masur that in male-authored erotic discourse 'lesbianism is a pretext for scenes of voyeurism, in which secret observation asserts the observer's superiority'.[59] In the Mont-jouvain episode of *Du Côté de chez Swann*, moreover, Proust seems to suggest that the lesbians themselves require the presence of a male watcher in order to achieve a full complement of pleasure,[60] implying that without a masculine spy, 'sapphic' sex might well not have taken place at all.

Mlle Vinteuil and her friend cannot, of course, be assured of the gaze of a human voyeur to stimulate their desire; they are, however, able to solicit voyeuristic scrutiny by using the picture of Vinteuil *père*, the dead music teacher. Before it, their caresses take on the character of a profanatory rite, yet their inclusion of the father in their erotic rituals suggests that they demand his approval, even as they desecrate his memory. As Randolph Splitter explains, 'the implication is not that Mlle Vinteuil is betraying her father for a "mother" but that even her betrayal expresses a need to be acknowledged, to be loved by the father'.[61] Proust therefore creates a complex scene with not one but two voyeurs in it; one of whom (Marcel, the narrator/protagonist of *A la Recherche*) is hidden from the lesbians but is aroused by them because he views their embraces as a sadoerotic performance, and the other of whom is vitally important to the lovers' sexual encounter, even though he is dead. The gaze of at least one of the voyeurs, if not both, is clearly presented as welcome to the lesbians.

It is difficult not to interpret the brothel episode in *Thérèse et Isabelle* as an intertextual reinscription of the account Proust gives the reader, in *Du Côté de chez Swann*, of the lesbian/voyeur relationship. Firstly, although based upon the same triangular situation as the Montjouvain incident, the voyeurism scene Leduc creates in her novella resolutely refuses the association of the voyeur's scrutiny and the arousal of lesbian desire which Proust sets up. As we saw in chapter three, Thérèse and Isabelle become the objects of a voyeur's gaze when they visit Mlle Algazine's 'maison de rendez-vous', hoping to experience a degree of sensual delight denied them within the bounds of their school. However, their pleasure is adulterated by Thérèse's fear of the disembodied eye she believes to be staring at them through an *œil de bœuf* — another Proustian detail, borrowed this time from the sadomasochism episode in Jupien's hotel in *Le Temps retrouvé*. The visit is damaging rather than liberating, and the lovers return, chastened, to the *collège*.

In contrast to Proust, then, Leduc presents voyeuristic scrutiny as the means by which lesbian desire is destroyed. Furthermore, her narrative undermines the centrality accorded to the male voyeuristic subject in Proust's Montjouvain episode. This is because the brothel scene in *Thérèse et Isabelle*, which is narrated from a first-person lesbian perspective, obviously foregrounds the dynamics of *feminine* homosexual exchange and not its arousing effect upon the *male* spy who observes it. The voyeur whose existence is suspected by

Thérèse, although a powerful element of disruption, is simply a ghostly, elliptical half-presence, half-absence, rather than a sexually stimulated narrator like Proust's Marcel, whose responses and reflections dominate the description of the events at Montjouvain. Consequently, the whole emphasis of Proust's version of the lesbian/voyeur topos is turned around. The voyeurism episode Leduc creates in *Thérèse et Isabelle* constitutes, in other words, a scene whose intertextual modifications 'correct', up to a point, Proust's vision of Gomorrah, and rescue lesbianism from a masculine literary field in which it represents a source of titillation for the male author/reader/voyeur.

Clearly, Leduc's creation of mimetic parallels enables her to 'write against' representations that belong to a deforming, male-authored erotic tradition, and indicates that in *Thérèse et Isabelle* she does evolve a kind of *écriture féministe*. If these parallels were the only evidence of an attempt on her part to produce a feminist text, the subversive potential of her novella would be rather restricted, since intertextual mimesis has its limitations. The value of 'borrowing' from the 'Fathers' is questionable, and, as Domna Stanton observes, 'the repetition of masculinist notions and images of the feminine does not necessarily have a ludic or subversive impact that points to an elsewhere'.[62] However, *Thérèse et Isabelle* is 'feminist' on other levels too. The techniques Leduc employs in it to write about the female body, for example, make it possible to read her text as a more radical assault upon masculine representational models. Leduc's 'body language', as we shall see in the next part of this chapter, constitutes another sort of *écriture féministe* which comes close to resembling an *écriture féminine*.

HEALING THE BODY: NAMING STRATEGIES

Fetichizing fragmentation of the female body is a key and enduring feature of (male-authored) erotic discourse. As Helena Michie points out, 'in Victorian literature and culture various parts of the body came to be fetichized sexually and representationally, as nameable, accessible parts of the body came to stand for the unnameable whole/hole. Twentieth-century sexual culture, the sexual "revolution", has produced an inversion of Victorian representational tropes, where the historically unnameable parts of the female body came to stand for the rest of it'.[63] Michie's observations concerning the treatment of the female form in the erotic texts/visual images of our period are borne out by, *inter alia*, the writings of Henry Miller, in which, for Kate Millett at least, what is achieved is 'a complete depersonalization of woman into cunt'.[64] In novels such as *Sexus*, the female body ceases to be an organic unity and is reduced instead to a limited number of objectified parts, which correspond to the erotic needs/fantasies of the (twentieth-century, Western) male subject. In the erotic texts produced by modern French male authors which Anne-Marie Dardigna analyses in *Les Châteaux d'Eros*, especially those of Robbe-Grillet and Klossowski, a similar tendency towards a *morcellement* or synecdochization of the body of the feminine object is apparent. It produces an 'anatomie fantasmatique du corps féminin',[65] which is in evidence, for instance, in the opening paragraph of Robbe-Grillet's *La Maison de rendez-vous*:

La chair des femmes a toujours occupé, sans doute, une très grande place dans mes rêves. Même à l'état de veille, ses images ne cessent de m'assaillir. Une fille en robe d'été qui offre sa nuque courbée — elle rattache sa sandale — la chevelure à demi renversée découvrant la peau fragile et son duvet blond, je la vois aussitôt soumise à quelque complaisance, tout de suite excessive. L'étroite jupe entravée, fendue jusqu'aux cuisses, des élégantes de Hong Kong se déchire d'un coup sous une main violente, qui dénude soudain la hanche arrondie, ferme, lisse, brillante, et la tendre chute des reins. Le fouet de cuir, dans la vitrine d'un sellier parisien, les seins exposés de mannequins de cire, une affiche de spectacle, la réclame pour des jarretelles ou pour un parfum, deux lèvres humides, disjointes, un bracelet de fer, un collier à chien, dressent autour de moi leur décor insistant, provocateur.[66]

Dardigna suggests that the masculine narrators/protagonists created by writers like Robbe-Grillet subject their female partners to bodily fragmentation in order to possess them more completely, and, in so doing, to confer upon themselves a quasi-superhuman status:

Il s'agit bien de les déposséder de leur corps, et à travers leur corps de leur identité. Cette expropriation/appropriation n'est possible pour le démiurge masculin qu'à condition d'une déconstruction radicale du sujet féminin — jusqu'à ce qu'il n'existe plus par lui-même. C'est alors la dernière phase de la possession.[67]

In erotic writing of the type cited above, the process of dismemberment and fetichization to which women are subjected constitutes a sustained assault on the integrity of the female body. It should come as no surprise therefore that modern women writers who have attempted to create their own erotic language(s) have sought to evolve new ways of treating the female anatomy. As Michie points out, 'a major although not always articulated task of feminist writing has, so far, been the full and responsible representation of the female body [. . .]. Since the early nineteen seventies, feminism has, in most of its manifestations, set out to do just that: to construct a female body in the face of patriarchal convention'.[68] In *Le Corps lesbien*, for example — probably the most radical erotic narrative written by a woman to date — Wittig periodically interrupts her poetic monologue in order to enumerate all the component elements of woman's body. This, as Martha Evans notes, is a strategy designed in part to illuminate the *morcellement* women suffer; it reminds the reader of how masculinist culture/language fragments and fetichizes (parts of) the female form, and in so doing repudiates this process:

The female body is a list: words next to each other, parts next to each other, without any apparent connections. By their syncopated appearances in an already discontinuous text, these lists represent the final reduction of the female to a selfless and random agglomeration of word-objects.[69]

Leduc's approach to writing the body differs from that adopted by Wittig — who, interestingly, cites Leduc as the only French woman writer she can acknowledge as a predecessor[70] — since it emphasizes healing and wholeness, rather than dismemberment. However, like Wittig, Leduc undoubtedly 'forces us to question our acceptance of male fragmentation of the body into discrete objects labelled "desirable" and "undesirable"'.[71] As we saw in chapter three, *Thérèse et Isabelle* indicates that the lesbian relationship, if it escapes the limitations of the heterosexual model and becomes genuinely 'other', allows the female body in its entirety to become eroticized. In making this apparent, Leduc names the whole of the body, with the result that a myriad of anatomical parts, usually absent from erotic discourse of the kind produced by Miller *et al.*, are insistently evoked in her novella. Arms, fingers, necks, legs, hair, bellies, hands, ankles, backs, shoulders, eyebrows, eyelashes, and faces all play a part in the sexual carnival and are resolutely cited by Leduc throughout the text. Instead of depicting a female body that is no more than a fetichized 'cunt', or presenting 'comme autant d'objets hétéroclites des *morceaux* de la chair des femmes',[72] Leduc names a feminine anatomy which is whole because her naming puts it back together and allows it to 'speak'. She consequently escapes the tradition of erotic *morcellement* and substitutes connection and unification for dislocation.

Leduc takes her (feminist) strategy of denominational subversion a stage further when she evokes the parts of the female body which *are* named (and fetichized) in contemporary erotic writing. Although she cites, insistently and directly, those elements of woman's anatomy which are obfuscated in male-authored texts, her references to the genitalia and breasts of her heroines are, on the whole, less explicit — she employs, for example, the word 'sexe' only ten times in the course of her novella (pp. 17, 50, 51, 52, 53, 77, 78, 92). Her treatment of these body parts takes two forms. Firstly, she employs figurative language in order to describe the clitoris, which is variously a 'perle' (pp. 52, 52, 105, 106) and a 'bourgeon précieux' (p. 35), and the vagina, which becomes for example a 'rosace' (p. 25), an 'agneau doré' (p. 50), a 'petit mongoli' or 'petit mordoré' (p. 50), a 'médaillon' (p. 50), 'de la nuit salée [. . .] de la nuit gluante [. . .] de la viande fragile' (p. 51), a 'carpe chérie' (p. 77), a 'bouche sousmarine adorée' (p. 77), a 'monstre rose' (p. 77), an 'anémone mouillée' (p. 77) and a 'sainte image' (pp. 77–78). Secondly, she resorts to a strategy of silence. In her evocation of Thérèse's 'ingestion' of Isabelle's breast, Leduc is elliptical rather than explicit:

– Mieux que cela, suppliait Isabelle.
Il ne quitta pas ma bouche lorsque nous tombâmes sur le parquet.

10

Je le gardais dans mes mains, je retenais son poids de tiédeur, de pâleur, de tendresse. Mon ventre était affamé de lueur.
– Caresse-le, dit Isabelle.
– Non!
J'ouvris la bouche, il entra. (p. 95)

and she uses the same, obscuring 'le' instead of an unequivocal *vagin/sexe/clitoris* elsewhere in her text:

Je le berçais, je l'aiguisais, je le sortais des replis de sa déchéance, je lui rendais confiance. Je ne me souviendrais pas de lui ainsi si je ne lui avais pas donné mon âme et ma vie. (p. 106)

J'ouvris ses lèvres et me suicidai avant de regarder. Mon visage le touchait, mon visage le mouillait. Je me mis à l'aimer de franche amitié. (p. 109)

Given her belief that women needed to 'oser' in order to represent their erotic experiences, it seems unlikely that Leduc's reluctance to name, explicitly, the most obviously sexual elements of the bodies of her heroines stemmed from a desire to veil those elements, in order not to shock. We do not need, either, to interpret her choice of metaphorical language to denote the female sexual organs as evidence of an incapacity on her part to elude the 'sépulture décorative', the 'couches de style ornemental',[73] the 'sinister "covering" of the female body'[74] which certain contemporary feminists — including Irigaray — view as symptomatic of a culture that cannot ultimately face/articulate the reality of the feminine (anatomy). Leduc's metaphorization of the female genitals can be read rather as part of her attempt to *déranger* a mode of erotic discourse, created by male writers, which exploits explicitation in order to 'damage' women's bodies. Her employment of metaphor distances an erotic rhetoric which focuses obsessively/exclusively on the female sexed parts, and presents them with a directness that renders them obscene. In the erotic writing of authors like Miller and Robbe-Grillet, obscene explicitation 'is a form of violence, a manner of conveying male hostility, both toward the female (who is sex) and toward sexuality itself (which is her fault)'.[75] By adopting a figurative mode, Leduc effectively repudiates the violence to which woman risks exposure, linguistically as well as physically, within the patriarchal system. In refusing to be sexually explicit/textually brutal in *Thérèse et Isabelle*, she evolves a non-violent discourse of the female body, which displaces denigratory bodily images found in erotic texts by men.

The codes Leduc employs in order to evoke the feminine genitals do not resemble the banal metaphors traditionally associated with the female anatomy in male-authored erotic writings which tend to the figurative rather than the explicit. In his *Dictionnaire historique, stylistique, rhétorique, étymologique de la littérature érotique*, Pierre Guiraud includes a list of those images which have commonly been used to figure feminine sexual parts in French erotic language. He suggests, moreover, that this language, which he too perceives as masculine-gendered, cannot adequately represent woman's body and sexuality:

Il est frappant de constater que ce langage — si on en juge au nombre des mots, des images et à leur pertinence et leur originalité — est très pauvre et souvent inadéquat quant à la description de la sexualité féminine dont nous commençons pourtant à soupçonner aujourd'hui qu'elle est physiologiquement et psycho-physiologiquement plus complexe et plus riche que celle de l'homme. Et cette carence du langage est une véritable castration [...].[76]

Only rarely do Leduc's genital metaphors constitute the kind of overworked, 'masculine' images listed in Guiraud's *dictionnaire*, images like *fournaise* (p. 53), *nid* (p. 31), *toison* (p. 108), or *pétales* (p. 109), for example. Leduc's imaginary is infinitely richer and, when she does resort to conventional codes, she transforms them by qualifying them in unusual or surprising ways, or by extending their scope. Isabelle's sex is not merely a *bouche*, for instance, but becomes instead a 'bouche sousmarine adorée', and the ubiquitous *rose* (a very common metaphor for the vagina) is variously replaced with 'rosace', 'cœur de rose' (p. 14) and 'monstre rose'. This suggests that Leduc's discourse of the female body, even when it comes close to falling into metaphorical banality, represents a stylistic regeneration of a pre-existent erotic/linguistic model she found inadequate.

Leduc's metaphorization of the sexed elements of the feminine form appears, like her use of intertextual mimicry, to be the product of a reaction against a (male) erotic rhetoric with which she was clearly familiar. Although less obviously marked by that rhetoric than her intertextual 'borrowings' are by the tradition of lesbian (mis)representation, her poetic body-writing none the less stands in (an antagonistic) relation to it. Leduc's figurative depiction of woman's sexual parts still represents therefore an *écriture féministe*, albeit of a more original kind that that constituted by her rewriting of male accounts of lesbianism. However, her employment of ellipsis suggests that *Thérèse et Isabelle* contains instances of a 'déconcertation du langage',[77] which (for the post-Lacanian feminist critic at least) arguably 'reinscribes' the feminine and may be taken as evidence of a kind of *écriture féminine*. Ellipsis involves the deliberate inclusion, within language, of 'blanks' or 'absences'; it places emphasis on, and gives value to, that which is left silent. In *Thérèse et Isabelle*, the 'unsaid' is used in connection with woman's sex and her breasts, i.e. with those features of her anatomy which signify the feminine difference/otherness that is denigrated or ignored within phallocentric culture. Leduc's ostentatious obfuscation of these anatomical elements, and the narrative 'disruption' this obfuscation produces, can be read as a textual strategy that is somehow 'feminine'.[78] Existing critical accounts of the work of another French woman writer, Marguerite Duras, help us to see how this might be the case.

Textual silences/gaps are much in evidence in Duras's *œuvre*. One explanation of this feature of her writing is that her use of ellipsis figures and celebrates
'la dimension fascinante du manque du pénis féminin: que Duras tente de [. . .]
faire "parler" comme cri (*Moderato cantabile*), ou comme "musique"'.[79]
Another interpretation, which constructs Duras's employment of ellipsis in a
more helpful way, suggests that by breaking up the smooth movement of her
narrative with gaps which point up the silencing of the feminine in 'phallic'
language and simultaneously undermine the coherence of that same language,
Duras creates, quite markedly, an 'other' style. Durassian ellipsis, Marcelle
Marini implies, brings into being a language which palpably illuminates the
masking of difference in discourse, and which represents, conceivably, a
language of the feminine:

[Les "blancs" dans les textes de Marguerite Duras] dessinent "les lieux de son
exclusion comme femme". [. . .] Dans le jeu des blancs avec les signes, du silence
avec le dit, s'opère, par effraction du texte-discours clôturant, un autre style
d'inscription-parole, au point que même le rapport de l'écrire au dire peut en être
changé.[80]

Marini is exploiting here an argument offered by Irigaray, in *Speculum, de
l'autre femme*. In the essay 'Toute théorie du sujet', Irigaray claims that by
manipulating 'ces *blancs* du discours qui rappellent les lieux de son exclusion' in
such a way that a syntactical/lexical 'bouleversement' is achieved, a woman can
'rouvr[ir] des chemins dans un (encore) logos qui la connote comme châtrée,
notamment et surtout de paroles'.[81] It is precisely the notion of a feminine
'reopening' of discourse which Marini is foregrounding when she evokes the
'autre style' Durassian ellipsis engenders. So how does her reading relate to
Thérèse et Isabelle? Leduc's novella is less obviously experimental than much of
Duras's *œuvre*. However, the fact that it contains examples of elliptical 'body
language' means that we can, if we accept the critical perspective outlined
above,[82] read it as marked by stylistic features which resemble those used by
Duras, which effectively reveal/undermine the exclusion ('castration') of the
feminine in language, and which can be viewed as emblematic of an 'other'
mode of discourse. In other words, in those parts of *Thérèse et Isabelle* where
Leduc resorts to a strategy of silence, and where her narrative becomes
disruptive and disrupted precisely as a result of her deliberate effacement of
that which signals woman's difference, she may be considered, paradoxically,
to produce a 'feminine-gendered' kind of writing. In the next part of my
discussion, which will examine Leduc's treatment of erotic sensation, further
potential manifestations of *écriture féminine* in *Thérèse et Isabelle* will be
scrutinized. In particular, Leduc's use of metaphor — which, according to
Cixous, 'drive[s] language mad', 'smashes language from all sides' and is
therefore related to the expression of unrepresented feminine 'otherness' and

to a feminine style that undermines the monolithic 'phallicity' of the linguistic realm — will be re-examined.[83]

Sexual Pleasure/Textual Difference?

Like her representations of the female genitalia, Leduc's treatment of feminine pleasure in *Thérèse et Isabelle* is highly figurative. Her metaphors of feminine erotic sensation fall into a number of central categories, the largest of which draws upon the world of nature. Her text contains fourteen images relating to flora and fauna, including:

Elle se dégagea, elle recula, elle revint, elle me changea en magnolia (p. 10)

Je creusais dans son cou avec mes dents, j'aspirais la nuit sous le col de sa robe: les racines d'un arbre frissonnèrent (p. 10)

Des lianes se détendirent, une clarté se propagea dans nos chevilles (p. 32)

Le nénuphar s'ouvrira dans mon ventre (p. 92)

Les feuilles de lilas déroulaient leur douceur (p. 106)

Les veilleuses se ranimaient, la pieuvre refaisait son travail d'accrochage (p. 100)

La mélopée tournait en rond dans mes coudes, dans mes genoux (p. 98)

Leduc also evokes other aspects of the natural realm, including the elements ('nous avons éventé les caresses, nous avons créé des motifs avec de la brise marine, nous avons enveloppé de zéphyrs nos jambes', pp. 31–32; 'J'avais un carambolage de nuages dans mes entrailles', p. 109), and the seasons ('Nous avons effleuré et survolé nos épaules avec les doigts fauves de l'automne', p. 31; 'le printemps me mettait à l'agonie', p. 106), and creates visions of explosions of light and heat ('nous avons lancé à grands traits la lumière dans les nids', p. 31; 'Mon ardeur gagna Isabelle, un soleil fou tournoya dans ma chair', p. 102; 'nous avons éte béantes de lumière', p. 107; 'une flamme de velours se tordit dans mes jambes', p. 107), in order to suggest the powerful character of the feelings her heroines enjoy.

A second key image-group involves nine metaphors which relate to death and present orgasm as a cessation of existence, a movement toward physical decomposition. It includes the following:

Nous avons roulé enlacées sur une pente de ténèbres. Nous avons cessé de respirer pour l'arrêt de vie et l'arrêt de mort. (p. 107)

Nos membres mûrissaient, nos charognes se décomposaient. Exquise pourriture. (p. 98)

J'étais amollie jusqu'à l'ineffable pourriture, je ne finissais pas de m'effondrer de félicité en félicité dans ma poussière. (p. 102)

[. . .] le printemps me mettait à l'agonie, la poussière des morts dansait dans ma lumière. (p. 106)

The above are only a sample of the numerous metaphorical phrases denoting feminine sexual pleasure — there are some eighty-seven in total — contained in Leduc's novella. Like her references to religion, food, music, madness, military activity, and a whole range of sense-related phenomena, they reveal the lyrical form her attempt to 'approcher un peu la sensation dans l'érotisme, la décrire' took. But do Leduc's metaphors engender the kind of language which feminist theorists have deemed to be an *écriture féminine*, i.e. a radical discourse of feminine difference? Can the reader justifiably conclude from them that *Thérèse et Isabelle* is a 'feminine' text?

The lyricism that characterizes those parts of Leduc's novella in which *jouissance* is evoked metaphorically recalls the writings of Anaïs Nin. Significantly, Nin explicitly related figurative, poetic language of the kind she and Leduc both evolved to a feminine form of writing which might, unlike that of Henry Miller, unlock the mysteries of women's sensuality.[84] Furthermore, the particular experience conveyed by some of Leduc's metaphors suggests that in *Thérèse et Isabelle* she was working towards (and achieved?) the creation of a language capable of representing feminine eroticism in a unique, and even 'gendered', way. The most striking thing about many of her images is that they foreground a dissolution of the boundaries between self and world, between the female subject and the material/natural environment, and indicate that sexual pleasure involves an attenuation of the limits and limitations of the individual being. This is particularly true of the nature images, which forcibly associate the erotic sensations Leduc describes with a blurring of rigid distinctions between self and non-self. The significance of this dissolution is highlighted by the fact that it is actively desired by Thérèse, as she and Isabelle become aroused:

Je ne suis que moi-même. C'est trop peu. Je ne suis pas une forêt. Un brin d'herbe dans mes cheveux, un confetti dans les plis de mon tablier, une coccinelle entre mes doigts, un duvet dans mon cou, une cicatrice à la joue m'étofferaient. Pourquoi ne suis-je pas la chevelure de saule pour sa main qui caresse mes cheveux? [...] Je modelais son épaule, je voulais pour elle des caresses campagnardes, je désirais sous ma main une épaule houleuse, une écorce. Elle fermait mon poing, elle lissait un galet. (pp. 8–9)

The osmotic mingling of self and world suggested by Leduc's metaphors may simply reflect the fact that, as Bataille observes, the essence of eroticism, for all human beings, 'est de substituer à l'isolement de l'être, à sa discontinuité, un sentiment de continuité profonde'.[85] Arguably, however, the central place occupied within her novella by images of pleasure that emphasize a confusion of the boundaries of self and non-self means that in her text Leduc evolves a poetic representation of a specifically *feminine* experience of the erotic. As we saw in the opening part of this chapter, woman — according to Hélène Cixous at least — is more open to that which is 'other', is less self-contained and closed off from the 'different', the 'outside', than man: 'La femme admet qu'il y ait de l'autre. Elle n'a pas effacé, dans son devenir-femme, la bisexualité latente chez la fille comme chez le garçon. [. . .] A l'homme, il est beaucoup plus difficile de se laisser traverser par de l'autre'.[86] We may attribute this 'openness', as Cixous does, to the enduring 'bisexuality' of the female subject, or, in Chodorowian mode, link it to the feminine ego boundary blurring/fluidity that is engendered by the complexities of mother/daughter bonding. Either way, it seems likely that if woman is able to 'se laisser traverser par de l'autre', as Cixous argues, then this facet of her nature will affect her sexuality, her relation to the erotic. In the light of this, sexual *language* which stresses, as Leduc's does, images of flux and dissolution and emphasizes an intermingling of self and non-self, a 'breaking down of boundaries, [a] fluidity whereby microcosm and macrocosm exchange places', may justifiably be taken to constitute what Alicia Ostriker (who notes the prevalence of such motifs in erotic writing by American women poets) has described as a 'gynocentric erotics'.[87] By creating a poetic discourse whose metaphors of pantheistic fusion embody what is possibly the core of woman's different erotic experience, Leduc may be said to evolve an *écriture féminine*.

A further justification for likening Leduc's language to an *écriture féminine* lies in the aural effects created within her narrative by the figure of metaphor. According to Cixous, 'woman-speak' is marked by an oral quality which is a consequence of the bond that exists between a woman's language and the voice/body of the mother, with which she never quite loses touch: 'Dans la parole féminine comme dans l'écriture ne cesse jamais de résonner ce qui de nous avoir jadis traversé, touché imperceptiblement, profondément, garde le pouvoir de nous affecter, le *chant*, la première musique, celle de la première voix d'amour, que toute femme préserve vivante'.[88] In *L'Ecriture-Femme*, Béatrice Didier, like Cixous, isolates an oral or musical style as characteristic of a specifically feminine discourse:

Or, précisément, [le] rapport à la littérature orale, [l'] "oralitude" (le mot est bien laid, tout au plus a-t-il l'avantage d'écarter les équivoques de l'"oralité"), est précisément un élément très positif de [la] spécificité féminine. Ecrire n'apparaîtra plus à la femme comme une sorte de trahison par rapport à la parole si elle sait créer une écriture telle que le flux de la parole s'y retrouve, avec ses soubresauts, ses ruptures et ses cris.[89]

Didier suggests moreover that it is metaphorical language in particular which permits the creation of the 'oral' *écriture* she and Cixous associate with linguistic/discursive femininity:

Le recours au style figuré prend alors un sens très particulier. J-J Rousseau avait bien vu que l'usage de la métaphore dans le texte écrit est un moyen de lui rendre cette chaleur, cette vie de la voix et du chant premiers . . . C'est qu'il savait bien que la voix fondamentale est maternelle. L'image dans l'écriture féminine renoue tout spontanément avec la tradition orale et permet au texte écrit de demeurer parlé ou chanté.[90]

Leduc's figurative descriptions of erotic sensation frequently possess a musical character which seems to endorse Didier's argument that not only is there an intimate link, in women's writing, between metaphor and musicality/*oralitude*, but that the former somehow gives rise to the latter. Leduc's images do not merely consist of evocative word pictures; they are also, simultaneously, sound pictures. Some are marked by alliteration ('Des tenailles me torturaient, mollement, mollement', pp. 13–14; 'Ce déferlement de douceur me finit', p. 32; 'Le plaisir sévère se propagea dans les pétales', p. 101; 'J'avais été frôlée par l'écharpe de la folie', p. 107). Others display assonance ('Le printemps dans sa toison fraternisait avec le printemps dans ma toison', p. 17; 'J'ai de la charpie dans les mollets, de l'espalier j'ai le poids de l'été', p. 99). As some of the above indicate, her metaphors are also characterized by a subtle rhyming, rhythmic harmony ('Vivantes, allongées, flottantes, séparées, nous pouvions croire au repos éternel', p. 23; 'deux gorges s'élancèrent, quatre foyers de douceurs irradièrent', p. 95; 'Mes yeux entendaient, mes oreilles voyaient', p. 101; 'Je fus tendue de gris. Mes jambes faiblirent dans leur paradis', p. 102). The metaphoricity of Leduc's erotic discourse indubitably bestows upon it the (feminine) 'privilège de la *voix*'[91] which a more prosaic or intellectual form of language, a direct, non-figurative discourse, would stifle. In consequence, her sustained employment of metaphor can be viewed as an attempt to come closer, in her account of feminine eroticism, to a 'feminine' form of language in which, as Cixous puts it, '*écriture et voix* se tressent, se trament'.[92]

Metaphor does not, however, simply infuse language with the oral quality Didier and Cixous associate with *écriture féminine*. More importantly, it forces a single word or phrase to convey simultaneously — and *incongruously* — literal and figurative levels of meaning, and is therefore predicated upon what Ricœur calls 'a semantic clash'.[93] Consequently, the trope introduces into discourse an element of contradiction, and generates within it a capacity for ambiguity and multivalence. As Donald Davidson explains, 'whether or not metaphor depends on new or extended meanings, it certainly depends in some way on original meanings; an adequate account of metaphor must allow that the primary or original meanings of words remain active in their metaphorical setting. Perhaps, then, we can explain metaphor as a kind of ambiguity: in the context of a metaphor certain words have either a new or an original meaning, and the force of the metaphor depends on our uncertainty as we waver between the two meanings'.[94] This is particularly true when, as in the case of Leduc's images (for example 'La vague vint en éclaireur, elle grisa nos pieds, elle se reprit', p. 32, or 'J'avais de la griserie en pleine pâte, j'avais un gazouillis d'épices, je m'élargissais jusqu'aux hanches', p. 101), the metaphor in question

s into being through 'simple replacement', i.e. via the absolute substitu-
of a (surprising) vehicle/metaphor for the tenor/proper term ('gazouillis
ces' or 'de la griserie en pleine pâte' for 'plaisir sexuel', for instance).[95]
ink between metaphor on the one hand and disruptive ambiguity on the
(a quality absent from, and 'hostile' to, the univocal, rational language
ay and Cixous categorize as phallocentric/morphic)[96] helps us to understand more clearly why metaphor has been perceived — by Cixous, at least —
as an integral element of *écriture féminine*, and encourages us to read *Thérèse et
Isabelle* as an example of this kind of *écriture*. The fact that the trope can
generate a 'vast potential of meanings',[97] and is therefore emblematic of the
heterogeneity which French feminism has associated with woman's body, her
libidinal make-up and her 'parole', renders the bond Cixous establishes
between metaphor and 'feminine-gendered' discourse all the more
comprehensible.

In summary, Leduc's metaphorical discourse of female pleasure corresponds
to my definition of what a 'feminine' language might entail in a number of ways.
Its allusive and elusive nature, together with the emphasis its images place
upon boundary dissolution, may be read as a sign that it represents authen-
tically that which has been obscured in masculinist culture, i.e. the reality of
female erotic sensation. Secondly, its musicality and its multivalent, disruptive
character can, like its elliptical aspect, be taken as evidence of a stylistic/
syntactical specificity that is, arguably, 'sexué féminin'. In other words, the fact
that Leduc's poetic text pre-dated the theoretical writings of women like
Cixous and Irigaray does not prevent it from having features in common with
the type of discourse their works indicate to be a 'langage autre'. In the light of
this, it seems justifiable, up to a point, to interpret *Thérèse et Isabelle* as an
example of *écriture féminine*, produced by Leduc in response to her awareness
of the masculine-gendered character of (erotic) language, as well as of *écriture
féministe*.

This kind of approach to Leduc's novel, although attractive, poses certain
problems however. For a start, because she 'borrows' in such an obvious (albeit
ironic) fashion from existing, male-authored works which deal with lesbianism,
and because the nature imagery she employs in order to convey *jouissance* is
conventionally associated with women and with feminine sexuality, her text
remains too close to the traditional/masculine literary order to allow a categori-
cal assertion of its discursive *féminité*.[98] Secondly, *Thérèse et Isabelle* shows
insufficient evidence of the syntactical 'bouleversement' Irigaray advocates,
and is far from constituting the kind of avant-garde work she apparently has in
mind when she talks of an 'autre écriture'.[99] Thirdly, the subversive/feminine
potential or a language that is so reliant upon the figure of metaphor needs to be
(re)considered carefully. If Cixous privileges the trope because it 'smashes'
(phallic) language, Irigaray views it with a greater degree of circumspection. In

Speculum, analysing woman's relation to metaphoricity, to the codes with which language surrounds the feminine, she presents the female 'subject' as being 'enfoui sous toutes ces métaphores survalorisantes ou dénigrantes', as stifling beneath '[des] revêtements dont le "sujet" habille, pudiquement, le "féminin"',[100] i.e. as a victim of what are essentially and inevitably deforming projections of the masculine imaginary. Moreover, as Margaret Whitford explains, Irigaray links metaphor — a trope of substitution, in which the vehicle replaces the tenor, rather than of contiguity — to a patriarchal/ masculine economy, whose basis is the son's (usurpatory) identification with the father and the 'movement of metaphoric substitution' which subtends that identification.[101] In other words, Irigaray views metaphor as part and parcel of a dominant phallic order, and as a 'phallomorphic' trope.[102] Metaphor dominates *Thérèse et Isabelle*, as we have seen. We are by no means obliged to accept an Irigarayan reading of metaphoricity, but if we do, then it is questionable whether we can go on attaching the label *écriture féminine* to Leduc's figurative discourse of *jouissance*. A further, major difficulty arises from the fact that, even if we conclude that her novella is polysemic, plural, and 'indeterminate' enough to justify a defence of its textual *féminité*, the whole concept of a separate, feminine aesthetics is hugely problematic. As numerous critics have argued, this notion is undermined by the fact that it is male rather than female authors who have tended to produce the type of writing in question. Moreover, as Rita Felski succinctly argues in her critique of the arbitrary, ahistorical character of much 1970s feminist theory, 'it is impossible to make a convincing case for the claim that there is anything inherently feminine or feminist in experimental writing as such; if one examines the texts of *l'écriture féminine*, for example, the only gender-specific elements exist on the level of content'.[103] In the light of this, however tempted we might be to restrict ourselves to the type of reading I have outlined so far, it seems both appropriate and necessary to find another way of understanding Leduc's discursive project, and specifically her recourse to a poetic form of language.

TRANSLATIONAL WRITING
('J'écrivais [. . .] pour les traduire, pour ne pas les trahir.')

Numerous metatextual observations contained in *La Folie en tête* suggest that Leduc felt that the writer's task was to translate into words, as accurately as possible, his or her experience of the world, to make palpable the precise nature of an urban scene or rural landscape, for example, or to convey the reality and immediacy of particular emotions, sensations, and perceptions. On one level, therefore, her search for the *mot juste* undoubtedly involved a quest after a form of language which, she believed, would act as a window onto the world — a belief which seems curiously outmoded today. She was convinced, however, that most writers, herself included, fail to produce 'translational', referential discourse, that they betray the realities they endeavour to evoke, and that this betrayal stems in part from the inadequacy of a linguistic medium which cannot embrace the richness, strangeness and unique character of the phenomena it is employed to describe:

Tendres nuances au ciel les premiers jours de mars, du côté de la Nation ... Revenez en décembre mes innocentes, revenez en janvier mes suaves, laissez vous prendre, je vais vous qualifier, je vais vous exploiter, je vais vous détruire puisque je vais vous trahir, tendres nuances au ciel, du côté de la Nation ... (*La Folie*, pp. 52–53)

Ecrire, en y réfléchissant, est malhonnête, nous trahissons. Nous trahissons quoi? Tout, tout ce qui est. Les choses, les êtres, les objets. Ils sont plus grands que nos suppositions. Nous ne pouvons pas forcer le silence d'une carrière de sable la nuit. (p. 87)

Ma plume n'est pas un pur-sang, elle ne franchit pas les obstacles des mots. (p. 16)

Leduc's awareness of linguistic *trahison*, of the impossibility of depicting the world in words which do not deform it, became acute when she sought to transcribe aspects of feminine sexuality and, concomitantly, to convey her own experience of *jouissance*. This, as one analyst of French erotic poetry has observed, may reflect the fact that the representation of eros, more than any other form of representation, forces the writer to confront the limitations we discover within language when we use it to reproduce reality:

De la description des serpents troublés par le bâton de Tirésias chez Malifâtre aux raisins sucés par le Faune de Mallarmé, la question de la représentation du corps érotique se confond avec la question des rapports entre parole et réalité, au point qu'on peut former l'hypothèse qu'il existerait une étroite analogie entre ces deux instances, et que savoir ce qu'un poète retient d'un corps serait du même coup préciser son rapport à la réalité. [...] Tout se passe comme si le corps érotisé jouait le rôle d'une métaphore du réel, comme si la représentation érotique était une figure de la représentation de la réalité. De même que cette dernière ne sera jamais que l'objet du *désir* du langage, de même l'éros ne sera-t-il jamais qu'*approché* par les ressources de la poésie.[104]

The nature of the obstacle language constitutes for the writer who, like Leduc, endeavours to translate *le réel* is illuminated by Henri Bergson in his *Essai sur les données de la conscience immédiate* (1889), which deals with the question of mental/emotional reality and the way we give an account of it. In this essay, the difficulties faced by the individual who tries to communicate private experiences in the public medium of words are analysed extensively. According to Bergson, there is a gulf between the unique, shifting world of perception, feeling and sensation that exists within each of us and the reifying words we employ in order to grasp and represent that world:

[. . .] nos perceptions, sensations, émotions et idées se présentent sous un double aspect: l'un net, précis, mais impersonnel; l'autre confus, infiniment mobile, et inexprimable, parce que le langage ne saurait le saisir sans en fixer la mobilité, ni l'adapter à sa forme banale sans le faire tomber dans le domaine commun.[105]

Bergson implies here that the opaque, impersonal, unequivocal character of language means that it must involve a betrayal of that which it is supposed to translate. He argues that when we use it in order to understand and articulate our experiences and perceptions, we inevitably find ourselves 'en présence de l'ombre de nous-mêmes: nous croyons avoir analysé notre sentiment, nous lui avons substitué en réalité une juxtaposition d'états inertes, traduisibles en mots, et qui constituent chacun l'élément commun, le résidu par conséquent impersonnel, des impressions ressenties dans un cas donné par la société entière'.[106] His position here is clearly a pessimistic one.

In *Le Rire* (1900), however, in which he explores the nature of creativity, Bergson indicates that artists are uniquely capable of conveying those realities which language, acting as a kind of veil, normally obscures or falsifies. Whereas in the *Essai* he casts doubt upon the possibility of communicating individual emotions in words, in this later work he suggests that creative beings who use language *poetically can* achieve this, because they are somehow 'detached' enough to see and express that which the 'commonality' of language conceals. For Bergson, the function of art is therefore revelatory:

Sous les mille actions naissantes qui dessinent au dehors un sentiment, derrière le mot banal et social qui exprime et recouvre un état d'âme, c'est le sentiment, c'est l'état d'âme [que les poètes] iront chercher simple et pur. Et, pour nous induire à tenter le même effort sur nous-mêmes, ils s'ingénieront à nous faire voir quelque chose de ce qu'ils auront vu: par des arrangements rythmés de mots, qui arrivent ainsi à s'organiser ensemble et à s'animer d'une vie originale, ils nous disent, ou plutôt ils nous suggèrent, des choses que le langage n'était pas fait pour exprimer.[107]

Bergson is distinguishing here between ordinary language, which serves only as a medium of practical communication, and poetry, which 'conveys individual moods and thoughts, by means of giving language a musical quality and thereby suggesting what it is not in the nature of ordinary language to be able to convey'.[108] His remarks offer insights into why Leduc found language a problem, and enable us to understand differently the nature of the discourse she creates in *Thérèse et Isabelle*. Although evidently troubled by the barriers erected by the genderization of the linguistic/creative sphere, her comments regarding the 'dishonesty' of language/writing indicate that she was exercised to a greater degree by the very issue Bergson raises in his *Essai*, i.e. the unsatisfactory *décalage* between our consciousness of the richness which characterizes *le réel* and our responses to it and the (limited) words we use in order to evoke this richness. In consequence, we can interpret the lyrical discourse contained in her novella less as an attempt to disrupt the 'masculinity' of the symbolic than as an assault upon the domination of language by 'mots banaux et sociaux' which cannot fully express the unique sexual ecstasy she and her lesbian heroines experienced. Leduc's development of a poetic mode of expression may, in other words, be read as evidence of her efforts to remedy the betrayals imposed upon the writer by a language which, in its normal form, is fit only for humdrum communication and is incapable of the kind of elevated translational function she required it to perform.

The discourse Leduc evolves in *Thérèse et Isabelle* corresponds to the Bergsonian vision of revelatory art in various ways. Firstly, her employment of alliteration, assonance and rhythm gives it precisely the kind of musicality and animation he recommends. Moreover, the hermetic, unusual character of some of her metaphors of pleasure ('Une musique orientale serpentait dans mes os', p. 98; 'la pieuvre refaisait son travail d'accrochage', 'Notre chair nous aimait, notre odeur giclait. Notre levain, nos bulles, notre pain', p. 32, for example), together with the fact that she employs the nouns 'plaisir' 'sensation' and 'orgasme', and the verb 'jouir' only sixteen times in the course of her novella,[109] means that her discourse is consistently allusive instead of directly denominational and, in Bergsonian terms at least, becomes therefore truly 'translational':

Ainsi, qu'il soit peinture, sculpture, poésie ou musique, l'art n'a d'autre objet que d'écarter les symboles pratiquement utiles, les généralités conventionnellement et socialement acceptées, enfin tout ce qui masque la réalité, pour nous mettre face à face à la réalité même.[110]

Nevertheless, it is debatable whether, in developing this kind of language, Leduc succeeded in overcoming linguistic opacity/banality and in translating, as adequately as she wished, private erotic reality. She herself was convinced that she had failed to realize her (unrealizable?) project. In *La Folie en tête*, she describes the sense of disappointment that overcame her as she finished the first version of *Thérèse et Isabelle* and confronted the degree to which the language of her text continued to misrepresent her subject matter:

J'ai écrit trois heures par jour *Thérèse et Isabelle* avec la chevelure-fleuve d'Isabelle dans ma bouche. Ce qu'Isabelle m'a apporté, ce que je lui ai donné, je l'ai rendu à mon cahier. J'ai sacrifié ma tenue et mes principes, c'était l'amour de ce que je voulais décrire. Je voulais tout dire, j'ai tout dit. C'est seulement en cela que je n'ai pas échoué. Mon texte est plein d'images. C'est dommage. Mes roses, mes nuages, ma pieuvre, mes feuilles de lilas, ma mouture, mon paradis du pourrissement, je ne les renie pas. Je visais à plus de précision, j'espérais des mots suggestifs et non des comparaisons approximatives. (pp. 350–51)

Leduc is implying here that even an elusive, suggestive discourse (of the kind she was clearly already employing to describe woman's *jouissance* in the mid-fifties and which finds its most complete form in the 1966 version of

Thérèse et Isabelle) may not enable the writer to give an accurate, 'transparent' account of individual, non-recurring or extreme experience. Indeed, she seems to indicate that while any attempt to do so necessitates a sustained use of images, these images themselves exacerbate the *trahison* inherent in language. She returns to this notion in her 1966 interview with Démeron, associating once again her failure to infuse erotic sensation into the language of her novella with the 'abus d'images' contained in that language ('J'avais une ambition: je voulais "fixer" mes sensations. C'est impossible, je n'y suis pas parvenue. [. . .] C'est pour cela qu'il y a peut-être un abus d'images, de comparaisons, peut-être de mauvaise poésie').[111] Leduc herself, therefore, seems both to endorse a Bergsonian vision of poetry as the means by which translational language may come into being and, paradoxically, to view her own poetic discourse as still inadequate to the task.

Leduc's preoccupation with questions of *style* ('Mourir en écrivant. Le style. L'hermétisme d'un style. La clarté d'un style. Les largesses d'un style. Lui donner ma peau, au style')[112] which is much in evidence in *Thérèse et Isabelle*, also suggests that she did not create (and was not, perhaps, in genuine pursuit of) a uniquely translational mode of expression. The poetic delicacy of many of her images, and the striking semantic combinations she introduces into her text (exemplified, for instance, by the phrase 'Infiltrations de langueur, lézardes de délices, marécages de sournoiseries . . . Les feuilles de lilas déroulaient leur douceur, le printemps me mettait à l'agonie, la poussière des morts dansait dans ma lumière', p. 106) reveal the extent of her self-confessed need to produce language which was formally distinctive as well as 'transparent'; to 'dire vrai' (i.e. to translate) but also to 'dire autre chose'.[113] She seems to have felt that the development of a stylistically perfect discourse might enable words to become less opaque, and to come closer to conveying the vividness of the real, which is destroyed by more prosaic language: 'Le style, c'est l'encens sur un cadavre. Les mots sont forts pendant que nous les cherchons'.[114] Yet her creation of just such a discourse means that *Thérèse et Isabelle* contains a model of language which, by virtue of the formal/poetic *justesse* of many of its *mots*, becomes at times entirely self-referential and displays the 'intransitivity' which, according to Jakobson, is precisely the essence of the poetic ('Poeticity is present when the word is felt as a word and not a mere representation of the object being named or an outburst of emotion, when words and their composition [. . .] acquire a weight and meaning of their own instead of referring indifferently to reality').[115] Leduc's discourse of sexual pleasure is one in which words emerge as important in their own right, rather than as mere windows through which the reader may look onto reality or life. In Barthesian terms, Leduc creates 'un nouvel état philosophal de la matière langagière; cet état inouï, ce métal incandescent, hors origine et hors communication', which ceases merely to be '*un* langage' and becomes instead '*du* langage'; something that is autonomous and, for Barthes, 'jouissif'.[116] Evidently, Leduc's preoccupation with style makes *Thérèse et Isabelle* a success rather than a failure as a work of *literature*. None the less, and in spite of Bergson's association of poetic language with the revelatory or translational, it is arguably the formal perfection of Leduc's narrative which undermines definitively her efforts to *traduire*. This explains perhaps why she came to view style as that which, paradoxically, combines 'clarté' and 'hermétisme'.

It is worth remembering too that, despite Leduc's efforts to create an original text, *Thérèse et Isabelle* can be linked to a broader, historically well-established corpus of erotic writing and cannot therefore be deemed an entirely successful translation of what Leduc believed to be a personal, unique experience of the sensual. The novella, like the majority of erotic narratives, 'remains firmly anchored to certain notions of the formal consummation of intense feeling',[117] and is marked by strategies/procedures belonging to (one 'branch' of) the erotico-discursive tradition which has flourished in France since the eighteenth century. In relation to the *galant* 'strand' of this tradition, Guiraud observes:

De même, à l'opposé de la gauloiserie, cette veine galante ne nomme pas directement les choses, mais procède par allusions, plus ou moins voilées. Il en résulte un système d'images conventionnelles et bientôt traditionnelles, une rhétorique — sous laquelle nous vivons toujours — qui a une double origine: humaniste et courtoise.[118]

Guiraud is suggesting here that the *tradition galante*, which was 'pratiquement fixée à partir du XVIIIe siècle' and produced a 'rhétorique désormais figée',[119] represents a euphemistic and highly precious mode of erotic expression — a mode described elsewhere as a discursive convention 'qui avoue la brûlure du désir et interdit la représentation directe de sa volupté, qui suggère l'éros et bride le langage érotique par le jeu des tabous ou plutôt des codes littéraires qui, bien loin de prétendre nommer directement l'éros, se font au contraire un *jeu* de multiplier les formules obliques d'une préciosité devenue à elle-même son propre but'.[120] Leduc's non-explicit, figurative erotic language, in which she herself discerned an 'abus d'images', undoubtedly belongs to the tradition Guiraud analyses, in spite of her modifications of conventional codes and metaphors. It seems, at times, *précieux* in the extreme, even ironically so — as if Leduc were articulating, through the (satirical?) employment of ostentatiously recondite or sophisticated metaphors ('ineffable pourriture', 'infiltrations de langueur' and 'lézardes de délices' spring to mind, pp. 102, 106), the impossibility of escaping the *rhétorique figée* Guiraud describes. Like the 'intransitive' aspect of her language, the ties binding *Thérèse et Isabelle* to the (impersonal) rhetorical conventions of the *tradition galante* make it difficult to read her text as a completely authentic 'translation' of what was in essence a private, individual experience of *jouissance*.

In common with other writers of her generation, Leduc was alive to the problems lying in store for the artist who grapples with language in the hope of maximizing its expressive potential. Her particular sense of the restrictions inherent in language may, as I have sought to demonstrate, be interpreted from a feminist and from a Bergsonian perspective. Moreover, the kind of discourse she evolves in *Thérèse et Isabelle* can be read as 'political'/feminist in nature, as an attempt at the production of a kind of textual *féminité*, and as an effort to rid language of its opaque, generalized banality so that it might say something new and revealing about the reality of specific, individual experiences and sensations. The presence, in *Thérèse et Isabelle*, of instances of *écriture féministe* seems clear. Ultimately, however, it is impossible to assert categorically that Leduc creates either an *écriture féminine* or an *écriture transparente/traductrice* in her novella. In the final analysis, is this so important? What counts is the beauty and strength of the text she produced, and the courage that accompanied its production, a courage which means that her writing merits a place alongside that of those better known French women writers — Colette, Duras, Beauvoir, Wittig — who have sought to represent women in innovative and ground-breaking ways.

NOTES

1. Kirsteen Anderson, 'Towards a New Reason: Guilt, Language and Nature in the work of Roland Barthes and Francis Ponge', in Harry Cockerham and Esther Ehrman (eds), *Ideology and Religion in French Literature — Essays in Honour of Brian Juden* (Porphyrogenitus, 1989), pp. 23–48 (p. 26).
2. Luce Irigaray, *Ce Sexe qui n'en est pas un*, pp. 71, 149.
3. Jacques Lacan, *Ecrits*, p. 655.
4. Jacqueline Rose, 'Introduction ii', in Juliet Mitchell and Jacqueline Rose (eds), *Feminine Sexuality: Jacques Lacan and the Ecole Freudienne* (Basingstoke and London: Macmillan, 1982), p. 38.
5. Deborah Cameron analyses the significance of the phallus and its relationship to language acquisition in the Lacanian schema as follows: 'Because of its function in the castration complex, the phallus is given two very powerful meanings. One of these is lack, for it symbolises the loss of the mother's body. After the prohibition of incest and the threat of castration there can never again be the closeness of mother and child that existed before the introduction of the third term. The other phallic 'meaning' is the Law of patriarchy, a social order in which incest is prohibited and castration threatened by the father. [. . .] For Lacan, it is precisely the awareness of lack that impels a child toward language. The idea that words can stand for things can only be grasped when the child has some concept of something missing or absent. Thus there can be no language until the mother/child dyad is broken, and language depends on the introjection of the phallus. This is why Lacan claims that the symbolic order is dominated by the phallus' (Deborah Cameron, *Feminism and Linguistic Theory* (Basingstoke and London: Macmillan, 1985), p. 121).
6. Lacan, *Encore: Le Séminaire XX* (Paris: Seuil, 1975), p. 68.
7. Susan Sellers, *Language and Sexual Difference* (Basingstoke and London: Macmillan, 1991), p. 97.
8. Marcelle Marini, op. cit., p. 95.
9. Lacan, *Encore: Le Séminaire XX*, p. 68.
10. Irigaray, *Ce Sexe qui n'en est pas un*, p. 145.
11. Irigaray, ibid., p. 77.
12. Ibid., p. 74.
13. Marini, op. cit., p. 53.
14. Fuss, op. cit., pp. 58–59.

15. Irigaray, *Ce Sexe qui n'en est pas un*, p. 26.
16. Margaret Whitford, 'Luce Irigaray's Critique of Rationality' in Margaret Whitford and Morwenna Griffiths (eds), *Feminist Perspectives in Philosophy* (Basingstoke and London: Macmillan, 1988), pp. 109–30 (p. 112).
17. Irigaray, 'Women's Exile', p. 64.
18. Irigaray, *Ce Sexe qui n'en est pas un*, p. 76.
19. Irigaray, 'Women's Exile', p. 65.
20. Ibid., p. 64.
21. Irigaray, *Ce Sexe qui n'en est pas un*, p. 24.
22. The notion of 'parler femme' is employed by Irigaray in *Ce Sexe qui n'en est pas un*, specifically to describe the kind of discourse which emerges when women speak together: 'Il est sûr qu'avec les-femmes-entre-elles (et c'est un des enjeux des mouvements de libération, quand ils ne s'organisent pas sur le mode du pouvoir masculin, et quand ils ne sont pas dans la revendication de la prise ou du renversement de "pouvoir"), dans ces lieux des femmes-entre-elles, quelque chose s'énonce d'un parler-femme. C'est ce qui explique le désir ou la nécessité de la non-mixité: le langage dominant est si puissant que les femmes n'osent pas parler-femme en dehors d'une non-mixité' (ibid., p. 133).
23. Jane Gallop, 'Quand nos lèvres s'écrivent: Irigaray's Body Politic', *Romanic Review*, 74 (1983), 77–83 (p. 78) (my emphasis).
24. Ibid., pp. 78–79. While Gallop's contention that we must 'beware too literal a reading of Irigarayan anatomy' (ibid., p. 78) and that 'the Irigarayan *poétique du corps* is not an expression of the body but a *poiésis*, a creating of the body' (ibid., p. 79) is an important one, Irigaray's anatomical references do lend themselves to literal interpretations — as Gallop herself acknowledges.
25. Irigaray, 'Is the Subject of Science Sexed', *Cultural Critique*, 1 (1985), 73–88 (p. 84).
26. Irigaray, *Ce Sexe qui n'en est pas un*, p. 28.
27. Cixous claims that exceptional beings of both sexes, beings who are open to otherness, can write bisexually: 'Il y a des exceptions. Il y en a toujours eu, ce sont des êtres incertains, poétiques, qui ne se sont pas laissés réduire à l'état de mannequins codés par le refoulement impitoyable de la composante homosexuelle. Hommes ou femmes, êtres complexes, mobiles, ouverts. D'admettre la composante de l'autre sexe les rend à la fois beaucoup plus riches, plusieurs, forts et dans la mesure de cette mobilité, très fragiles. [. . .] Ainsi sous le nom de Jean Genêt, ce qui s'inscrit dans le mouvement d'un texte qui se divise. se met en pièces, se remembre, c'est une féminité foisonnante, maternelle' (Cixous, *La Jeune Née* (Paris: Union générale d'éditions, 1975), pp. 153–54).
28. Ibid., p. 158.
29. Ibid., p. 175.
30. Ibid., p. 174.
31. Monique Plaza argues that Irigaray adopts a resolutely essentialist/naturalistic position because her writings suggest that 'all that "is" woman comes to her in the last instance from her anatomical sex, which touches itself all the time' (Plaza, '"Phallomorphic Power" and the Psychology of "Woman"', *Ideology and Consciousness*, 4 (1978), 4–36 (p. 32)). Toril Moi refers to Cixous's biologism and suggests that although she seems to adopt a deconstructive, anti-essentialist stance in her accounts of woman's discourse, this stance 'is opposed and undercut by a vision of woman's writing steeped in the very metaphysics of presence she claims she is out to unmask' (Toril Moi, *Sexual/Textual Politics* (London and New York: Methuen, 1985), p. 110).
32. Leduc's desire to 'fixer' and 'traduire' and her faith in the 'mot juste' suggest that she held the (old-fashioned) view that the relationship between elements of reality — whether it be that of the external world or that of feeling and emotion — and the words used to evoke them can be a stable/'fit' one. Yet, as Terence Hawkes points out, Saussurean linguistics demonstrates the arbitrariness of the linguistic sign, and reveals that 'there exists no necessary "fitness" in the link between the sound-image, or signifier "tree", the concept, or signified that it involves, and the actual physical tree growing in the earth' (Hawkes, *Structuralism and Semiotics* (London: Methuen, 1983), p. 25).
33. Interview with Pierre Descargues, *Tribune de Lausanne*, 18 October 1964, p. 8.
34. Interview with Madeleine Chapsal, *L'Express*, 19 October 1964, pp. 70–71 (p. 71).
35. Colette avoids explicit descriptions of women's pleasure, particularly lesbian pleasure, explaining in *Le Pur et l'impur* that she does so because of taboos surrounding feminine homoeroticism: 'On trouvera que je fais la part petite au fiévreux plaisir, dans ce chapitre où passent et repassent, liées par paires, des femmes. C'est, d'abord, parce que le libertinage saphique est le seul qui soit inacceptable. Il n'y aura jamais assez de blâme sur les saphos de

rencontre, celle du restaurant, du dancing, du train bleu et du trottoir, celle qui provoque, qui rit au lieu de soupirer. Il n'y aura jamais trop de crépuscule ménagé, de silence et de gravité sur une étreinte de femmes' (Colette, *Œuvres complètes*, 9 (Paris: Flammarion, 1949), pp. 5–137 (pp. 91–92)). Elaine Marks stresses Colette's reticence: 'Unlike her successors in the examination of the "dark continent" of female sexuality, Violette Leduc or Monique Wittig, Colette does not focus on love-making or the celebration of the female body. [. . .] Women who love women come together in Colette's world because they are fleeing from a painful experience with a man and are looking for a *retraite sentimentale*' (Marks, 'Lesbian Intertextuality', in Marks and Stambolian (eds), op. cit., pp. 353–77 (p. 369)).

36. Interview with Pierre Démeron, *Candide*, 5–11 September 1966, pp. 35–37 (p. 36).
37. Irigaray, *Ce Sexe qui n'en est pas un*, p. 75.
38. Ibid.
39. Marie Cardinal, *Autrement Dit* (Paris: Livre de poche, 1977), p. 89.
40. Irigaray, 'Women's Exile', p. 62.
41. Hélène Cixous, 'Entretien avec Françoise van Rossum-Guyon', *Revue des Sciences humaines*, 44 (1977), 479–93 (p. 485).
42. Guiraud argues that (French) erotic language is particularly marked by the masculine, and implies that this renders it infinitely less accessible to women: 'Il est bon de relever — c'est un fait culturel considérable et qui dépasse notre sujet — que [la] représentation de la sexualité et le langage qui en découle est [. . .] d'origine entièrement masculine. Ces images et ces mots reflètent une expérience qui, à de rares exceptions près, est vécue et traduite uniquement par des hommes' (Guiraud, op. cit., p. 113).
43. See, for example, Shari Benstock, *Women of the Left Bank* (London: Virago, 1987); Jeanette Foster, *Sex Variant Women in Literature* (Tallahassee: Naiad Press, 1985); Lillian Faderman, *Surpassing the Love of Men: Romantic Friendship and Love between Women from the Renaissance to the Present* (London: The Women's Press, 1985); Sandra M. Gilbert and Susan Gubar, *No Man's Land 2: Sexchanges* (New Haven and London: Yale University Press, 1989); Elaine Marks, 'Lesbian Intertextuality'.
44. Foster talks of Diderot's 'clinical accuracy' and described *La Religieuse* as 'a landmark in the literature of female sex variance' (Foster, op. cit., p. 55).
45. 'While Diderot the Encylopedist urged greater freedom and self-determination for man, he did not urge the same for woman. The idea of a society ruled entirely by them, the convent, was probably as distasteful to him for that reason as it was for more progressive political and philosophical reasons. In a convent, women were almost entirely self-sufficient, and the head of the community was another woman. [. . .] To Diderot, the convent was a place where the blind led the blind, and where the depraved led the innocent into perversity. It was the one French institution where women, who were at best incapable children, actually ruled' (Faderman, op. cit., p. 45).
46. See 'The Rise of Antifeminism' in Faderman, op. cit., pp. 233–38.
47. Havelock Ellis, *Studies in the Psychology of Sex: Volume One, Sexual Inversion* (Watford: London University Press, 1897), pp. 99–100.
48. Marks, 'Lesbian Intertextuality', p. 361.
49. Benstock, op. cit., p. 51.
50. Colette, op. cit., pp. 105–06.
51. Roland Barthes, *Le Plaisir du texte* (Paris: Seuil, 1973), p. 59.
52. For an account of the link the image of the 'femme damnée' establishes between Diderot and Baudelaire, see Georges May, 'Diderot, Baudelaire et les femmes damnées', *Modern Language Notes* (June 1950), pp. 395–99, and Antoine Adam (ed.), in Baudelaire, *Les Fleurs du Mal* (Garnier: Paris, 1961), pp. 411–13. The image originates from the words Suzanne overhears her lesbian superior address to her confessor: 'Mon père, je suis damnée . . .' (Diderot, *La Religieuse* (Paris: Flammarion, 1968), p. 198).
53. It seems likely that Leduc knew the works of all three writers well. As her autobiographies indicate, she was an avid reader of Proust. Her decision to entitle her original draft of *Ravages*, which included the first version of *Thérèse et Isabelle*, *Les Verts Paradis* suggests that she was also familiar with Baudelaire's poetry, since his 'Mœsta et Errabunda' evokes 'le vert paradis des amours enfantines'. There are no direct references to Diderot in Leduc's autobiographical writing. However, the intertextual parallels that bind *Thérèse et Isabelle* to *La Religieuse* and Leduc's explicit dismissal of the lesbian/'femme damnée' association, which Diderot establishes, indicate that she must have read it.
54. Diderot, op. cit., p. 169.

55. Baudelaire, *Œuvres complètes* (Paris: Gallimard (Pléiade), 1961), pp. 134–39. All the page references for Baudelaire in the main body of my text come from this edition.

56. Claude Pichois (ed.), in Baudelaire, *Œuvres complètes* (Paris: Gallimard (Pléiade), 1975), p. 1061.

57. The lesbianism/vampirism link signals a (masculine) rejection of the authenticity of feminine homoeroticism and of the right of lesbians to indulge in violent forms of erotic exchange acceptable within heterosexual sex: 'Derrière cette vision, c'est le refus [...] d'une sexualité qui aurait, parce qu'elle est authentique, ses formes de violence dans l'étreinte, sa jouissance propre, même si comme dans l'hétérosexualité elle peut revêtir une composante sado-masochiste [...]' (Claudine Brécourt-Villars, *Petit glossaire raisonné de l'érotisme saphique 1880–1930* (Paris: Pauvert, 1980), p. 34). Faderman notes that, in the first half of the twentieth century, writings on lesbianism by women evidenced a disturbing internalization of the image of the lesbian vampire. These include Clemence Dane's *Regiment of Women* (1915) and Francis Brett Young's *White Ladies* (1935) (Faderman, op. cit., pp. 341–44).

58. In his other '*Femmes damnées*' (*OC*, 1961, pp. 107–08) Baudelaire is less hostile to his lesbian heroines and becomes positively sympathetic, telling them: 'Vous que dans votre enfer mon âme a poursuives/Pauvres sœurs, je vous aime autant que je vous plains/Pour vos mornes douleurs, vos soifs inassouvies/Et les urnes d'amour dont vos grands cœurs sont pleins!' (p. 108). These lines suggest that Baudelaire's lesbians, like his other sinners, pursue their 'vice' out of a thirst for the infinite (a 'soif inassouvie') stemming from a disgust at the banality of human existence which he shared, and that they are to be admired as much as condemned. According to Antoine Adam, 'dans ces femmes demeurées fidèles aux rites antiques de Sapho [Baudelaire] découvre quelque chose de sacré, de primitif, de mystérieux. Il retrouve en elles [une] quête de l'infini, [une] recherche épuisante et inapaisée d'un *au-delà* de la condition humaine'. See Adam (ed.), *Les Fleurs du Mal* (Paris: Garnier, 1961), p. 412. Consequently, the hostility towards Delphine, Hippolyte and the inhabitants of Lesbos present in the other poems I have considered may be interpreted as an (ironic) mimicry of the world's condemnation of lesbianism, rather than a true indication of the poet's own sentiments.

59. Lucienne Frappier-Masur, 'Marginal Canons: Rewriting the Erotic', *Yale French Studies*, 75 (1988), 112–28 (pp. 115–16).

60. – Laisse donc ouvert, j'ai chaud, dit son amie.
   – Mais c'est assommant, on nous verra, répondit Mlle Vinteuil.
      [...]
   – Quand je dis nous voir, je veux dire nous voir lire; c'est assommant, quelque chose insignifiante qu'on fasse, de penser que des yeux nous voient.
      Par une générosité instinctive et une politesse involontaire elle taisait les mots prémédités qu'elle avait jugés indispensables à la pleine réalisation de son désir. Et à tous moments au fond d'elle-même une vierge timide et suppliante implorait et faisait reculer un soudard fruste et vainqueur.
   – Oui, c'est probable qu'on nous regarde à cette heure-ci dans cette campagne fréquentée, dit ironiquement son amie.
      Et puis quoi? ajouta-t-elle (en croyant devoir accompagner d'un clignement d'yeux malicieux et tendre ces mots qu'elle récita par bonté, comme un texte qu'elle savait être agréable à Mlle Vinteuil, d'un ton qu'elle s'efforçait de rendre cynique) "quand même on nous verrait, ce n'en est que meilleur".
   Marcel Proust, *Du côté de chez Swann* (Paris: Gallimard (Folio), 1954, p. 190.

61. Randolph Splitter, *Proust's Recherche: A Psychoanalytic Interpretation* (Boston: Routledge and Kegan Paul, 1981), p. 35.

62. Domna C. Stanton, 'Difference on Trial', in Nancy K. Miller (ed.), *The Poetics of Gender* (New York: Columbia University Press, 1986), pp. 157–82 (p. 172).

63. Helena Michie, *The Flesh Made Word* (New York and Oxford: Oxford University Press, 1987), p. 141. Béatrice Didier suggests that the French literary tradition has treated woman's anatomy analogously: 'Le corps féminin — beaucoup plus que le corps masculin — était, dans la littérature, un corps morcelé. S'il faut bien convenir que le corps masculin est souvent peu présent également dans la littérature, le personnage masculin y conserve cependant l'unité d'un sujet, tandis que le personnage féminin y subit le morcellement de l'objet' (Didier, *L'Ecriture-Femme* (Paris: Presses Universitaires de France, 1981), p. 36).

64. Kate Millett, *Sexual Politics* (New York: Ballantine Books, 1978), p. 439.

65. Anne-Marie Dardigna, *Les Châteaux d'Eros, ou l'infortune du sexe des femmes* (Paris: Maspero, 1980), p. 254.

66. Robbe-Grillet, *La Maison de rendez-vous* (Paris: Editions de minuit, 1965), p. 9.
67. Dardigna, op. cit., p. 254.
68. Michie, op. cit., pp. 125–26.
69. Martha Noel Evans, *The Masks of Tradition*, pp. 200–01.
70. 'Male homosexual literature has a past, it has a present. The lesbians, for their part, are silent — just as all women are as women at all levels. When one has read the poems of Sappho, Radclyffe Hall's *The Well of Loneliness*, the poems of Sylvia Plath and Anaïs Nin, *La Bâtarde* by Violette Leduc, one has read everything.' (Monique Wittig, *The Lesbian Body* (preface), trans. David LeVay (New York: William Morrow, 1975), p. 9.)
71. Diane Crowder, 'Amazons and Mothers', *Contemporary Literature*, 24 (1983), 117–44 (p. 121). This article contrasts the approaches Cixous and Wittig take to the relationship between sexuality, gender and discourse.
72. Dardigna, op. cit., p. 133.
73. Irigaray, *Speculum, de l'autre femme*, p. 177.
74. Michie, op. cit., p. 145. I shall return to the issue of feminist reservations regarding metaphor, and its relation to the feminine — which Michie discerns in the work of Adrienne Rich and Audrey Lorde, and which is also present in Wittig and Irigaray — in the next part of this chapter.
75. Kate Millett, op. cit., p. 430.
76. Guiraud, op. cit., p. 113.
77. Irigaray, *Speculum, de l'autre femme*, p. 178.
78. Leduc may have derived her sense of the 'subversive' nature of ellipsis from Colette. A lucid discussion of Colette's manipulation of the unsaid, which argues that it can be interpreted, despite the capitulation to social censorship it represents, as a feminine ploy destined to disrupt, is provided by Sherry Dranch: 'Colette is obscure on the topic of female sexuality, and yet her text demands that one perceive what lies beyond her subterfuges. Since the unsaid in a literary text is established in contrast to what is said, we can detect the features, the contours, of the unsaid by identifying patterns of ellipses, through a hermeneutic reading of a censored style. Ellipses are the connection [. . .] between Colette's style — the subliminal style of the flesh — and a forbidden obsession. A sub-text, consisting of the clearly-stated unsaid, or more precisely of an "inter-said" [interdit: forbidden] is indicated through ellipsis and metaphor [. . .]' (Dranch, 'Reading through the Veiled Text: Colette's *The Pure and The Impure*', *Contemporary Literature*, 24 (1983), 176–89 (p. 177)).
79. Michèle Montrelay, 'Recherches sur la féminité', *Critique* (July 1970), pp. 654–74 (p. 666).
80. Marcelle Marini, op. cit., p. 69.
81. Irigaray, *Speculum, de l'autre femme*, pp. 176–77.
82. Not all Durassian critics accept Marini's reading of ellipsis. Trista Selous comments: 'I do not think such a way of using language can be called specifically "feminine" in itself; for it works in the same way as innuendo or jokes, by controlling and using the power of unconscious links between signifiers, and I do not see why or how such universally found phenomena can be gendered. Furthermore, I do not think it is possible to see [Duras's blanks] as disrupting the rules by which (masculine) language or literature works' (Selous, *The Other Woman: Feminism and Femininity in the Work of Marguerite Duras* (New Haven and London: Yale University Press, 1988), p. 137).
83. Cixous, 'Rethinking Differences', p. 71.
84. 'At the time we were all writing erotica at a dollar a page, I realized that for centuries we had had only one model for this literary genre — the writing of men. I was already conscious of a difference between the masculine and feminine treatments of sexual experience. I knew there was a great disparity between Henry Miller's explicitness and my ambiguities — between his humorous, Rabelaisian view of sex and my poetic descriptions of sexual relationships [. . .]. As I wrote in volume three of the *Diary*, I had a feeling that Pandora's box [poetry] contained the mysteries of woman's sensuality, so different from man's, and for which man's language was inadequate.' (Anaïs Nin, *Delta of Venus* (London: W. H. Allen, 1978), pp. 13–14.)
85. Bataille, op. cit., p. 21.
86. Cixous, *La Jeune Née*, p. 158.
87. Alicia Ostriker, *Stealing the Language: the Emergence of Women's Poetry in America* (London: The Women's Press, 1986), pp. 174, 166.
88. Cixous, *La Jeune Née*, p. 172.
89. Didier, op. cit., p. 32.
90. Ibid.

91. Cixous, *La Jeune Née*, p. 170.
92. Ibid.
93. Ricœur, 'The Metaphorical Process as Cognition, Imagination and Feeling' in Sheldon Sacks (ed.), *On Metaphor* (Chicago and London: University of Chicago Press, 1979), pp. 141–57 (p. 144).
94. Donald Davidson, 'What Metaphors Mean', in ibid., pp. 29–45 (pp. 32–33). Winifred Nowottny concurs, commenting that ambiguity 'is now associated with such concepts as ambivalence, tension, paradox and irony, and with interest in metaphor and symbol as means by which the poet can evade or transcend unequivocal assertion' (*The Language Poets Use* (London: The Athlone Press, 1962), p. 147).
95. 'Ambiguity is, of course, the great strength of metaphor by Simple Replacement, and I am not suggesting that we have to decode it into one specific proper term and one only'. (Christine Brooke-Rose, *A Grammar of Metaphor* (London: Secker and Warburg, 1958), pp. 28–29.)
96. In 'The Epistemology of Metaphor', Paul de Man examines the 'damage' metaphor specifically inflicts upon philosophico-rational (i.e. univocal, 'phallocentric/morphic') language: 'Metaphors, tropes, and figural language in general have been a perennial problem and, at times, a recognized source of embarrassment for philosophical discourse and, by extension, for all discursive uses of language, including historiography and literary analysis' (de Man, in Sacks, op. cit., pp. 11–18 (p. 11)). He goes on to explain that Locke, who wrote 'An Essay concerning Human Understanding' in order to condemn the employment of rhetorical devices, associated metaphor etc. with femininity. According to de Man, Locke's argument is that 'it is clear that rhetoric is something one can decorously indulge in as long as one knows where it belongs. Like a woman, which it resembles [. . .], it is a fine thing as long as it is kept in its proper place. Out of place, among the serious affairs of men [. . .], it is a disruptive scandal' (ibid., p. 13).
97. Nowottny, op. cit., p. 162.
98. 'Because the gynaeceum and schoolgirl love are so heavily invested with intertextual connotations and because Violette Leduc uses traditional nature codes for metaphoric support, *Thérèse et Isabelle* is not nearly as original or as disturbing a text as *Le Corps lesbien*.' (Elaine Marks, 'Lesbian Intertextuality', p. 375.)
99. Gallop suggests when she evokes an 'other' kind of language/writing, Irigaray envisages the inscription 'of the multiplicity of the female genitals as a textual production, [. . .] in accord with our modernist conception of writing' (Gallop. 'Quand nos lèvres s'écrivent: Irigaray's Body Politic', p. 79).
100. Irigaray, *Speculum, de l'autre femme*, p. 177.
101. Margaret Whitford, *Philosophy in the Feminine*, p. 180.
102. Whitford (ibid.) explains that if metaphor represents, for Irigaray, an emblem of the masculine economy/genealogy, metonymy, predicated on contiguity, on 'that which touches, associates or combines' instead of substitution/replacement, signifies in Irigarayan terms 'a figure for the vertical and horizontal relationships between women, the maternal genealogy and the relation of sisterhood' and stands for a different/feminine economy. There is a close link, in Irigaray's work, between metonymy and the motif of the 'two lips', which Irigaray associates variously with women's autoeroticism and with her (unacknowledged) love of the self/same.
103. Rita Felski, *Beyond Feminist Aesthetics* (London: Hutchinson Radius, 1989), p. 5.
104. John E. Jackson, *Le Corps amoureux* (Neuchâtel: A La Baconnière, 1986), p. 13.
105. Henri Bergson, *Œuvres* (Paris: Presses Universitaires de France, 1963), pp. 85–86.
106. Ibid., p. 88.
107. Ibid., pp. 461–62.
108. Anthony Pilkington, *Bergson and his Influence* (Cambridge: Cambridge University Press, 1976), p. 14.
109. See pp. 98, 100, 32, 23, 52, 53, 56, 76, 78, 101, 102, 107, 111.
110. Bergson, op. cit., p. 462.
111. *Candide*, 5 September 1966, p. 36.
112. *La Folie en tête*, p. 117.
113. *La Chasse à l'amour*, p. 46.
114. Ibid., p. 295.
115. Roman Jakobson, *Language in Literature* (Cambridge Mass.: Harvard University Press, 1987), p. 378.
116. Barthes, op. cit., p. 51.
117. Susan Sontag, 'The Pornographic Imagination' in Georges Bataille, *Story of the Eye* (Harmondsworth: Penguin Books, 1982), pp. 83–118 (p. 96).

118.   Guiraud, op. cit., p. 112.
119.   Ibid., p. 114.
120.   Jackson, op. cit., p. 27.

CONCLUSION

What kind of a writer is Violette Leduc? What view of her creative skills does a close reading of *L'Asphyxie*, *Ravages* and *Thérèse et Isabelle* afford us?

Firstly, these texts show that Leduc was able to understand and represent the intricacies of female relationships in a remarkable way. Readers may come to differing conclusions regarding the 'femininity' of her discourse, but it is undoubtedly the case that Leduc offers us a 'distinctly female vision' of the way in which familial and sexual bonds between women work.[1] What is perhaps most significant about her account of these bonds is that it illuminates the 'perfect moments' they can engender, even as it reveals the difficulty of achieving such moments, and highlights their transitory, (irretrievably) archaic, or fantasmic character. We are left with the feeling that Leduc never loses sight of the possibility that an ineffable, strife-free feminine union might exist, even if the odds are stacked against its realization. For all the bleakness of much of her writing, the reader senses that Leduc privileges female relationships because, unlike those that obtain between women and men, they do not preclude the chance of happiness.

In the final analysis, can Leduc be viewed as a writer whose work is 'recuperable' for feminism, in the same way that certain women authors of the nineteenth and twentieth centuries (Colette, for example) have proved to be? The answer is undoubtedly yes. Whatever ambivalence Leduc may have felt regarding feminist politics, her account of female bonding undermines the state of representational exclusion to which women are subject within patriarchal culture. Irigaray argues that in the symbolic/cultural order as it stands, 'la femme dispose [. . .] de trop peu d'images, de figurations, de représentations, pour pouvoir s'y re-présenter'.[2] Moreover, she relates the fact that women have no identity in the symbolic (save that of defective, castrated men, or mothers) to the unsymbolized character of the mother/daughter bond, i.e. to what Margaret Whitford describes as 'an absence of linguistic, social, cultural, iconic, theoretical, mythical, religious, or any other representations of that relationship'.[3] Irigaray's suggestion that the creation of positive conceptualizations of the tie between mothers and daughters (modern versions of the Demeter/Kore myth, for instance)[4] seriously endangers the stability of the patriarchal symbolic order may arouse scepticism, even in feminists. None the less, literary or artistic depictions of joyful relations between women, when they elude enclosure by and within a masculine imaginary, do, arguably, have a 'disruptive' impact. Because Leduc offers us at least one representation of the mother/daughter bond which is not predicated upon the Freudian notion that this union becomes redundant after the intercession of the paternal male, and because she creates, in *Thérèse et Isabelle*, a vision of lesbian relations which escapes containment within a heterosexual/masculine model, she must ultimately be considered a textual feminist, albeit (perhaps) an unconscious one.

What of her formal/discursive achievement? It is apparent in all of the texts I have discussed that Leduc is a stylist of the first order, possessed of the ability to push language far beyond its everyday, 'communicational' limits. Yet her autobiographical works, particularly *La Folie en tête*, reveal the degree to which she doubted her own capacity to overcome 'les obstacles des mots' (*La Folie*, p. 16) and to weave the kind of resonant, formally consummate discourse she longed to evolve. Her sense of creative inadequacy was misplaced. Leduc's language indubitably displays 'poeticity', as it is defined by Jakobson. Hers is an art which is informed by her awareness of, and ability to exploit, the non- or self-referential, 'plastic' quality of words. Her texts convey an unforgettable impression that their signifiers serve as aesthetic artefacts, and do not merely represent 'windows' onto the real. Leduc is not simply 'une femme [qui] descend au plus secret de soi et [. . .] se raconte avec une sincérité intrépide',[5] or a (proto-) feminist novelist whose work illustrates the feminine condition in a new and revealing way. Although she is both of these things, she is also a poet, and critics who neglect the poetic dimension of her writing inevitably produce partial and impoverished accounts of her work.

For those of us who have been captivated by Leduc's *œuvre*, it is hard to understand why critical acclaim eluded her for most of her lifetime and continues to do so today. Various explanations for the obscurity in which her work still languishes offer themselves. Firstly, as Beauvoir succinctly puts it, 'Violette Leduc ne veut pas plaire; elle ne plaît pas et même elle effraie. Les titres de ses livres — *L'Asphyxie*, *L'Affamée*, *Ravages* — ne sont pas riants'.[6] Leduc's texts are frequently depressing; they can seem rebarbative and critics have undoubtedly been deterred by their bleakness. Furthermore, as my discussion of *Ravages* has indicated, her works do not lend themselves easily to interpretation. Leduc is 'difficult', and 'difficult' authors, particularly when they are also women authors, do not always attract the critical attention they deserve.[7] Above all, however, Leduc has been neglected because she is hard to 'place' — a fact of which she herself was painfully aware.[8] While it is possible to approach her as a feminist writer, or a modernist, or an autobiographer bent on a quest for self-understanding, or a 'poète maudit(e)',[9] attempts to attach exclusive and definitive labels to her work inevitably come to grief. It is to be hoped, nevertheless, that her writing will not be forgotten. She may have perceived herself as a 'désert qui monologue' but, as Beauvoir states in her preface to *La Bâtarde*, the 'desert' of Leduc's *œuvre* contains 'des beautés innombrables' (*La Bâtarde*, p. 7).

NOTES

1. Elaine Showalter, 'Toward a Feminist Poetics', in Showalter (ed.), *The New Feminist Criticism* (New York: Pantheon Books, 1985), pp. 125–43 (p. 137).
2. Luce Irigaray, *Speculum, de l'autre femme*, p. 85.
3. Margaret Whitford, 'Rereading Irigaray', p. 108.
4. For Irigaray, the Demeter/Kore myth offers a unique vision of a privileged mother/daughter union that (partially) avoids the 'taint' of the patriarchal system and the masculine imaginary. She views the bond between these two mythic figures as 'a good mother/daughter relationship outside the patriarchal regime', and implies that Demeter and Kore resist the exile upon which 'normal' femininity, as it is constructed in our masculinist, œdipal culture, is predicated (Luce Irigaray, 'Interview', in Janet Todd (ed.), *Women Writers Talking* (New York and London: Holmes and Meier, 1983), pp. 232–45 (p. 239)).
5. Beauvoir, *La Bâtarde* (preface), pp. 7–8.
6. Ibid., p. 7.
7. De Courtivron argues forcefully that if critics have refused to make the necessary effort to penetrate Leduc's hermetic textual world, it is because she is female, and 'women's deviance from accepted cultural or literary patterns does not lead — as it has in the case of many male writers — to the recognition of innovative or visionary pronouncements and to their eventual assimilation into the literary canon' (De Courtivron, *Violette Leduc*, p. 16).
8. De Courtivron discusses Leduc's 'unplaceability' at length in 'A Life and Work that Resist Tradition', in ibid., pp. 1–17.
9. De Courtivron concludes that while the comparison does not hold perfectly, 'if one were to associate Violette Leduc with any tradition, it would most likely be with the lineage of *poètes-maudits*, with the naysayers of literature, the self-appointed destroyers of literary and social rules, the decadent, semi-mad geniuses who created beauty from their fantasies and visions. [. . .] Violette Leduc's defiance of social and literary conventions, her flagrant departure from accepted life-styles, and the intensity of her visions — all of which she re-creates in her writing — parallel those of earlier writers in this particular line' (ibid., pp. 14–15).

BIBLIOGRAPHY

PRIMARY SOURCES

Novels and *récits*

L'Asphyxie (Paris: Gallimard (Collection 'Espoir'), 1946).
L'Asphyxie (Paris: Gallimard (Collection Blanche), 1973).
L'Asphyxie (Paris: Gallimard (Collection 'L'Imaginaire'), 1988).

L'Affamée (Paris: Jean Jacques Pauvert, 1948).
L'Affamée (Paris: Gallimard (Collection Blanche), 1948).
L'Affamée (Paris: Gallimard (Folio), 1974).

Ravages (Paris: Gallimard (Collection Blanche), 1955).
Ravages (Paris: Gallimard (Folio), 1975).

La Vieille fille et le mort (Paris: Gallimard (Collection Blanche), 1958).

Trésors à prendre (Paris: Gallimard (Collection Blanche), 1960).
Trésors à prendre (Paris: Gallimard (Folio), 1978).

La Bâtarde (Paris: Gallimard (Collection Blanche), 1964).
La Bâtarde (Paris: Gallimard (Folio), 1972, re-edited 1991).

La Femme au petit renard (Paris: Gallimard (Collection Blanche), 1965).
La Femme au petit renard (Paris: Gallimard (Folio), 1976).

Thérèse et Isabelle (Paris: Gallimard (Collection Blanche), 1966).
Thérèse et Isabelle (Paris: Gallimard (Folio), 1972).

La Folie en tête (Paris: Gallimard (Collection Blanche), 1970).
La Folie en tête (Paris: Gallimard (Folio), 1973).

Le Taxi (Paris: Gallimard, 1971).

La Chasse à l'amour (Paris: Gallimard (Collection Blanche), 1973).

All page references in this study are to the 'Collection Blanche' editions, unless otherwise stated.

Short stories published in *Les Temps modernes*

'Une mère, un parapluie, des gants', *Les Temps modernes*, November 1945.
'Le Dézingage', ibid., December 1945.
'Train Noir', ibid., March 1946.
'Les Mains sales', ibid., December 1946.
'L'Affamée', ibid., October 1947.
'Au Village', ibid., March 1951.
'Désirée Hellé', ibid., June 1952.
'Le Tailleur anguille', ibid., November 1961.
'La Bâtarde', ibid., August–September 1963.

Magazine Articles

'L'Ecole buissonnière en classe', *Pour Elle*, 11 September 1940.
'Je me tourne vers la lumière', *Pour Elle*, 30 October 1940.
'Tendez les mains', *Pour Elle*, 19 March 1941.
'Brigitte Bardot', *Adam*, June 1966.

'The Great Craftsmen of Paris', *Vogue*, 15 March 1965 (translated by Antonia White).
'Scene Stealing with Hepburn and O'Toole', *Vogue*, 1 April 1966 (translated by Antonia White).

Correspondence

'Lettres à Simone de Beauvoir', *Les Temps modernes*, October 1987 — twenty-nine letters are published here, covering the period 1945–56. They represent only a fragment of Leduc's correspondence with Beauvoir, the rest of which has not been made public by Sylvie Le Bon de Beauvoir.

Interviews

Combat (with Jean Paget), 7 July 1960.
Le Figaro Littéraire (with Jean Chalon), 1–7 October 1964.
Les Lettres françaises (with Claude Couffon), 15–20 October 1964.
La Tribune de Lausanne (with Pierre Descargues), 18 October 1964.
L'Express (with Madeleine Chapsal), 19–25 October 1964.
Candide (with Pierre Démeron), 19–25 November 1964.
L'Illustré (with Danielle Gilman), 3 December 1964.
Candide (with Pierre Démeron), 21–28 January 1965.
Le Figaro littéraire (with Jean Chalon), 19–25 August 1965.
L'Express (with Madeleine Chapsal), 25–31 October 1965.
Candide (with Pierre Démeron), 25–31 October 1965.
Le Nouvel Observateur (with Katia Kaupp), 10 November 1965.
Candide (with Pierre Démeron), 5–11 September 1966.
Candide (with Pierre Démeron), 28 August 1967.
Le Figaro littéraire (with Jean Chalon), 30 March–5 April 1970.
France-Inter ('Radioscopie', with Jacques Chancel), 25 April 1970.
Radio France-Culture (with R. Vigny and J. Brenner), 21 June 1970.
Radio France-Culture (with P. Lhoste), 8 July 1970.

SECONDARY SOURCES

Articles in Journals

Dominique Aury, 'Violette Leduc', *La Nouvelle revue française* (March 1974), 114–16.
Barbara J. Bucknall, 'Anne Hébert et Violette Leduc: lectrices de Proust', *Bulletin de la société des amis de Marcel Proust et de Combray*, 27 (1977), 410–18; 28 (1978), 662–68.
Isabelle de Courtivron, 'Violette Leduc: The Courage to Displease', *L'Esprit Créateur* (Summer 1979), 95–102.
Marilyn Yalom, 'They Remember Maman', *Essays in Literature*, 8 (Spring 1981), 73–90.
René de Ceccatty, 'Violette Leduc', *Masques* (Autumn 1981), 39–56.
Martha Noel Evans, 'La Mythologie de l'écriture dans *La Bâtarde* de Violette Leduc', *Littérature*, 12 (May 1982), 82–92.
Jean Snitzer Schoenfeld, '*La Bâtarde* or Why the Writer Writes', *French Forum*, 7 (September 1982), 261–68.
Michèle Respaut, 'Femme/Ange, Femme/Monstre', *Stanford French Review* (Winter 1983), 365–74.
Pièr Girard, '*L'Affamée* de Violette Leduc', *Topique*, 34 (January 1985), 113–28.
Isabelle de Courtivron, 'From Bastard to Pilgrim: Rites and Writing for Madame', *Yale French Studies*, 72 (1986), 133–48.
René de Ceccatty, 'L'Insistance d'une morte', *La Nouvelle revue française* (March 1989), 33–38.

Essays in Books

Simone de Beauvoir, *Préface*, in *La Bâtarde*, 1964, pp. 7–18.
Elaine Marks, '"I am My Own Heroine": Some Thoughts about Women and Autobiography in France', in Sidonie Cassirer (ed.), *Female Studies IX: Teaching about Women in the Foreign Languages* (New York: Feminine Press, 1975), pp. 1–10.

Jane Rule, 'Violette Leduc', in *Lesbian Images* (Garden City, New York: Doubleday, 1975), pp. 139–46.

Margaret Crosland, 'Violette Leduc', in *Women of Iron and Velvet: French Women Writers after George Sand* (New York: Taplinger Publishing Company, 1976), pp. 201–10.

Elaine Marks, 'Lesbian Intertextuality', in Elaine Marks and George Stambolian (eds), *Homosexualities and French Literature* (Ithaca and London: Cornell University Press, 1979), pp. 353–77.

Martha Noel Evans, 'Writing as Difference in Violette Leduc's Autobiography', in Shirley N. Garner et al. (eds), *The (M)Other Tongue: Essays in Feminist and Psychoanalytic Criticism* (Ithaca and London: Cornell University Press, 1985), pp. 306–17.

Martha Noel Evans, 'Violette Leduc: The Bastard', in *Masks of Tradition: Women and the Politics of Writing in Twentieth-Century France* (Ithaca and London: Cornell University Press, 1987), pp. 102–22.

Colette Trout Hall, '*L'Ecriture féminine* and the Search for the Mother in the Works of Violette Leduc and Marie Cardinal', in Michel Guggenheim (ed.), *Women in French Literature* (Saratoga: Anma Libri and Co., 1988), pp. 231–38.

Michael Sheringham, 'Dealing with the Reader' and 'Existentialist Autobiography', in *French Autobiography: Devices and Desires* (Oxford: Oxford University Press, 1993), pp. 137–64 and 202–45.

Monographs on Leduc's Writing

Isabelle de Courtivron, *Violette Leduc* (Boston: Twayne's World Authors Series, 1985).

Pièr Girard, *Œdipe masqué* (Paris: Des Femmes, 1986).

Academic Theses of note

Jacob G. Stockinger, 'Violette Leduc: the Legitimizations of *La Bâtarde*', unpublished PhD dissertation, University of Wisconsin–Madison, 1979.

René de Ceccatty, 'Evidence de Violette Leduc', unpublished *thèse du troisième cycle*, University of Paris I, 1980.

Colette Trout Hall, 'Les Mères chez les romancières du XXe siècle', unpublished PhD dissertation, Bryn Mawr College, 1983.

Ghyslaine Charles-Merrien, 'Violette Leduc ou le corps morcelé', unpublished *thèse de doctorat*, University of Rennes II, 1988.

REFERENCES AND FURTHER READING

Critical/Literary Theory

Roland Barthes, *Essais critiques* (Paris: Seuil, 1964).

——, *Le Plaisir du texte* (Paris: Seuil, 1973).

Terry Eagleton, *Literary Theory: An Introduction* (Oxford: Blackwell, 1983).

Gérard Genette, *Figures III* (Paris: Seuil, 1972).

Gayle Greene and Coppelia Kahn (eds), *Making a Difference — Feminist Literary Criticism* (London and New York: Methuen, 1985).

Terence Hawkes, *Structuralism and Semiotics* (London: Methuen, 1977).

Maggie Humm, *Feminist Criticism — Women as Contemporary Critics* (Brighton: Harvester Press, 1986).

Mary Jacobus, *Reading Women: Essays in Feminist Criticism* (London: Methuen, 1986).

Morton Kaplan and Robert Kloss, *The Unspoken Motive: A Guide to Psychoanalytic Literary Criticism* (New York: The Free Press, 1973).

Nancy K. Miller (ed.), *The Poetics of Gender* (New York: Columbia University Press, 1986).

Toril Moi, *Sexual/Textual Politics* (London and New York: Methuen, 1985).

Shlomith Rimmon-Kenan, *Narrative Fiction: Contemporary Poetics* (London and New York: Methuen, 1983).

——, (ed.), *Discourse in Psychoanalysis and Literature* (London and New York: Methuen, 1987).

Jean Rousset, *Forme et Signification* (Paris: José Corti, 1962).

Elaine Showalter (ed.), *Speaking of Gender* (London: Routledge, 1989).
John Sturrock, *The French New Novel* (London: Oxford University Press, 1969).
——, (ed.), *Structuralism and Since: From Lévi-Strauss to Derrida* (Oxford: Oxford University Press, 1979).
Elizabeth Wright, *Psychoanalytic Criticism: Theory in Practice* (London and New York: Methuen, 1984).

Feminist Theory

Simone de Beauvoir, *Le Deuxième Sexe* (Paris: Gallimard, 1949).
Catherine Clément/Hélène Cixous, *La Jeune Née* (Paris: Union générale d'éditions, 1975).
Claire Duchen, *Feminism in France from May '68 to Mitterrand* (London: Routledge and Kegan Paul, 1986).
Diana Fuss, *Essentially Speaking* (New York and London: Routledge, 1989).
Luce Irigaray, *Ce Sexe qui n'en est pas un* (Paris: Editions de Minuit, 1977).
Luce Irigaray, *Ethique de la différence sexuelle* (Paris: Editions de minuit, 1984).
Elaine Marks and Isabelle de Courtivron (eds), *New French Feminisms* (Brighton: Harvester, 1981).
Kate Millett, *Sexual Politics* (New York: Ballantine Books, 1978).
Margaret Whitford, *Luce Irigaray: Philosophy in the Feminine* (London: Routledge, 1991).
——, *The Irigaray Reader* (Oxford: Blackwell, 1991).

Femininity, Feminism and Linguistics

Deborah Cameron, *Feminism and Linguistic Theory* (London and Basingstoke: Macmillan, 1985).
Luce Irigaray, 'L'Ordre sexuel du discours', *Langages* (March 1987), 81–123.
Marina Yaguello, *Les Mots et les Femmes* (Paris: Payot, 1987).

Psychoanalysis

Gaston Bachelard, *L'Eau et les rêves* (Paris: José Corti, 1947).
Sigmund Freud, 'On the Transformation of Instincts with Special Reference to Anal Eroticism' (1917), *Standard Edition*, 17, pp. 125–33.
——, 'The Taboo of Virginity' (1918), *Standard Edition*, 11, pp. 191–208.
——, 'The Uncanny' (1919), *Standard Edition*, 17, pp. 217–53.
——, 'Fetishism' (1927), *Standard Edition*, 21, pp. 147–57.
Havelock Ellis, *Studies in the Psychology of Sex*, 1 (*Sexual Inversion*) (Watford: London University Press, 1897).
Melanie Klein, *The Selected Melanie Klein*, edited by Juliet Mitchell (Harmondsworth: Penguin, 1986).
Julia Kristeva, *Histoires d'amour* (Paris: Denoël, 1983).
——, *Soleil noir: dépression et mélancolie* (Paris: Gallimard, 1987).
Jacques Lacan, *Ecrits* (Paris: Seuil, 1966).
Jacques Lacan, *Speech and Language in Psychoanalysis* (translation and commentary by Anthony Wilden) (Baltimore and London: Johns Hopkins University Press, 1968).
Anika Rifflet-Lemaire, *Jacques Lacan* (Brussels: Dessart, 1970).
Hanna Segal, *Introduction to the Work of Melanie Klein* (London: Hogarth Press, 1988).

Psychoanalysis, Femininity and Feminism

Carolyn Burke, 'Irigaray through the Looking Glass', *Feminist Studies*, 7 (1981), 288–306.
Sigmund Freud, 'Female Sexuality' (1931), *Standard Edition*, 21, pp. 223–43.
——, 'Femininity' (New Introductory Lecture on Psychoanalysis 33, 1933), *Standard Edition*, 22, pp. 112–35.
Jane Gallop, *Feminism and Psychoanalysis: The Daughter's Seduction* (Basingstoke and London: Macmillan, 1982).
Luce Irigaray, *Speculum, de l'autre femme* (Paris: Editions de minuit, 1974).
——, 'Women's Exile' (interview with Couze Venn), *Ideology and Consciousness*, 1 (1977), 62–76.
——, *Le Corps-à-corps avec la mère* (Montreal: Editions de la pleine lune, 1981).

——, 'Interview', in Janet Todd (ed.), *Women Writers Talking* (New York and London: Holmes and Meier, 1983), pp. 232–45.
——, 'Is the Subject of Science Sexed?', *Cultural Critique*, 1 (1985), 73–88.
——, 'La Limite du transfert' and 'Misère de la Psychanalyse', in *Parler n'est jamais neutre* (Paris: Editions de minuit, 1985), pp. 293–305 and pp. 253–79.
Jacques Lacan, *Encore: Le Séminaire XX* (Paris: Seuil, 1975).
Juliet Mitchell, *Psychoanalysis and Feminism* (Harmondsworth: Pelican Books, 1975).
Juliet Mitchell and Jacqueline Rose, *Feminine Sexuality: Jacques Lacan and the Ecole Freudienne* (Basingstoke and London: Macmillan, 1982).
Michèle Montrelay, 'Recherches sur la féminité', *Critique* (July 1970), 654–74.
Monique Plaza, '"Phallomorphic Power" and the Psychology of "Woman"', *Ideology and Consciousness*, 4 (Autumn 1978), 4–36.
Margaret Whitford, 'Luce Irigaray and the Female Imaginary: Speaking as a Woman', *Radical Philosophy*, 43 (Summer 1986), 3–8.
——, 'Rereading Irigaray', in Teresa Brennan (ed.), *Between Feminism and Psychoanalysis* (London and New York: Routledge, 1989), pp. 106–26.

Stylistics, Linguistics and Poetics

Henri Bergson, *Œuvres* (Paris: PUF, 1963).
Christine Brooke-Rose, *A Grammar of Metaphor* (London: Secker and Warburg, 1958).
Donald Davidson, 'What Metaphors Mean', in Sheldon Sacks (ed.), *On Metaphor* (Chicago and London: University of Chicago Press, 1979), pp. 29–45.
Roman Jakobson, *Language in Literature* (Cambridge Mass.: Harvard University Press, 1987).
Paul de Man, 'The Epistemology of Metaphor', in Sacks (ed.), op. cit., pp. 11–28.
Winifred Nowottny, *The Language Poets Use* (London: Athlone Press, 1962).
Anthony Pilkington, *Bergson and His Influence* (Cambridge: Cambridge University Press, 1976).
Paul Ricœur, 'The Metaphorical Process as Cognition, Imagination and Feeling', in Sacks (ed.), op. cit., pp. 141–57.
Stephen Ullman, *Style in the French Novel* (Oxford: Blackwell, 1964).

Women, Language, and Writing

Verena Andermatt, 'Hélène Cixous and the Uncovery of a Feminine Language, *Women and Literature*, 7 (1984), 38–48.
Rachel Blau Duplessis, 'For the Etruscans: Sexual Difference and Artistic Production — the Debate over a Female Aesthetic', in Alice Jardine and Hester Eisenstein (eds), *The Future of Difference* (New Brunswick and London: Rutgers University Press, 1987), pp. 128–56.
Madeleine Borgomano, *Duras: une lecture des fantasmes* (Paris: Astre, 1988).
Germaine Brée, *Women Writers in France* (New Brunswick: Rutgers University Press, 1973).
Hélène Cixous, 'Entretien avec Françoise van Rossum-Guyon, *Revue des sciences humaines* (October–December 1977), 479–93.
——, 'Rethinking Differences' in George Stambolian and Elaine Marks (eds), op. cit., pp. 70–86.
——, *Entre l'écriture* (Paris: Des Femmes, 1986).
Diane Crowder, 'Amazons and Mothers', *Contemporary Literature*, 24 (1983), 117–44.
Béatrice Didier, *L'Ecriture-Femme* (Paris: PUF, 1981).
Sherry Dranch, 'Reading through the Veiled Text: Colette's *The Pure and the Impure*', *Contemporary Literature*, 24 (1983), 176–89.
Marguerite Duras and Xavière Gautier, *Les Parleuses* (Paris: Editions de minuit, 1974)
Rita Felski, *Beyond Feminist Aesthetics* (London: Hutchinson Radius, 1989).
Jane Gallop, 'Quand nos lèvres s'écrivent: Irigaray's Body Politic', *Romanic Review*, 74 (1983), 77–83.
Claudine Herrmann, *Les Voleuses de langue* (Paris: Des Femmes, 1976).
Ann Rosalind Jones, 'Writing the Body: Towards an Understanding of *l'écriture féminine*', *Feminist Studies*, 7 (1981), 247–63.
Adèle King, *French Women Novelists: Defining a Female Style* (Basingstoke and London: Macmillan, 1989).

'Questions à Julia Kristeva' (interview with Françoise van Rossum-Guyon), *Revue des sciences humaines* (October–December 1977), 495–501.
Marcelle Marini, *Territoires du féminin* (Paris: Editions de minuit, 1977).
Helena Michie, *The Flesh Made Word* (Oxford and New York: Oxford University Press, 1987).
Jan Montefiori, *Feminism and Poetry* (London and New York: Pandora, 1987).
Alicia S. Ostriker, *Stealing the Language* (London: The Woman's Press, 1986).
Susan Sellers (ed.), *Writing Differences* (Milton Keynes: Open University Press, 1988).
Susan Sellers, *Language and Sexual Difference* (London and Basingstoke: Macmillan, 1991).
Trista Selous, *The Other Woman: Feminism and Femininity in the Work of Marguerite Duras* (New Haven and London: Yale University Press, 1988).
Domna C. Stanton, 'Difference on Trial', in Nancy Miller (ed.), *The Poetics of Gender* (New York: Columbia University Press, 1986), pp. 157–82.
Virginia Woolf, *A Room of One's Own* (London: Grafton Books, 1977 (1929)).

Eroticism and Erotic Discourse

Roland Barthes, *Sade, Fourier, Loyola* (Paris: Seuil, 1971).
Georges Bataille, 'L'Erotisme', in *Œuvres complètes X* (Paris: Gallimard, 1987), pp. 11–270.
Jessica Benjamin, 'The Bonds of Love: Rational Violence and Erotic Domination', in Jardine and Eisenstein (eds), op. cit., pp. 41–70.
Anne-Marie Dardigna, *Les Châteaux d'Eros ou l'infortune du sexe des femmes* (Paris: Maspero, 1980).
Andrea Dworkin, *Pornography: Men Possessing Women* (London: The Women's Press, 1981).
Lucienne Frappier-Masur, 'Marginal Canons: Rewriting the Erotic', *Yale French Studies*, 75 (1988), 112–28.
Pierre Guiraud, *Dictionnaire historique, stylistique, rhétorique, étymologique de la littérature érotique* (Paris: Payot, 1975).
John E. Jackson, *Le Corps amoureux* (Neuchâtel: A la Baconnière, 1986).
Anaïs Nin, *Delta of Venus* (London: W. H. Allen, 1978).
C. J. Rawson, 'Cannibalism and Fiction', *Genre*, 2 (1978), 227–313.
Susan Sontag, 'The Pornographic Imagination', in Georges Bataille, *Story of the Eye* (trans.) (Harmondsworth: Penguin Books, 1982), pp. 83–118.
Susan Rubin Suleiman, '(Re)writing the Body: The Politics and Poetics of Female Eroticism', *Poetics Today*, 6 (1985), 43–65.
Evelyne Sullerot, *Histoire et mythologie de l'amour* (Paris: Hachette, 1974).

Lesbianism

Shari Benstock, *Women of the Left Bank* (London: Virago, 1986).
Claudine Brécourt-Villars, *Petit glossaire raisonné de l'érotisme saphique 1880–1930* (Paris: Pauvert, 1980).
Martha Noel Evans, 'Monique Wittig: The Lesbian', in *Masks of Tradition: Women and the Politics of Writing in Twentieth Century France* (Ithaca and London: Cornell University Press), 1987, pp. 185–219.
Lillian Faderman, *Surpassing the Love of Men: Romantic Friendship and Love between Women from the Renaissance to the Present* (London: The Women's Press, 1985).
Jeanette H. Foster, *Sex Variant Women in Literature* (Tallahassee: Naiad Press, 1985).
Sigmund Freud, 'The Psychogenesis of a Case of Homosexuality in a Woman' (1920), *Standard Edition*, 18, pp. 147–72.
Sandra Gilbert and Susan Gubar, *No Man's Land 2: Sexchanges* (New Haven and London: Yale University Press, 1989).
Georges May, 'Diderot, Baudelaire and "les femmes damnées"', *Modern Language Notes* (June 1950), 395–99.
Esther Newton, 'The Mythic Mannish Lesbian: Radclyffe Hall and the New Woman', *Signs*, 9 (1984), 557–75.

Mother/Daughter Bonding

Nancy Chodorow, 'Family Structure and Feminine Personality', in Michelle Rosaldo and Louise Lamphere (eds), *Women, Culture and Society* (Stanford: Stanford University Press, 1974), pp. 42–66.

——, *The Reproduction of Mothering: Psychoanalysis and the Sociology of Gender* (Berkeley and Los Angeles: University of California Press, 1978).

——, 'Gender Relation and Difference in Psychoanalytic Perspective', in Jardine and Eisenstein (eds), op. cit., pp. 3–19.

Jane Flax, 'The Conflict between Nurturance and Autonomy in Mother-Daughter Relationships and within Feminism', *Feminist Studies*, 4 (February 1978), 171–89.

——, 'Mother-Daughter Relationships: Psychodynamics, Politics and Philosophy', in Jardine and Eistenstein (eds), op. cit., pp. 20–40.

Marianne Hirsch, 'A Mother's Discourse: Incorporation and Repetition in *La Princesse de Clèves*', *Yale French Studies*, 62 (1981), 67–87.

——, 'Mothers and Daughters: Review Essay', *Signs*, 7 (1981), 200–22.

——, *The Mother/Daughter Plot: Narrative, Psychoanalysis, Feminism* (Bloomington and Indianapolis: Indiana University Press, 1989).

Luce Irigaray, *Et l'une ne bouge pas sans l'autre* (Paris: Editions de minuit, 1974).

Adrienne Rich, *Of Woman Born* (London: Virago, 1977).

Ronnie Scharfman, 'Mirroring and Mothering in Simone Schwarz-Bart's *Pluie et vent sur Télumée Miracle* and Jean Rhys's *Wide Sargasso Sea*', *Yale French Studies*, 62 (1981), 88–106.

Hélène Wenzel, 'Introduction to Luce Irigaray's "And the One Doesn't Stir without the Other"', *Signs*, 7 (1981), 56–59.

Reflections, Mirrors, and Doubles

Robert Rogers, *A Psychoanalytic Study of the Double in Literature* (Detroit: Wayne State University Press, 1970).

M-C. Schapira, *Le Regard de Narcisse* (Lyon: Presses universitaires de Lyon, 1984).

Naomi Segal, *The Unintended Reader* (Cambridge: Cambridge University Press, 1986).

——, *Narcissus and Echo: Women in the French Récit* (Manchester: Manchester University Press, 1988).

Voyeurism, the Eye, and the Gaze

Michel Erman, *L'Œil de Proust: écriture et voyeurisme dans 'A la recherche du temps perdu'* (Paris: Nizet, 1988).

Jacques Lacan, *Les Quatre concepts fondamentaux de la psychanalyse: Le Séminaire XI* (Paris: Seuil, 1973).

Randolph Splitter, *Proust's 'Recherche': A Psychoanalytic Interpretation* (Boston: Routledge and Kegan Paul, 1981).

INDEX